THE BILL CLINTON STORY

THE
BILL CLINTON STORY

WINNING THE PRESIDENCY

John Hohenberg

Syracuse University Press

Copyright © 1994 by John Hohenberg

First Edition 1994
94 95 96 97 98 99   6 5 4 3 2 1

The paper used in this publication meets the minimum requirements of American National Standard for Information Sciences—Permanence of Paper for Printed Library Materials, ANSI Z39.48-1984. ∞™

Library of Congress Cataloging-in-Publication Data

Hohenberg, John.
    The Bill Clinton story : winning the presidency / John Hohenberg.
        p.   cm.
    ISBN 0-8156-0284-7 (cloth). — ISBN 0-8156-0285-5 (p.b.)
    1. Presidents—United States—Election—1992. 2. Clinton, Bill, 1946–   3. United States—Politics and government—1989–1993. I. Title.
    E884.H64   1994
    324.9730928—dc20   93-47406

Manufactured in the United States of America

Another for Jo Ann

Contents

Contents

Part Three—The Election

An Acknowledgment

Ever since I helped cover the arrival of President Harding in Seattle from Alaska in 1923 on my first assignment as a seventeen-year-old reporter, the presidency and its occupants have fascinated me. In the seventy years that have elapsed since, I have known some of them and written about nearly all of them, which is why this book about Bill Clinton is so close to my heart.

I am grateful to Syracuse University first of all for my two years as a Newhouse Distinguished Professor in 1983–84 and 1984–85 and to my colleagues there who encouraged me to do this book. For the care with which publication has been managed, I am thankful as well to Syracuse University Press, to Robert A. Mandel as its director, and Cynthia Maude-Gembler as its executive editor.

To my own first lady, Jo Ann Fogarty Hohenberg, I owe the greatest debt of all for seeing me through still another book with her many thoughtful and useful suggestions. If she wasn't very impressed the first time she was ushered into the White House press room, I can't blame her. The home that she has maintained for both of us these lovely fifteen years, including my study, is much more her style.

John Hohenberg

Prologue

A Time for Renewal

It seemed like a national holiday. American flags, large and small, were fluttering everywhere in the nation's capital that crisp and sunny January day. A big brass band was pumping away at patriotic airs. Every now and then, there would be a cheer from the huge crowd for no reason except exuberance for the sheer joy of being together and making history.

A choir of children began singing to the encouraging hand waving of the bandmaster:

> My country, 'tis of thee
> Sweet land of liberty,
> Of thee I sing . . ."

Before the gleaming white dome of the national Capitol, great masses of people had assembled for as far as the eye could see. Batteries of television cameras transmitted animated views of the colorful scene for the vast American home audience. For this was January 20, 1993, in Washington, D.C., Inauguration Day, when a new president of the United States would be sworn in promptly at noon.

As the ceremonial hour approached, the chatter and movement in the crowd seemed to ease off. The distinguished and the undistinguished took their places in rows of chairs on a platform facing the crowd to witness this solemn transfer of power.

Now the black-gowned chief justice of the United States, William H. Rehnquist, moved to the front of the platform. Beside him stood the new president, Bill Clinton, humbly born forty-six years ago in the village of Hope, Arkansas. Like the chief justice, he was bareheaded and seemed unnaturally solemn in his dark clothes.

At one side of the new chief executive, the family Bible in her hands, was his first lady, Hillary Rodham Clinton, a vivid figure in blue; at the other, their twelve-year-old daughter, Chelsea, who seemed to be enjoying the thrill and excitement of the moment.

Nearby, the new vice president, Tennessee's former senator, Al Gore, looked on with benign assurance. His wife, Tipper, also in blue like the first lady, was beside him with their four children, three girls and a boy. Seated to one side, almost unnoticed among the dignitaries packed together on the platform, was the outgoing president, George Bush, whose many years of outstanding service to the nation were about to end.

Against the background of the sunlit and now silent crowd, the chief justice asked the new president to repeat after him the constitutional oath of office precisely as it had first been uttered by George Washington in 1789. Placing his left hand on the Bible held by the first lady and slightly raising his right hand, Clinton did so in a loud, clear voice:

"I, William Jefferson Clinton, do solemnly swear that I will faithfully execute the office of President of the United States, and will, to the best of my ability, preserve, protect and defend the Constitution of the United States." He added, as the chief justice had done before him, "So help me God."

The crowd roared in triumph. The politically elect on the platform joined in the applause regardless of partisan loyalties. The band pounded out "Hail to the Chief" with brassy precision while an honor guard stood at attention, presenting arms. The new president and his wife embraced and both hugged their little daughter.

In this manner the incredible, the unbelievable, the hundred-to-one shot came to pass. The man from Hope, third youngest in the history of the nation, now was the president of the United States and already was addressing his inaugural call to the American people for a renewal of faith in the nation and in themselves. And far beyond, as the new leader of the free world, his message of courage and confidence in the democratic ideal was being carried to the ends of the earth.

It was a time for reflection, to look back over the terribly rough road this newcomer to national and world power had traveled in the campaign that had just ended, to consider as well the enormous difficulties that lay directly ahead.

Within two years at the congressional elections, the American people would decide whether this utterly different and venturesome new leader merited a vote of confidence at the polls. Within four years, barring accident and ill health, he also would know whether he and his administration had been able to move the nation sufficiently ahead to merit reelection.

For now, though, that golden day in January was his to savor and to enjoy with his loved ones and the close friends who had believed in him. This, then, becomes the story of how he fashioned his stunning victory at the polls—a classic in the annals of American democracy—that so many had believed to be impossible. From it, both friend and foe will have to draw their own conclusions as to whether he can do it again.

THE BILL CLINTON STORY

PART ONE
CHOICES FOR AMERICA

1

Election in Paradise

Cold sunlight glinted on the hard-packed snow. Across the distant white hillsides of New Hampshire, the icy fingers of winter had tightened their grip. Nearby, beside a well-worn trail of rutted snow, a sparkling icicle dropped soundlessly from the bared branch of a lone maple tree and shattered on the frozen surface.

It was near zero that morning, February 18, 1992.

Along many such trails throughout the state, crowds of bundled-up out-of-state visitors were gliding into the bluish-white haze on their skis. Here and there, on short downhill courses, the excited cries of children could be heard as they rode their sleds—going belly-buster, they called it—under the watchful supervision of their elders.

Throughout this snowy paradise that day, the people of New Hampshire were undertaking a much more important task than the visitors at play who were their paying guests. They were casting the first votes of all in America in that year's presidential election against the background of this midwinter carnival, and a mildly interested nation was awaiting the outcome.

This was likely to provide the first clue to whether President George Bush, then completing his fourth year in the White House, could be as easily reelected as both he and nearly everybody else of importance expected at the time. Truly, he seemed to be unbeatable: the commander in chief who had seen America's greatest foe, the Soviet Union, collapse at the end of the forty-five-year Cold War, who had led a coalition force to a quick victory in the Persian Gulf War, and who had been the beneficiary of the economic boom created during the regime of his predecessor, Ronald Reagan.

Even Bush's most determined enemies among the Democrats had given up opposing his reelection although they still controlled both houses of Congress. Against an apparently invincible president, some of the best-known Democratic leaders were not seeking the party's presidential nomination. Only five little-known candidates had entered the Democratic primary in New Hampshire in quest of that seemingly empty honor. For that matter, the only Republican who had dared oppose Bush in the party's primary that day was a neophyte, Patrick J. Buchanan, a television figure and columnist.

If there was a signal of trouble ahead, it was the slackening of the economy that had begun in July 1990. Unemployment was now inching up, especially in New England, but that danger sign was overshadowed by the booming stock markets. Still, some leading economists were cautioning that the downturn might become serious if something wasn't done to make the country more competitive abroad. Only nobody appeared to be listening at the White House. The position there was that the lower business indicators were just a blip in the fortunes of a great power.

For now in New Hampshire, President Bush shrugged off all warnings about the chance of a reversal before election day, November 3, when he was confident he would be voted four more years in power.

•   •   •

It was not exactly a coincidence that New Hampshire was counting more than ever on its winter tourism industry during the first of the state campaigns in the long presidential primary season of voting or caucusing in the fifty states for both major party nominations. The father figures of the Granite State had realized that making it the earliest to vote, especially in midwinter, might also serve as promotion for their expanding winter tourism industry. And so it turned out. At the onset of the 1992 campaign, hordes of news people and all-important television crews invaded the northland. As a result, tourists also followed the politicians to New Hampshire, offsetting to some extent the state's damaged economy.

This, however, was not the only coincidence that marked the presidential campaign in the state that was the first to vote. On January 23, less than a month before the primary, a checkout counter grocery tabloid, *Star*, had printed an allegation by a former nightclub singer, Gennifer Flowers, that she had had a twelve-year romance with Governor Bill Clinton of Arkansas. Clinton promptly denied it.

To those who bought the tabloid, Clinton may not have meant much. When Republican politicos quickly picked up the story, however, and relayed it to the nation, they stressed that the Arkansas

4

governor was a candidate for the Democratic presidential nomination in the New Hampshire voting.

That did it. Other newspapers picked up the *Star*'s story and amplified it through news conferences with Flowers. Next, television further embroidered the sex charges, leaving the fight for the Democratic nomination to four other primary challengers. Clinton, however, simply refused to quit faced with such personal attacks.

With his wife, the Arkansan went on CBS's "60 Minutes" to refute the Flowers account, but Hillary Clinton, apparently, made the difference. For by standing up for her husband and defending both their marriage and the future of their daughter, Mrs. Clinton helped make him a national figure. Now it remained to be seen how this political soap opera would play in the New Hampshire primary.

Whether the Republican spin doctors liked it or not, they had brought the governor of one of the poorest states in the union to national attention as a possible Democratic contender against President Bush. The matchup still was a long shot and the Bush forces, stymied because the Arkansan refused to fold up, piled on more charges in the so-called character issue.

The other four Democratic candidates in the primary in New Hampshire meanwhile had become side issues, virtually ignored by both the news people and the public at large.

Clinton was accused of smoking marijuana, which he admitted, saying he had tried pot once as a young man but, he added seriously, he hadn't inhaled. The net result was merriment among the nighttime television comics and still more public attention for Clinton, although the publicity remained decidedly negative. Then, the Republican high command came up with something much more serious: an allegation that the governor had been a draft dodger during the Vietnam War.

Clinton's response was that he had had a high draft number, which was true. Moreover, when the accusation was viewed against the antiwar sentiment of many of the college students and other youth of his generation, the draft-dodging charge also failed to impress a lot of people across the land.

So far, at least, Clinton had taken all that the Republicans had been able to throw at him and come back for more. He was the reverse of his predecessor in 1988, then Governor Michael Dukakis of Massachusetts, who had failed to effectively protest Republican charges that he had given furlough privileges to a convicted killer. In consequence, Dukakis had frittered away a seventeen-point lead over Bush and lost the election.

Clinton at least had established himself as a far more determined candidate but it remained to be seen what the voters of New Hampshire would think of him and Hillary.

As for President Bush, he was relatively untouched by the time the first voters went to the polls that cold February day. True, a Dallas newspaper reported in an interview with the president that he had complained bitterly about charges from unspecified sources that his sons and other relatives had been involved in the $50 billion savings-and-loan scandals. Then, too, there were continual rumors in the nation's capital about what had been called "carryings-on" by the president in years long past, something Hillary Clinton once referred to in a moment of anger but immediately apologized for.

That, however, was the extent of the Democrats' negative campaigning against the president. For New Hampshire, at least, Bush still went before the electorate as an odds-on favorite for reelection, and his Republican cohorts, in seeming unanimity, trumpeted his virtues to the populace. No responsible pollster or reporter believed the president could lose and only a few lonely souls in the news business even thought he was vulnerable.

. . .

The first signal that New Hampshire sent to the nation when the primary election returns were complete that February 18 was discouraging for President Bush. In his first test, his victory for renomination over a minor challenger had been unexpectedly narrow. A columnist and television broadcaster, Pat Buchanan, had taken 40 percent of the Republican vote away from him.

In the sobering aftermath, the White House's apologists admitted that there had been a bad break in the Republican party's ranks. The principal excuse was that unspecified conservatives on the far right had vowed to punish the president for failing to keep his 1988 campaign pledge against greater taxation, especially of the wealthy. It was a promise that had been colorfully phrased: "Read My Lips—No New Taxes!" Even the president himself, in a postprimary confessional, conceded the tax increase had been his biggest mistake.

However, there was much more to the president's weak showing in New Hampshire than that. On television and in the press, there was a steady drumfire of criticism of the president's failure to move to strengthen the steadily sinking economy. More and more Republicans, and not only conservatives on the far right, came forward to question both Bush's judgment and his resolve.

This was not necessarily something that Clinton or other Democrats had started. It appeared to be a shift within the Republican party itself—the first symptoms of public concern, even anger, over the status quo that was to take shape in America. As the mood developed, it was to assume an antiincumbent, antigovernment attitude among much of American public opinion.

.   .   .

The verdict on Clinton in New Hampshire also seemed indecisive. He finished second to a better-known New England favorite, former Senator Paul E. Tsongas of Massachusetts, but both were well ahead of the other three candidates in the Democratic primary who were given little chance thereafter of challenging either of the leaders. It was important, too, that 62 percent of New Hampshire's voters, both major party members and independents, had gone to the polls in the election—more than twice as many on the average as usually cast ballots in other states.

The conclusion, greatly in Clinton's favor, was that he had not only survived an all-out Republican attack but also seemed increasingly to become the most formidable of the candidates for the Democratic presidential nomination. From a little-known governor of a Southern state that had gone Republican for Bush in the 1988 presidential election along with all the other states of the old Confederacy, Clinton had become the man of the hour for the Democrats.

It had been years since anybody as strong, savvy, and goodlooking as Clinton had made a major presidential bid in America. However, he was by no means a favorite of the always skeptical news crowd and he did not automatically draw large numbers of people to his cause as he left New England for campaigns for primary elections and caucuses in the rest of the fifty states.

The doubt that more discriminating voters had about him, despite his strength and demonstrable competence, was his lack of experience in national government and in dealings with key nations abroad as well as international organizations. That had been Bush's strength and it would be difficult for any newcomer, no matter how talented and determined, to overcome.

However, the demand for a government that would pay major attention to the ills of America instead of the worries of the world became Clinton's most telling argument for the support of Democratic voters for the party's presidential nomination. Even more significant, the demand produced a slow but meaningful increase in his standing in the polls.

There still were many miles to go for the Democratic nomina-

tion, let alone a victory over an experienced sitting president in November, but Clinton was on his way. After this initial surprise of the
1992 presidential election year, the feeling already was spreading
through the land that there would be many more surprises arising
from the subdued cries of protest first heard in New Hampshire.

.   .   .

The contrast between President Bush and his challenger was
symbolic of the clash of interests between the candidates and the
virtually opposite directions in which they proposed to lead the nation
toward century's end.

The president, now in his sixty-ninth year, had been born to
wealth and power as the son of one of the most prominent New En-
glanders of his time, Prescott Bush, who had been a U.S. senator
from Connecticut. Governor Clinton, then forty-five, was no child of
privilege, having been born to hard-working parents in the small
town of Hope, Arkansas.

Ordinarily, someone with as fortunate a heritage as George
Bush's would have gone straight through prep school and university,
but the Japanese attack on Pearl Harbor had led directly to Bush's
enlistment in the navy and a distinguished career as a fighter pilot in
World War II that brought him three air medals and a Distinguished
Flying Cross. When he returned to classes at Yale, he couldn't qual-
ify for his B.A. in economics until he was twenty-four.

Clinton's course as a youth was different. He had been a baby
boomer, born after World War II, and had completed his education
through hard work and scholarships—a B.A. from Georgetown, later
a Rhodes scholarship at Oxford, and finally a law degree from Yale
Law School after three more years of study.

As a Texan, having established an oil business in the Lone Star
State, Bush made his late beginning in public life. By being elected
twice to the House of Representatives, starting in 1967 from the Sev-
enth District, the World War II veteran soon was a dominant force in
the Republican party. He became successively the U.S. ambassador
to the United Nations, chairman of the Republican National Committee, chief of the U.S. Liaison Office in Communist China, director of
the Central Intelligence Agency, and Ronald Reagan's two-term vice
president.

Clinton, belonging to a newer and different generation in a Solid
South that had repeatedly supported Republican presidents, began
more modestly. He practiced law for two years in Little Rock before

becoming attorney general of Arkansas and, latterly, the state's governor for eleven years as well as the chairman of the national Democratic Leadership Council. He was still governor when Bush was elected president in 1988, but, when the Democratic elders backed away from contesting the president's second term, he hesitated not at all to make a run for the White House.

The political storm that had swirled about Clinton from the outset would have destroyed a less gritty candidate. The Arkansan, however, hung on after his second-place finish in New Hampshire, hoping for a break. On March 11, "Super Tuesday," it finally happened when eleven states held primary elections or caucuses. Less than a month after all the anxiety in New Hampshire, the Republican allegations of character failings in Clinton's past were rejected by the voters.

What happened was this: mainly in the Southern states, the Arkansas governor became the favorite for the Democratic presidential nomination. He triumphed in Texas and Florida over his chief rival at the time, former Senator Tsongas, who had to be satisfied with victories in his native Massachusetts and Rhode Island. In this remarkable manner a seemingly fatally wounded candidacy was revived.

After that, there was no question of Clinton's leadership. He became the man to beat in the race for the Democratic nomination. In addition, he steadily narrowed the gap between him and a deflated President Bush in the opinion polls.

It would not be long before the protests against Bush that first had been noted in New Hampshire would burst into a full-throated roar by Democratic voters for change in America. Curiously, the greatest argument for change came from neither Clinton nor Bush, but from a new voice. It belonged to an impetuous man from Texas with an occasionally bad temper and several billion dollars—Henry Ross Perot. Unlikely as it may have seemed at the time, this quirky and combative person was to change the entire course of the presidential campaign of 1992.

2

The Apostle of Change

SKiP

Ross Perot once compared himself to a few grains of sand that cause an oyster to produce a pearl, saying: "That's what I am, an irritant. I stir things up."

It didn't take the sixty-one-year-old Texas billionaire very long to stir up the American electorate. Once he began his independent campaign for president, pollsters reported that millions of complaining voters were dissatisfied with the prospective choices of both major parties for the highest office in the land. As if that hadn't been discouraging enough for Messrs. Bush and Clinton, both soon were outdistanced by Perot in the polls—and this from a holdover of the Know-Nothings of the last century who had no political party and no other organization of consequence.

Even so, the self-made image that Perot projected was a puzzle. Sometimes, he liked to pose as the successful businessman who'd restore order from chaos in Washington merely by applying disciplined business methods. If that seemed a bore to him, he also could present himself as a crusader for the public interest, a patriot intent on restoring damaged American prestige, even a simple citizen willing to spend much of his acquired wealth to benefit his fellow Americans.

To the sophisticated, he undoubtedly seemed like a caricature straight out of a Sinclair Lewis novel of the 1920s: a satiric portrait of an impatient commoner of great wealth who believed all the ills of humankind in the land of his birth could be dispelled with a wave of his hand. However, with his fabulous riches, he might well have ignored his satiric critics by quoting George S. Kaufman, the master of the Broadway stage, who once observed that satire was something that closed on Saturday night.

. . .

The incredible Perot presidential venture seemed to begin purely by happenstance. It originated in the unlikeliest place, a televised interview on "Larry King Live" of the Cable News Network on February 20, just two days after the New Hampshire primary. Lacking a planned script, which was the nature of the show, King had been prodding the billionaire about the possibility of an independent run for the presidency without much success when his guest suddenly made this qualified offer:

If he could be placed on the ballot by petitions signed by legally qualified citizens in the fifty states, he would agree to run as an independent candidate for president.

King was satisfied, Perot seemed relieved, and so the discussion ended. The next day, though, probably to Perot's utter astonishment, the response to what seemed like a desperation offer to stall an inconvenient proposal was taken seriously by a surprisingly large section of the American people. As Tevye, the Broadway milkman, had exclaimed in the musical, "Fiddler on the Roof," such things could happen only in America.

Both the Republican and Democratic high commands were taken by surprise. Neither President Bush nor Governor Clinton, both still preoccupied with the contests in their respective primaries or caucuses in forty-nine other states after New Hampshire, were not inclined at first to be diverted from their campaigns. Despite Perot's autocratic personality and his "father knows best" attitude, his apparently accidental and still undeclared presidential candidacy had caught the public's fancy. Volunteers were flocking to organize his campaign in the fifty states without much urging.

If Perot was surprised by the initial results, he didn't show it. Instead, he encouraged still more people to work for him by popularizing his cause over the televised talk and call-in show circuit. His delighted on-the-air hosts, quick to seize on a new attraction for their programs, gave him free rein. He found it a lot easier to deal with them and their call-in questioners than the pesky professional reporters who didn't take kindly to his manner and his political inexperience.

To be sure, he made some questionable statements and sometimes contradicted himself. Despite his mistakes, though, he became an almost overnight television sensation. Stimulated by the public acceptance of his candidacy even though he wouldn't make a formal declaration, he pledged to spend $100 million of his own money if necessary to win the presidency. The response was so favorable that he soon was doubling and tripling the estimated amounts he might spend in his campaign. Yet, even though he had a fortune estimated at $2.5 to $3.5 billion, he thriftily accepted all gifts that came his way.

In America, it was still true, as it had been in the time of Bernard M. Baruch, that big money commanded respect. Baruch, the fabled adviser to presidents, had been Perot's forerunner in public life but had declined to run for public office. Once, when asked what various presidents had done with his advice, he grumbled, "They didn't pay much attention to it."

In the excitement of a grass-roots presidential movement, however, Perot couldn't seem to restrain his enthusiasm. All at once, in making his almost daily television rounds, he came up with a single word that rumbled across the country like thunder: "change." That became his theme—a changing America, a better America, an America more responsive to the needs of its people, to the ideals of its founders. From the American heartland, there was a tremendous roar of response from a disheartened, even a fearful segment of the electorate.

The billionaire, in trying to justify the mass movement he had touched off across the land, had come up with a rationale for his independent campaign that enthused his volunteers and brought him still more followers day after day. Governor Clinton and the Democrats, who had been much more timid in sounding the call for change, now seized upon it avidly in the knowledge that they were losing people to the Perot movement. The Republicans—disunited and quarrelsome—still sat on their hands, as did President Bush in the White House.

However, the quest for change had taken hold among the public. No matter what President Bush did in trying to ignore Perot, the mass movement grew to threatening proportions even for the Republicans in just a few weeks.

.   .   .

The puzzle to Perot's friends and associates, and to his family in all probability, was why he had let himself be drawn into the 1992 presidential campaign when he had refused for many years to have anything to do with politicians except when they were useful for his purposes. At one time, he even had turned aside the notion that he might run for president by saying good-naturedly that he wasn't suited for the job temperamentally.

Repeatedly, while the Perot drive was being organized, there were stories in the press and on television about a supposed feud of long standing between the billionaire and President Bush. Although the president had nothing to say about that, the first lady, Barbara Bush, had guessed on a television talk show that ill feeling between the two might have originated with an offer from Perot to hire Bush when both were much younger and separately engaged in business in Texas. At any rate, nothing came of the supposed offer, if it had ever been made.

A more plausible source of hard feeling between the president and his newest rival was the belief, often expressed by Perot's closest associates, that Bush as vice president had asked Perot in 1986 to try to do something about frequent reports that some American prisoners of war still were being held in Southeast Asia years after the end of the Vietnam War. However, according to one published version of events thereafter, the Reagan-Bush administration failed to give Perot adequate support when he did try to do the work assigned to him. Perot seldom could be drawn out on that discouraging point when questioners referred to it before his own presidential campaign.

Whatever version of the differences between the two may be correct, subsequent events even before the 1992 presidential campaign frequently showed them to be at odds. That, over the long run, may have done more to increase the split in the once-solid Republican front for Bush than it did to generate opposition to the Clinton candidacy in the Democratic campaign.

A poll taken in the early stages of the Perot drive demonstrated how little faith the public had in the two-party system just then. Only 28 percent of the respondents were willing to admit they were Republicans, a scant three percent more identified themselves as Democrats, 35 percent were straight-out independents, and the remaining six percent gave no response.

It was this situation on which Perot's undeclared quest for the presidency capitalized. Although other candidates had used television over the years, what the Texan did amounted to a blitz because of the way he continued to make his talk show appearances. The formal speech was not for him as a rule. He went for the sound bite. Instead of stiff poses for the camera, he preferred the photo op. He seemed to hate the probing questions of professional reporters because, as he sometimes explained, he feared being misquoted.

However, few talk show hosts or hostesses demanded a definitive answer to such troublesome questions as what to do about the economy, unemployment, crime, drugs, abortion, the environment, and all the other issues of consequence to the future of the nation.

.   .   .

The Horatio Alger-type story of Perot's rise to fame, fortune, and an undeclared presidential campaign began conventionally with his birth on June 27, 1930, to a tightly knit middle-class family in Texarkana, Texas. He developed into a reasonably diligent student at a small private school and at nineteen entered the U.S. Naval Academy at Annapolis, from which he was graduated in 1953 as the president of his senior class and a prospective naval career officer.

After two years of life aboard ship, he'd had enough of the navy and promptly applied for an honorable discharge but was turned down. Still, he persisted and eventually was separated from the service under honorable circumstances. Despite his dislike for the stiff discipline of the armed services, he associated forever after whenever necessary with professional police, the CIA, and military types. He also tried to instill the military discipline and obedience he'd successfully avoided in most people who worked for him.

After leaving the navy and breaking in with IBM as a computer salesman, he went into business for himself on his thirty-second birthday in 1962 by writing a $1,000 check, now suitably framed in his office in Dallas, with which he founded Electronic Data Systems (EDS), one of the earliest computer service companies. It was the foundation of his fortune.

EDS took off with the creation of the Medicare and Medicaid programs. As grateful millions swamped the federal government with medical bills, the panicky bureaucracy couldn't handle the load but Perot managed to do so. When he couldn't finish his work by day with his small staff and few computers, he rented computers from other companies at night and kept going with the processing of still more claims. Before long, he'd earned enough to expand his setup and was handling all the business the federal government could give him.

By the time Richard Nixon took office, Perot already was a millionaire. He did it by going public with EDS shares with an opening price of $16.50 a share, more than a hundred times earnings. If that seemed overpriced, the results failed to indicate it because EDS shares rose to $23.00 by the end of the first day during which they were traded. Within eighteen months, EDS was being traded at the whopping price of $162.50 a share, quite a windfall for the speculator from Texarkana. Because he himself then owned 9.5 million shares of his company, he suddenly was worth $1.5 billion on paper. It would have been impossible after that for anybody, including the Texan's most determined detractors, to call him a simpleton.

By reason of the continued profits EDS kept piling up as a favored computer firm that dealt with the federal government, Perot sold his company in 1984 to General Motors for $2.5 billion and accepted a seat on the corporation's board of directors. His GM association didn't last long; evidently, when he couldn't have his way, he wanted to get out—but always, if possible, at a profit. That is the way it worked at GM, because he quarreled continually with the management and after only about nine months decided to resign from the board of directors over his rejected demands for business reforms.

When GM bought him out, he added another $700 million to the fortune he had already accumulated, then looked around for new opportunities for money making. To help him in his quest, he started a new firm, Perot Systems, Inc., but that evidently wasn't enough of a challenge to occupy him. He also embarked on new adventures outside his regular orbit that brought him into public prominence as a venturesome billionaire.

.   .   .

One of the most daring of Perot's exploits occurred in Iran after two of his agents, who had gone there to look for business opportunities for him, ended up in a Tehran prison instead. That was an immediate challenge for the Texan. Disregarding possible danger to himself, he flew to the Iranian capital without wasting time on appeals to the State Department for help and conferred with his agents in their prison before trying to set them free. However, when the Iranian authorities turned down his pleas to liberate them, he conceived the idea of organizing a paramilitary force to rescue them at his expense and on his responsibility.

Just how he managed it has been told several times in different ways, but what the whole business added up to was that guards to the Iranian prison where Perot's agents were held had a seeming lapse of memory one night and left its gates open. Evidently, the prison itself also had been similarly neglected so the result was that the Perot agents, along with some other prisoners, were able to escape at night. The paramilitary force the Texan had created picked up his men and spirited them back to the United States.

If the American government participated in this exploit or was even informed in advance of what was to happen, all that was kept a secret. Some time later, when President Carter tried to free American hostages from Iran with the full force of the nation at his command, he failed.

·   ·   ·

Thereafter, Perot developed a patriotic interest in finding out what had happened to American prisoners of war and American combatants reported missing in action after the Vietnam War. Despite the years that had elapsed, he soon turned up with information that some listed POWs and MIAs had been sighted in North Vietnam and that others were believed to have been sent to the Soviet Union.

However, after several visits to Hanoi and subsequent testimony before a congressional committee, once again he could not produce a favorable result. What he did do was to proceed despite President Richard Nixon's announcement of March 29, 1973: "For the first time in twelve years, no American military forces are in Vietnam. All our American POWs are on their way home."

The families who charged that their loved ones had been left behind refused to believe him. Perot, after so many others had failed to prod the government into action, became their champion over almost a quarter century beginning in 1969. He kept their hopes alive. He also bedeviled successive presidential administrations for stronger action to force Hanoi's cooperation even though he never could produce a single ex-serviceman who'd been abandoned.

The restless billionaire meanwhile took on other causes. One, in which he confessed he had lost $60 million, was an attempt to save the Wall Street brokerage firm of duPont, Flore and Forgan from bankruptcy. Despite his effort to reorganize and revitalize the business over four years, he ultimately failed there, too.

All these activities turned out to be preliminaries to Perot's greatest adventure: his undeclared independent quest for the presidency. No matter how or why he accepted the challenge of a television talk show host, what happened thereafter made history. The 1992 presidential campaign would have been different without him.

3

A Question of Morals

A passionate argument over legalized abortion became the first cause to test the presidential candidates.

No moral decision since the adoption of the Twenty-first Amendment to the Constitution, repealing nationwide prohibition in 1933 after Franklin Roosevelt's election, had aroused such emotion and created so much tumult from coast to coast.

This time, too, a fight over a constitutional amendment was shaping up. President Bush had endorsed a proposed Republican platform plank calling for the adoption of such an amendment outlawing abortion, which Governor Clinton and the Democratic party fiercely opposed.

In his undeclared independent candidacy, Ross Perot also favored continued legalized abortion.

This was far more than a political and social issue. It had divided a whole generation of American women, who formed 53 percent of the population, and deeply affected both their families and their religious beliefs. The candidates, therefore, were well aware that this struggle, together with high unemployment and the continued economic slump, could determine the outcome of the election.

In his commitment to the pro-life, or antiabortion, cause, President Bush also had given warning that he would authorize the solicitor general of the United States, at an appropriate time, to ask the Supreme Court to upset a more liberal high court decision in 1973 that created legalized abortion in the case of *Roe* vs. *Wade*. It was another way of approaching the goal of the antiabortion cause, which intensified the differences between the major party presidential candidates.

No one, however, could predict whether the honorable justices of the present day would delay action until after the election on any government move to obtain an immediate rehearing on *Roe* vs. *Wade*. There still was a considerable following for the informal doctrine once voiced by Finley Peter Dunne's "Mr. Dooley": "No matter whether th' Constitution follows th' flag or not, th' Supreme Court follows th' illicition returns."

The antiabortionists argued furiously that the high court wouldn't want to disgrace itself by stalling a decision of such importance. It was a belief that President Bush shared.

．　　　．　　　．

The president originally had advocated a woman's right to decide whether to have an abortion, but he had long since switched sides. Even though most polls now showed that legalized abortion was favored by most Americans, he refused to change his mind. However, like his vice president, Dan Quayle, he tried to put a more human face on his proposed prohibition of abortion in a constitutional amendment by agreeing that he would support a decision by a woman relative if she sought an abortion.

That, however, did not ease the conflict between the president and his probable Democratic opponent, Governor Clinton, who charged that the president was trying to have it both ways: antiabortion by law, proabortion on a personal basis. This truly was a cause that would have to be decided either in the Supreme Court or on election day, possibly both.

．　　　．　　　．

The way the battle over abortion was fought from the beginning was fascinating in itself.

President Bush made good his threat to go to the Supreme Court for a reversal of *Roe* vs. *Wade* on the eve of the significant primary elections in New York and Pennsylvania from which Governor Clinton hoped to emerge as the top-heavy favorite for the Democratic presidential nomination. What the president did was to indicate that the expected challenge to *Roe* vs. *Wade* would come during a Supreme Court hearing on a pending Pennsylvania law limiting the right to an abortion.

There was no immediate political danger for the president in making this announcement. No real challenge to his renomination had been mounted in any Republican primary to date and none was expected for the remainder of the primary period. For Governor Clinton, however, there was a possibility of a fight, for the new governor of Pennsylvania, Robert Casey, a Democrat, was a violent antiabortionist and wanted to challenge Clinton on the issue.

Countering Bush's move, leaders of the proabortion cause decided to demonstrate the strength of their movement to the president by staging a mass march on the White House, with marchers from all parts of the nation, just before the New York primary. By press estimates, a half-million people showed up (the estimate of the national park police was two hundred fifty thousand) but the most important part of their audience, President and Mrs. Bush, already had departed that day for Camp David, their retreat in Maryland.

Once the leaders of the march realized the president had eluded them, they changed plans and led the marchers toward the Mall near the Capitol to concentrate on carrying their message to Congress instead. That started the serious business of the demonstration featuring the president's chief Democratic challenger, Governor Clinton.

Putting in an appearance at the nation's capital to address the proabortion rally had been considered by the Democratic high command to be important enough for the youthful Arkansan to interrupt his New York campaign. Not only did he do so with an effective attack on the president's position but former Governor Edmund G. Brown, Jr., of California, now his principal remaining rival for the Democratic nomination, also came from New York to denounce the president's position.

This was intended as an added demonstration that public opinion was swinging away from the antiabortionists, despite the president's leadership, and toward Clinton's support of a woman's right to choose what she believed to be best for her. However, even though Clinton's rivals in New York agreed with him on the abortion issue, he narrowly won the state Democratic party's endorsement at the subsequent presidential primary.

After 162 New York delegates to the Democratic National Convention were safely committed to him, the Arkansas governor was more than half way toward a majority of the 2,145 delegates he needed to clinch the nomination. With 1,279 delegates safely for him, he was far ahead of his remaining rivals, former Senator Tsongas, who had added 100 New York delegates to increase his total to 520, and former Governor Brown, whose 98 added New York delegates gave him a total of 272. Not surprisingly after that, Tsongas dropped out of the race but Brown stubbornly continued what seemed to be a hopeless struggle for the Democratic nomination.

All signs pointed to a showdown on the abortion issue leading up to the succeeding primary in Pennsylvania on April 28. As expected, Governor Casey mounted a scathing attack on Clinton's position as a proabortionist but he didn't enter the primaries against the Arkansan. In effect, therefore, what Casey did was merely a demonstration and it had no effect on the outcome of the voting.

The antiabortionists, however, did determine to show their strength in the area despite Clinton's triumph in Pennsylvania and they did so in a completely unexpected manner.

.   .   .

On April 19, shortly after the New York primary, the Bush administration finally asked the Supreme Court to nullify the legality of abortion. The solicitor general of the United States, as expected, presented the government's position to the high court on the Pennsylvania law that had put new limits on the right of abortion in that state. What the government did in effect was to ask the court to go beyond the legality of the Pennsylvania statute and undo its 1973 decision instead.

As was their custom, the nine justices heard testimony and arguments from all sides before concluding the hearing and taking the case under advisement for an unspecified period before returning a decision.

Next day, one of the worst disturbances over abortion occurred just across the Pennsylvania border in New York's second largest city, Buffalo. There, a number of women with some male support including a few clergy surrounded five legal abortion clinics in what seemed like an attempt to close them by force.

These tactics had been used elsewhere for some time to try to move public opinion toward the antiabortion cause, but without any indication of a favorable result. But there was no doubt of the zeal and the determination of the demonstrators who tried to block the entrances to the besieged clinics.

To oppose them, a crowd of women committed to legalized abortion, with a fringe of male support, tried to keep the clinics open. When the attackers sprawled before the entrances, the Buffalo police carried them away and placed them under arrest. Hours later, the clinics still remained open for patients, a few of whom safely made their way through the opposing factions and were treated inside.

Scores of arrests were made that day, mainly of antiabortionists charged with disorderly conduct and other minor offenses, but without breaking the spirit of the attackers. The scenes outside the clinics continued sporadically day after day, but the Buffalo police saw to it that street warfare would not prevail no matter how violently the anti-abortion women tried to maintain their offensive. Nevertheless, it lasted through the Pennsylvania primary but apparently without effect on the outcome even though Governor Casey participated in antiabortion demonstrations within that state.

When the Pennsylvania votes were tallied, Governor Clinton appeared to have scored his greatest victory of the primary campaign —and this faced with Governor Casey's criticism of him as a weak and indecisive candidate who had minuscule support and was "unelectable." In fact, when Clinton emerged from the Pennsylvania primary he had 1,439 delegates and needed only 706 more to clinch the Democratic presidential nomination. His sole remaining challenger, former Governor Brown, had only 326 and couldn't possibly have beaten him.

It was then at last that the Democratic congressional leadership invited the Arkansas governor to the nation's capital as the presumptive titular head of the party and its next presidential candidate. Nobody mentioned the "electability" issue at that figurative love feast on April 29, the day after the Pennsylvania vote. Instead, the House majority leader, Richard A. Gephardt of Missouri, said, "Pennsylvania may have broken the ice, and I think his [Clinton's] numbers are going to grow very quickly now."

To that forecast, Clinton responded with the essence of the stump speeches he had been making around the country in his drive for the presidential nomination: "We're not going to turn this country around until we have a president and Congress jointly committed to change—change in the lives of this country and restoring the leadership of this country economically."

Whether Clinton and his party's congressional leadership realized it, the line coincided with the basis of Perot's still undeclared independent presidential campaign. In it, the impulsive Texan had repeatedly varied his demand for change in the country's leadership with a caustic denunciation of what he called the "gridlock" in Washington: the Republican presidency and the Democratic Congress that were almost continually at odds with each other.

At the time Clinton first began sounding the same note in his campaign, he was still lagging in the polls. More often than not he was third—four or five points behind either President Bush or Perot, who seemed virtually tied in most polls, only a point or two separating them. This in effect had become the basis for the criticism made of Clinton by Governor Casey of Pennsylvania and others among the antiabortionists, the theme being that he still was "unelectable."

The stern political reality at that early stage in the campaign was that, for as long as Clinton could manage to stay fairly close to the president and Perot, there was at least a mathematical chance that no one could gain a majority in the November 3 election. Thereby, under the Constitution, the decision still could go to Clinton for as long as the Democrats maintained their leadership in the House of Representatives. However, neither the Bush nor the Clinton campaign people dared even guess at what would happen if the unpredictable Perot should drop out of the race before election day.

This was what complicated the position of both major parties as well as their presidential and congressional candidates. Perot's still undeclared drive had made it virtually impossible to predict what type of government would emerge from so scrambled a mixture of conservatives, moderates, liberals, and unclassified independents in November.

Despite President Bush's easy string of primary victories after New Hampshire and Clinton's emergence at the top of the Democratic list of the president's rivals, therefore, nothing seemed settled except that an aroused electorate now was insisting on change. And regardless of how the Supreme Court finally ruled on the abortion issue, it then seemed unlikely to be a decisive influence in the outcome of the presidential and most congressional elections.

Nothing remotely resembling so chaotic a situation at the peak of government had developed in this century since the 1912 presidential campaign. Ex-President Theodore Roosevelt, in a vengeful attack against President William Howard Taft's reelection, had been decisive in throwing the presidency to the Democtratic nominee, former Gov. Woodrow Wilson of New Jersey.

Toward century's end, the latest presidential campaign was far more complex, even if it was three-sided for the time being, for it was being played out in a far different country and a strange world of which no one could even have dreamed in that era of fourscore years ago.

·   ·   ·

A postscript to the public struggle over the abortion issue was touched off by President Bush's decision to seek a Supreme Court reversal of the legality of abortion. After failing to close the five Buffalo clinics, the leaders of the antiabortion movement called off the offensive that had brought them nothing but defeat, ridicule, and what appeared to be a shift in public opinion against their cause. Even among the Catholic laity in Buffalo, who ordinarily would have been sympathetic to the antiabortion cause, there was criticism of the way the demonstration against the five clinics had been conducted in their city. In all, more than five hundred people had been arrested during the strife.

The last gasp in that conflict, Operation Mercy, came on May 1 in nearby Amherst, New York, when several hundred antiabortionists tried to close an abortion clinic there with a back-door blockade. Once again, however, the attempt was broken up by a combination of effective police work and proabortionist defenses. In all, about a hundred more people had been arrested at Amherst. Afterward, the defeated crusaders took refuge in prayer and antiabortion television ads while awaiting the Supreme Court's decision on the president's appeal to outlaw abortion by repealing the decision in *Roe* vs. *Wade*.

When the high court's judgment was announced on June 29, the surprise was that *Roe* vs. *Wade* was upheld by a vote of 5–4, but parts of the Pennsylvania law further restricting the right of women to have an abortion also were approved. In effect, therefore, the honorable justices passed this legal puzzle along to the states where it now appeared possible to curb abortion practice as long as the burden did not become unbearable, but no one could say exactly where that line could be drawn.

Still, the court's majority insisted the "essence" of *Roe* vs. *Wade* had been validated and that, in giving states the right to limit access to abortions, an important precedent had been set. After that it appeared certain, as some constitutional experts predicted, that lawyers would be given considerable employment for a long time to come in both state and federal courts in battling over the meaning of the high court's latest decision. Restrictions such as forcing women to undergo waiting periods for an abortion, to seek parental consent where applicable, and other requirements not considered an "undue burden" softened what apparently had seemed to be a White House defeat.

Southey's lines about the "Battle of Blenheim" seemed to apply:

> "But what good came of it at last?"
> Quoth Little Peterkin.
> "Why, that I cannot tell," said he;
> "But 'twas a famous victory."

.   .   .

There was no doubt now that this issue would be fought during the remainder of the presidential campaign and determined—at least for the next four years—on the day the victor was inaugurated in 1993.

4

A Crisis in Black and White

$\mathbf{A}$merica has teetered on the precipice of racial turmoil for much of this century. Everybody who was trapped in the rotting inner cores of the nation's largest cities knew it. So did those nearby who saw what was happening and either prepared to face the consequences or fled to the suburbs while there still was time.

The rioting in the 1960s was the warning of worse yet to come. In the Kerner report of 1967, the people of America were told bluntly of what was about to happen to them: "Our nation is moving toward two societies, one black, one white—separate and unequal. . . . Discrimination and segregation have long permeated much of American life; they now threaten the future of every American."

Yet, there was very little movement to try to meet the developing crisis, much less to avert it. In so desperate a situation, one would have thought that an issue of such consequence would have been of overwhelming importance in the presidential elections of the 1970s and 1980s, but the subject was rarely mentioned, and then only in passing.

It was as if a whole great nation had given in to the reality of a decline in a substantial part of its society. It was either that or sheer indifference to the plight of millions of deprived peoples who had been consigned to an underclass—uncared for, unwanted, and abandoned by the comfortable and the well-fed, who imagined the hardships of their neighbors were none of their business.

The romance of the immigrant peoples who swarmed to these American ghettos early in this century was still being taught in the nation's schools to the deprived children of the poor who still lived there. Again and again, the new generation in the ruined inner cities heard how their immigrant predecessors helped build the country into a great force for freedom. They were taught to respect the Irish who created a new Boston, the Jews who inhabited the Lower East Side of

Manhattan and contributed to New York's greatness, the east Europeans who transformed Chicago, and all the rest.

What these new children of the ghetto were seldom told was that the way out of poverty for many of them, in a much larger country with more diversified urban areas, would take more time and more government assistance than was generally available except in emergencies. Except for the strongest, most ambitious, and determined among them, the rest would often have to live for years in crime-ridden neighborhoods that had been abandoned by the immigrants who had preceded them in the earlier years of this century.

This, to a very large extent, was the position when Los Angeles exploded in three days and nights of the worst rioting in many years beginning on April 29, 1992, in the middle of that year's presidential primary campaigns. Not only in California but also across the land, there was a concerned reaction. People inside and outside the affected areas fully realized something had to be done at once; but beyond the restoration of law and order, no one—including the presidential candidates—had any patent long-term answer to the plight of American minorities in urban areas.

President Bush, Governor Pete Wilson of California, and Mayor Tom Bradley of Los Angeles all came to the aid of the beleaguered and outnumbered Los Angeles police. The president ordered fifteen hundred Marines and three thousand army personnel into Los Angeles. Governor Wilson called out units of the National Guard. Mayor Bradley declared a state of emergency and imposed a dawn-to-dusk curfew.

In addition, the president said that the state jury's verdict in the King case had "sickened" him. He directed the Department of Justice to reopen an investigation into King's beating, the step that eventually led to federal action against the four officers and a trial in a federal court, in which two of the four were found guilty of violating King's civil rights.

Another nationally publicized incident in the rioting, videotapes by passersby that were shown on TV in the beating of a white truck driver by a few blacks, also resulted eventually in arrests and court trials.*

*On April 17, 1993, a federal jury in Los Angeles found Police Sgt. Stacey C. Koon and Officer Lawrence M. Powell guilty of violating King's civil rights after which both were sentenced to thirty months in prison. The other two police defendants were freed. In the case of Reginald Denny, the beaten white truck driver, a black defendant, Damien N. Williams, was given a maximum ten-year sentence, but could serve less than four years under California law. His codefendant, Henry K. Watson, who already had served seventeen months, was freed on parole.

25

According to Los Angeles police figures, the casualties in the riots included at least sixty dead, almost twenty-five hundred injured, and property damage estimated at $850 million. There also was a police figure of eighteen thousand arrests, which was never officially confirmed. City Attorney James J. Hahn said his office had handled about eight thousand cases but he had no knowledge of what happened to the ten thousand others in the statistics listed by the police. In any event, for many weeks after the riots, grand juries were busy with indictments and the courts were clogged with cases arising from the Los Angeles calamity.

Out of a 1990 census population of 3,425,000 in the nation's second-largest city, most of the rioting, arson, and looting was confined to the inner city's south central district with a much smaller total of people, businesses, and dwellings. The police estimated the population in that area at the time of the riots consisted of 48 percent blacks, 45 percent Hispanics, and a much smaller percentage of Asian Americans and non-Hispanic whites. It was charged long afterward that the damage attributed to looting in the south central district had hurt a group of Korean-owned shops most of all.

With few exceptions, communities outside the most severely affected areas were spared. In the much larger area covering suburban Anaheim and Riverside as well as Los Angeles's central district, the 1990 census figures gave a population of 14,500,000. Of that, the black population was given as 8.5 percent, Asians 9.2 percent; Hispanics 33 percent with the rest being non-Hispanic whites.

. . .

In addressing the nation on the night of May 1 from the White House, the president said he believed the rioting in Los Angeles had been due to "the brutality of the mob" and added, "Let me assure you I will use whatever force is necessary to restore order."

On May 7, after a thirty-eight-hour tour of the city to see for himself what had happened, he told reporters that he wanted to find out what had gone wrong in Los Angeles. He added, "Things weren't right before. . . . Things aren't right in too many cities across the country. And we must not return to the status quo. Not here, not in any city where the system perpetuates failure and hatred and poverty and despair."

What the president proposed immediately, in addition to the use of federal funds to help damaged shops and homeowners to make necessary repairs and provide food and shelter for those who needed it, consisted mainly of the following:

—The creation of "tax-free enterprise zones" for the restoration of totally ruined businesses and factories in blighted areas.

—More money for children's educational "head start" programs.

—Larger home-relief funding.

Governor Clinton, as the prospective Democratic nominee for president, also toured the city but not at the same time as the president once calm had been restored. What he suggested was more social planning based on using funds diverted from the nation's military budget to make a beginning on rebuilding the ruins of south central Los Angeles and thereafter attacking the requirements of other inner cities across the land with problems as severe as those of the California metropolis.

In response to a White House spokesman's charge that the riots could have had a deep-seated cause in the "Great Society" programs sponsored by President Lyndon Baines Johnson in the 1960s, the Democratic candidate counterattacked by blaming twelve years of inaction by the Reagan and Bush administrations.

Such exchanges as these between the prospective major party candidates for the presidency in the fall campaign served to emphasize the lack of a serious political dialogue to try to relieve the spread of urban blight in America and its effect on the millions of people who were trapped in the inner cities through no fault of their own.

This, after all, was not South Africa. In the United States, there was no apartheid, no law legally separating the races that had produced years of rioting and revolutionary activity in South Africa. Still, it was common knowledge among all parties that the unspoken barriers between the races in America, as the Kerner Commission had found, had led to discrimination and segregation that "have long permeated much of American life" and "now threaten the future of every American."

To this, after the Los Angeles rioting, Senator Bill Bradley of New Jersey added, "The fire next time is going to engulf all of us."

Many in American urban areas feared this, too, even though they had in large part retreated from the cities to what they believed to be the safer redoubts of the suburbs. However, relatively few such people along with many millions of other Americans were willing to pay in higher taxes for the kind of costly radical change that was believed necessary. Nor could they be blamed if an element of trust between the minorities themselves and the non-Hispanic white majority did not follow when there was no assurance that the situation could be improved no matter how much money was spent.

The more fortunate people of the greatest metropolis in the land,

New York City, could not forever look down on the black community of Harlem or live beside the even larger black center of Brooklyn, Bedford-Stuyvesant, and merely shake their heads at the human misery that was exposed to them daily. Nor could the White House, regardless of which party was in power, do more than spread a little money around in the massive black community in the nation's capital. The same was true of the slums in many another urban area, where millions of people had to struggle every day against deprivation, hunger, and crime merely to stay alive.

There were many more publicized issues in this latest presidential campaign—the economy and unemployment, crime and the life-threatening drug traffic, abortion, the environment and education, among others—but attempts to close the racial breach appeared to many to be a prerequisite to advances on all other fronts. Until the American people and their chosen leaders recognized it, many a social scientist argued, very little of permanent advantage to the country could be expected despite all the promises and proposals of the presidential candidates.

. . .

Nothing of consequence beyond a fresh allotment of federal funds happened after the riots in Los Angeles to ease the desperate condition of the people of the inner city who had absorbed the largest casualties and suffered the greatest damage. Long after the federal troops and National Guard had been withdrawn, the main government objective seemed to be the maintainence of an uneasy calm mainly through enlarged city police patrols in specified areas.

Despite the proposals that were still being made and discussed in connection with the presidential campaign and the promise of further action by Congress, what most people outside the most damaged areas seemed to want was enlarged protection against a possible revival of the terror of those April nights of rioting. And so, despite all President Bush's goodwill efforts and his warnings that the nation must not return to the status quo, that inevitably was what happened in Los Angeles.

Still, agencies of the federal government continued to produce warning statistics that calm could not be forever guaranteed in the inner cities either in Los Angeles or elsewhere.

The Census Bureau had found that, throughout the country, unemployment among blacks was more than twice as high as it was among whites. The median income for black households, too, was not comparable, being only 59 percent of that for whites. Among black children, it was estimated that 44 percent lived in poverty as compared with 16 percent of white children.

Discrimination also had been documented in other fields such as housing, education, and employment. For example, the Congressional Budget Office found disabled blacks were more often rejected than whites for aid from the $43.2 billion program that annually was voted to support the disabled.

The Congressional Budget Office also estimated that 44 percent of the after-tax income of all Americans went to one percent of the people, the wealthiest in the land. Calculating the gains of this group, the same source estimated that their profits had jumped from 7 percent in the 1980s to 12 percent a decade later.

By contrast, the Census Bureau issued a report in 1992 showing that 18 percent of all full-time workers in this country in 1990 had earnings below the most recently established federal poverty level of $12,195 annually (or $6.10 an hour for a forty-hour week during the fifty-week working year). That, the Census Bureau said, was up from 12.1 percent in 1979—a measure of the gap in income between the working poor and the affluent regardless of minority status. If these statistics meant anything at all, it was that the path to reduced unemployment and the maintenance of a living wage was far distant for the average American family.

The encouraging aspect of such surveys as these was the emergence of a substantial black leadership after the self-sacrifice of such courageous leaders as the assassinated Rev. Dr. Martin Luther King, Jr. Now there were about three hundred black mayors in American cities. The first black governor, L. Douglas Wilder, had been elected in Virginia. The first black chairman of the Joint Chiefs of Staff, Gen. Colin Powell, had distinguished himself both as a strategist and wise counselor on military affairs in successive Republican and Democratic administrations.

If young black youths needed role models, they were on view in TV throughout much of the year in college football and even more so in professional baseball and football teams where many commanded salaries in the millions of dollars annually. And for years, since the time of Jesse Owens in 1936 and his sprinting triumphs in Berlin that had embarrassed Hitler, black American athletes had been among the nation's most admired Olympic champions.

In Congress and state and city legislatures, too, the number of black and other minority representatives was steadily increasing; and it was just as true in annual surveys of the professions, including law, medicine, education, social science, and communications. But much still remained to be done to encourage minority children to try to make something of themselves despite the discouragement of their beginnings.

.   .   .

When federal relief finally came to battered Los Angeles, it was part of a package deal between President Bush and his Democratic opponents in Congress to grant emergency aid to the nation's distressed cities. Each side, maneuvering cautiously in a presidential election year to deflect further public criticism of the Washington Establishment from an angry electorate, could then rightfully claim credit for pet programs here and there.

The president won his "enterprise zones" to try to restore ruined businesses in the ghetto as well as his law-and-order initiatives, including a renewed war on inner city drug dealers. The Democrats in Congress took credit for new or improved social programs such as the extension of unemployment benefits, job training, better basic education for millions of children, and greater relief efforts to help the poor.

The unanswered question, in view of the already large annual budget deficits and the national debt of $4 trillion, was how the government expected to pay for these programs. Except for Governor Clinton's suggestion of tax increases for the wealthy and a five-year plan for cutting the national debt, it seemed certain that future generations, for the most part, would be handed much of the total bill for rebuilding the inner cores of America's most damaged cities.

Despite all the publicity for President Bush's initiatives and Governor Clinton's claims to produce more funding for relief than the current occupant of the White House, there was a recognizable limit to what both could do and what Congress could reasonably be expected to appropriate.

The president had already accomplished all that he could possibly expect Congress to concede to him in appropriations of sufficient size to produce benefits for even a minimum of minorities in the nation's inner cities. As for Governor Clinton's hope of cutting the budget deficit in half through his program of reducing government expense and taxing the rich, budgetary experts had already given warning that the Democratic candidate's projections for success were questionable. And that, all too soon, was verified when he was elected and took office to face the same limitations for help to the nation's inner cities that had frustrated his predecessor.

Such realistic experiences in politics in America, too, were part of the consequences of the Los Angeles riots. Over many years, such financial and social efforts might well ease at least some of the nation's problems in the inner cities, but there was general agreement among most leaders of minority peoples as well as the majority that the healing process in America would have to be given a much higher priority than it had generally received in the latter part of this century.

In his first year in the White House, Clinton caught something of the needed changes in heart and mind when he spoke from the pulpit in Memphis that Dr. King used the night before he was assassinated in 1988. The new president uttered what he imagined Dr. King would have said to the American people about their social crisis had he lived: "I did not live and die to see the American family destroyed. . . . I fought to stop white people being so filled with hate that they would wreak violence on black people. I did not fight for the right of black people to murder other black people . . ."

It follows that for the nation to break out of its current mind-set will take courage, enormous patience, and time well into the next century.

5

As California Goes . . .

Millions of people in California were disturbed by a slumping economy before the Los Angeles riots shook the state as well as much of the American west. Afterward, as public concern turned into public anger, George Bush's reelection campaign faltered.

The reason was simple, tough, and readily understandable. In more than a hundred years, any Republican who couldn't win California also lost the presidency.

This was what brought President Bush flying to the Golden State a half dozen times during the primary election season of 1992 although he had clinched his renomination. Neither he nor the Republican veterans running his campaign could be sure how the state would go in the election in November. That situation, as they fully realized, would persist for as long as Ross Perot remained an undeclared independent presidential candidate, something most polls confirmed at the time.

The Democrats, however, did not take advantage of their opportunity at once to make gains in the state at the president's expense. After failing to be elected to the White House for twenty of the previous twenty-four years, they had been slow to unite behind the presidential candidacy of Governor Clinton although he had maintained and extended his lead in the primaries after New Hampshire. Still, the Washington leadership hesitated about embracing his cause. Clinton himself, shying away from the traditional Democratic leaning toward liberalism to try to conciliate old-line party conservatives, hadn't provided much in the way of inspiring leadership.

As a result, while the president and Perot were fighting each other in California and elsewhere, Clinton was still finishing third in some important polls. It was an extraordinary situation for an ever-shifting presidential campaign, but then, California is an extraordinary state.

.   .   .

Elderly Republicans of another era often referred to their Gilded Age of the last century with the expression, "As Maine goes, so goes the nation." That was because Maine then voted in September and invariably went Republican.

California's claim to leadership in electing American presidents was based on more substantial evidence. It had long since become the largest state in the union with almost 30 million people, 12 percent of the nation's population, and it cast one fifth of the votes in the electoral college out of the 270 needed to elect a president.

Although Republican candidates such as Eisenhower, Nixon, and Reagan had had little trouble taking California in recent presidential elections, Bush in 1988 had barely squeaked through against a weak opponent. Now he was in trouble in the greatest Republican stronghold in the state, Orange County. At one stop in late spring, he had conceded to an outdoor crowd of dissatisfied voters that he was facing "a hurricane out there." It was all of that. With an effort, however, he regained his self-possession and concluded defiantly, "I'm not going to be their spear-catcher for the rest of the year."

The White House public relations people tried to help by producing what they called a "new" Bush. Sometimes, it was a pretty hammy performance with the sixty-eight-year-old president shamelessly working crowds, tieless and in shirtsleeves, grabbing at myriads of outstretched hands for a brief touch that constituted a political handshake plus a firmly pasted-on smile. He also could vary the performance now and then by patting the heads of somewhat apprehensive small children. (Bill Clinton had gone him one better by playing the saxophone with almost professional skill at a late night television appearance with Arsenio Hall's band.)

Still, for all his folksy corn-muffin attitudes, the "new" Bush wasn't changing the numbers in the opinion polls. If anything, as the spring progressed, the numbers were getting worse instead of better. That reflected in general the downward slope of the state's once-booming economy during the Reagan era's sponsorship of immense military hardware production. Sadly enough for the Bush White House, this was now history and nothing much could be done to re-create it unless Saddam Hussein of Iraq or some other public scourge could be depicted as a threat to the nation.

During the Cold War, the existence of the Soviet Union as a rival global superpower had made it easy for conservatives to dispose of inconvenient opponents by linking them, fairly or not, with the Communist enemy. But with the Soviet collapse, that weapon no longer was available although President Bush hopefully experimented for a time by associating his foes with something called the "Big L," supposedly a liberal menace. Only it didn't go over very well with the public in a damaged economy.

In California, moreover, the damage was mounting. It was becoming known throughout the state that Governor Wilson and his Democratic legislative opponents were facing a budgetary shortfall of $10 billion or more for the new fiscal year. Because the state's reserve funds now were exhausted, it followed that payless paydays for state employees and unpaid state bills for services would result amid a presidential campaign unless the governor somehow could win agreement on a combination of tax increases and drastically reduced services.

It wasn't likely with unemployment in the state exceeding 9 percent, more than a national average that was already being considered disastrous. In vain, President Bush complained that all this was the fault of the Democratic-controlled Congress that he tried to credit with powers beyond that of his high office. It didn't impress the electorate any more than the image of the "new" Bush unhappily working crowds in the Golden State.

.   .   .

All imagery and other heavy-handed political pretense aside, the numbers in California provided a fixed political equation that all the hippety-hop air tours, speeches, and presidential exploits in crowds couldn't change. To win California, what the president had to do was to try to hold down traditional Democratic majorities in the state that were supplied mainly from San Francisco and Los Angeles, then stimulate majorities in excess of 60 percent in the great Republican stronghold of down-state Orange County. In 1988, Bush had been able to win narrowly over a hard-pressed Michael Dukakis primarily because Orange County gave the then vice president a majority of almost 40 percent of the total vote. Even the most enthusiastic old-line Republican four years later, however, couldn't see that happening again.

In that reelection year, Orange appeared to be hurt economically despite its reputation as the stronghold of wealth and privilege in the state. It was out of the question, therefore, that the president could repeat his feat in 1988 of overcoming Dukakis's statewide lead with a

540,000-vote Orange County majority that enabled him to take California by a mere 350,000 votes out of nearly 10 million cast.

To be sure, before California's June primary in 1992, the president still was reputed by reliable polls to be leading Clinton but not by much. The *Orange County Register,* widely read in the area, had taken an unfriendly view of some of the president's statewide campaigning as ineffective. Then, too, the Bush campaign organization seemed to be in a continually jittery condition, and the president was criticized by some of his supporters who believed his leadership to be weakened.

This was not, by any means, because of some imagined superiority of either Governor Clinton and his Democratic organization or the almost completely disorganized volunteer group trying to handle Perot's still undeclared independent drive. A well-managed, capably directed Republican organization in the Reagan or Nixon years would have bowled over the Democrats and independents in short order. However, in a sinking economy, the Republicans supporting Bush seemed in disarray—much of the president's problem in California.

When the Los Angeles riots exploded and some critics charged that the president had hesitated in handling the crisis, his position in California became critical. It remained so while Perot appeared to be gaining strength without much of an organization and the Clinton campaign began to show signs of coming alive.

. . .

It was then that California's fiscal problems developed with a profound shock that was felt across the land and deeply affected the presidential contest.

Regardless of whatever was happening in that campaign, an unbelieving nation learned that as of July 1 the largest and supposedly the richest state in the union would run out of cash and thereafter would have to pay its employees and its bills with IOUs while standing up its creditors. No one in authority could say when that crisis would be resolved.

Every segment of life in the state was affected, even the students at California's once superior state educational system headed by the University of California itself. Unpaid faculty people served notice of departure. Some classes had to be canceled. Some specialties couldn't be offered for lack of an instructor.

Concern spread across the land. For if this could happen to California, lesser states also knew they would feel the pinch sooner rather than later. Public confidence in government, already near an all-time low, plummeted sharply as the energency in the once Golden State tightened.

Among Republican and Democratic campaigners in the presidential struggle, and Perot's undeclared campaign as well, everybody agreed that new soundings had to be taken to try to assess what effect the fiscal crisis would have on how California's fifty-four electoral votes would go in the November election. In the June 2 California primary, almost a month before the emergency took hold, there had been no surprises; Bush, as expected, had come through the Republican primary unscathed, and Clinton, despite a challenge from former Governor Brown of California, also had done well in the Democratic voting.

Now, however, with the Democratic majorities in both houses of the California legislature solidly against the Republican governor, Pete Wilson, and even conservative Republicans in Orange County wavering in their loyalty to the state's chief executive, any prediction about how the voters of the Golden State would respond in the voting for president on November 3 was bound to be hazardous.

So the nation watched, waited, and worried over California's future as an indication of what might yet be in store one day in the future for others among the remaining forty-nine states. There was no movement in Sacramento, California's capital. Despite the emergency, neither Governor Wilson nor his Democratic-controlled legislature would budge on adopting a budget that would, however temporarily, break the impasse.

So, week after week as the presidential campaign changed direction, California was still a reckless IOU state in a depressed economy. The banks within the state warned that there would be a limit to how long it would be possible to honor the IOUs and the state's credit in general.

During the previous fiscal year, a similar emergency had been resolved when the Democratic legislators persuaded the Republican governor to raise state taxes by $7 billion to resolve a major budget gap. As a result, Governor Wilson took the hit from the electorate instead of his Democratic opponents; even in the Republican stronghold of Orange County, the governor was denounced for giving in to boosting taxes still more.

That was the prime reason the governor had refused new Democratic suggestions for another tax increase this year, which, had he acceded, would have slammed the door on any possibility that President Bush could carry the state in November. Even so, because of the

36

new IOU crisis, California already had begun to tilt toward the Democrats and Governor Clinton.

As the situation stood well into the spring, the state would not be restored to fiscal health, however temporarily, until the governor and the legislature adopted a budget somewhere around $57 to $60 billion for the fiscal year that would start on July 1. Because the governor had stood fast against another tax boost, it followed that deep cuts would have to be made in state services, including education, public welfare, health insurance, especially for poor people, and grants to local governments.

Nobody among the state's scrappy band of politicians, least of all those in the governor's office, wanted to be held responsible for such reductions, the boosting of state fees for various services (instead of personal taxes), and a big squeeze on local governments. In the legislature in particular, both Democrats and Republicans were nervously aware that an embittered electorate already had limited their terms in office and they knew full well that they could be hurt by still more such initiatives and referendums, a feature of the California system of government.

.   .   .

California was paying dearly for its rapid growth earlier in the century. It no longer could afford to provide the generous state services it had made available for its 30 million people in the best of times. Belt tightening meant pain for all concerned—both the governors and the governed.

What had happened, in brief, was that California, like so many other states, had been caught between forced assumption of some former federal services and the allocation of former local government responsibilities to the state as well. As if that hadn't been bad enough, the continual expansion of California's population also had required greater spending for more police, firemen, sanitation workers, health and welfare needs, and, more than all else, education paid for by the state.

It could not have been much of a surprise, therefore, that not enough money could be found in a major recession to satisfy everybody's needs. It would be most difficult for the governor and legislators to explain to the voters why two hundred thousand new pupils in California primary and secondary schools would receive less per pupil than at present, when California had already slipped to thirty-fourth among the fifty states in public education spending.

The easy answer was higher taxes. Except for a boost in state fees on various services, such as automobile licenses, the governor already had been burned once and he wasn't about to go for higher taxation again when the presidential election might well be at stake. So it happened that the state was in a bind with its IOU payments and both the governor and the legislators were unyielding on budgetary issues, each being determined to protect their own turf in the immemorial manner of politicians pinned against the wall.

This stand-off continued for sixty-three days after the onset of the emergency when a postmidnight session of the legislature finally gave in to the governor. The state was given a tight $57.4 billion budget and arrangements at last were made to substitute cash for IOUs and unpaid bills. The tragedy, as nearly every informed public source outside the circle of combatants agreed, was that the whole mess could have been resolved on the deadline, avoiding all the agony.

Still, for President Bush and his rivals, the Congress and the governments of the other forty-nine states, California's grim experience pointed to a lesson the country would have to learn all too soon. Either taxes and payment for services would go up or there would be a cut in entitlements and other benefits because of the drawn-out recession, the huge cost of the unemployed, and other heavy expenses for the sick, the disadvantaged, and the aging.

The national cornucopia of benefits was not inexhaustible.

.   .   .

Who was hurt in California? Although it does not automatically follow that the same portion of the population would suffer similarly elsewhere or at the federal level either in this recession or the next, the temporary solution of the problem in the Golden State may give some indication of what lies ahead for state governments and people caught in straitened circumstances elsewhere.

What went first under the new state budget was welfare, in which grants were cut by at least 8 percent. A single mother with two children, for example, had to get along on $625 a month, a $38 drop. The state's grants to the aged and the disabled had almost as deep a slash, being cut $37 to $608 a month. Health insurance for the poor also was hard hit with reductions in reimbursement for surgery, radiology, and anesthesia as well as a limitation on prescriptions.

Public education took a reduction as well by maintaining state spending per pupil the same as the previous year even though attendance had increased by two hundred thousand, thus dropping California from thirty-fourth to thirty-ninth among the fifty states, a notch better than South Carolina. Community college fees were boosted from $6 to $10 a credit with an 11 percent cut in state support for the University of California and an 8 percent reduction at California State University.

It told the public something else about the legislature, however, when the Senate denied the necessary two-thirds majority to a measure calling for a reduction in the bureaucracy including the elimination of 108 public relations people.

It also told the public something about the governor when it developed that the final budget he approved, after so much finagling with his legislative opponents, allowed the state controller only $435 million in cash, an amount so small that it virtually put all concerned on notice that another fiscal crisis could be expected within the following year.

Who, then, was hurt? Mainly, those who could least stand it.

It turned out, therefore, to be a hollow victory for the governor when he could report to the people of the state that there would be no further increase in taxes for the fiscal year. Technically, that was true, but it developed that the state, by having deprived local governments of $1.3 billion in their property taxes, had put many local officials in the position of being forced to raise taxes, fees, or both.

The 2½–month exercise in budget balancing in California, therefore, wasn't altogether as honest a performance as had been claimed. What it also meant to the federal and forty-nine other state governments was that no amount of budgetary juggling could disguise the heightened cost of government services henceforth, especially in a recession.

That was another lesson an ill-prepared public had to absorb during the presidential campaign of 1992.

6

Ending the Primaries

W hen the presidential primary season ended on June 2, the non-candidate, Ross Perot, overshadowed the victors, President Bush for the Republicans and Governor Clinton for the Democrats.

Both major party candidates were wounded. The electorate was even angrier than before with government as usual. The economy was still in a bind. The United States, the world's sole remaining superpower, seemed to be adrift in a rapidly changing world.

Perot had become the vortex of this swirling political storm. Without a party and mainly through self-advertisement on televised talk and call-in shows, the billionaire had made himself such an attractive national figure that many voters in the concluding six state primaries had said they'd have voted for him, had he been on the ballot, rather than Bush or Clinton.

This was not malarkey dreamed up by lazy reporters or over-zealous pollsters. Exit polls in California, Ohio, and four other states had shown that anywhere from a quarter to a half of those questioned would have preferred Perot. The White House's anti-Perot offensive, far from knocking him out of competition, seemed for the time being to have reinvigorated him.

There was something more to this than the antigovernment, anti-incumbent phenomenon that had been characteristic of the elections and caucuses in the fifty states that had just concluded. A dropout in previous Democratic primaries, former Senator Tsongas, may have guessed right when he called the rebellion at the polls a referendum for change—change in government, change in the economy, but change above all else.

The two-party establishment, he said, was so cautious "that they're missing what's in their faces."

For President Bush, the primaries had meant nothing at all. He had quickly disposed of his sole challenger, the columnist and television figure, Pat Buchanan, after the shock of his 40 percent protest vote in the New Hampshire primary. But the operation against Perot outside the primary voting booths had to date been a disaster. Already, the early calls for more aggressive leadership in the president's campaign were being intensified despite a White House reshuffle in which Samuel K. Skinner, the secretary of transportation, had replaced John Sununu as chief of staff.

Once again, rumors were spreading that the secretary of state, James A. Baker, would be drafted to put vigor into the sagging Bush campaign as he had done for the previous one in 1988. But Baker showed no inclination to give up his diplomatic post for the hurly-burly of domestic politics when the president's prestige was sinking to an all-time low.

A *New York Times*–CBS poll, the first with the approach of a long, weary summer, showed the president's disapproval rating had mounted to 78 percent, within four points of the adverse showing for President Carter in June 1980, when that unfortunate Democratic president already was being marked down as a loser. The same poll had Perot virtually tied with the president with a three-point margin of error—32 percent for Bush, 30 percent for Perot, 24 percent for Clinton, and the remaining 14 percent undetermined.

However, not all was sweetness and light for Perot. The respondents in the poll, by close to half who were questioned, said they were dissatisfied with all three. After that, Perot's own disapproval rating suddenly doubled for no apparent reason except the public's changeable moods. Nevertheless, it marked the first time that the Texan had shown that he, too, was vulnerable in this passing strange election year.

About two weeks after the end of the primaries, on June 17, a CBS television documentary concerning the Watergate scandal and President Nixon's forced resignation didn't help matters. On the twentieth anniversary of the break-in at Democratic National Headquarters in the Watergate complex by Republican burglars, the scandal as recalled could only have fed the public's increased doubts about government in general and presidential performances in particular.

There was little comfort for any thoughtful American voter in the booming voice that asked at the end of the televised Watergate memoir: "Could it happen again?" The answer was yes, cold and unqualified.

.　　.　　.

If there was any relief for President Bush in his position that June, it was that Governor Clinton, his Democratic rival, also had troubles. The Arkansan appeared to be portrayed to the electorate, despite his triumph in the primary elections and caucuses, as a loser mainly because he continued to trail his two rivals. This may not have been fair, considering all the obstacles Clinton had overcome, but it was ingrained in the rough-and-tumble of presidential politics in America, which assumed that the candidates were always beetle-browed primitives who would slug and batter and berate each other to occupy the highest office in the land for four years. Those who tried to run a respectable campaign, literate and reasonable in the manner of an Adlai Stevenson or a Hubert Humphrey, a Wendell Willkie or a Tom Dewey, were bound to be criticized by their detractors as born losers.

That also wasn't fair but it was quintessentially in the American political tradition. When candidates of superior intellectual attainment burst through this political underbrush to impress the electorate and win the presidency, their feat deserved to be called a political miracle. In so seemingly hopeless a position, Clinton made his first important bid for the attention of thoughtful voters with an appeal to reason rather than the usual rock 'em and sock 'em approach. That took both sensitivity under stress and an unusual brand of political courage.

Although an early series of position papers the Arkansas governor had put out on national problems had been lost in the uproar over abortion and the Los Angeles riots, he issued a new series on what he proposed to do if elected. It should not be imagined that these were pounced on with delight and featured on television and the better newspapers as the work of a genius; in the television age, political genius was in short supply and ranked far below soap operas and midnight comedians. What impressed me, for example, was the suggestion that a relatively untried candidate for the White House had enough trust in the rebellious public disposition to resort to reason rather than the mailed fist in an emergency not of his own making. By contrast, at that same period. President Bush was flailing away at the Democratic Congress for all his faults and Ross Perot was refusing to issue his program for the nation except to demand the public trust in whatever he chose to do.

The first of Clinton's new position papers was far from brilliant, however. Mainly what he proposed to heal an ailing economy was to pull back on two of his previous proposals, one to give the middle class a tax cut and the other to sweep aside the enormous federal deficit within four years. Both these had been criticized previously by economic experts as pie-in-the-sky efforts.

Clinton deserved good marks for trying again, this time with more agreeable results. What he hoped to do in his latest position paper on the economy was to cut federal government spending by $150 billion a year and increase taxes by the same amount, primarily on those most able to bear the heavier load, people earning more than $200,000 a year and large, prosperous corporations.

In this manner, he said he hoped to spare the elderly and the poor from reductions in Social Security, Medicare, and other entitlements. Atop that, he also proposed a $200 billion program of shakily defined projects to increase employment. Later still, he promised a more adequate public health program, improvements in public education, and greater efforts in other domestic areas.

Among the Democratic faithful—the officeholders, party officials, and the more liberal-minded press (of which a minority had survived)—there was a buzz of favorable comment on Clinton's latest show of good sense in his presidential campaign. But even they had to concede that his economic planning was too optimistic compared with the enormity of the problem.

Despite such stumbling blocks, Clinton still managed to end his primary campaigning with enough Democratic National Convention delegates to win the party's presidential nomination. He had gone into the last six primaries in Alabama, Montana, New Mexico, and New Jersey, besides California and Ohio, needing only 167 delegates to win the nomination. The outcome put him well past the 2,145 delegates he required.

However, Clinton's triumph didn't put him in an exultant mood. Now, as he said, he would have to go to the "larger electorate" to defeat an incumbent president and a billionaire. To the public, he made this appeal: "If you want an outsider, if you want someone who's passed a program, taken on interest groups, got a plan for the future, that's my campaign."

Almost immediately, he modified his grandiose plan for disposing of the national debt within four years as far too ambitious. He also was much more prudent about announcing in advance whom he intended to tax and for how much. He wanted to sound more conservative.

So the Clinton campaign changed course amid an apparent shift of opinion in his favor that couldn't have been forecast in the snows of New Hampshire. He knew, though, that his gains were temporary and warned they could just as easily vanish.

.   .   .

It would be simplistic to blame the weakness of the once stable two-party system in the United States on what might very well have been called Perotism for want of a better term. For all his faults, the erratic Texan did not create the shaky position in which both major parties found themselves at the height of his undeclared independent presidential drive. Nor did he, to any considerable extent, widen the internal divisions within each party that made them both an ill-assorted collection of clashing political and social interests.

What Perot did do was to expose the fundamental problems within the American body politic that had led to well-nigh three decades of divided government, a Republican presidency except for the four Carter years against a largely Democratic-controlled Congress. It was a position in which presidents applied their veto to the wishes of the congressional majority, especially in the Bush years when that president exercised thirty-one vetoes, and the Democratic leadership in Congress replied in kind. This, basically, was what contributed to an almost habitual mistrust among large sections of the American public in big government.

It was not a situation in which the parties had become so much alike, as they did in the disastrous 1930s when Franklin Roosevelt ridiculed them as "Tweedledum and Tweedledee," then led the Democrats perceptibly to the left with his New Deal reforms. Thirty-two years later, Barry Goldwater began what turned out to be an equally drastic shift of the Republican party to the right by capitalizing on the public's fear of Soviet-style communism and Soviet challenges to America.

However, despite the Republicans' string of presidential election successes in the latter twentieth century, this did not mean that the GOP had become a stronger and more cohesive party any more than that FDR had permanently solidified the Democratic coalition of convenience. The Reagan Democrats—the largely big city Democratic conservatives—turned away from their mild liberalism in the 1980s to support Ronald Reagan and George Bush, marking the first big break in the respective coalitions supporting each major party.

It was to be expected, once Perot gave them an alternative to Bush's reelection, that many of the Democratic Reaganites would desert to Perot's undeclared presidential cause. They did with a whoosh that unsettled the remains of the Reagan-Bush Republican coalition.

At the same time, not many former Democratic Reaganites skipped over the Texan billionaire to return to the Democratic party with its various ill-assorted combinations. The party included a big-city combination of liberal-minded intellectuals plus large groupings of minorities including Hispanics, blacks, and Asians, millions of stranded blue-collar labor union members, a few surviving Norman Thomas Socialists, and an even smaller group of always dissatisfied younger radicals, a scattering of suburban liberals, and the remains of the New Deal farm belt vote.

Unlike the Republicans, whose disparate composition held together mainly because of repeated presidential victories, the Democrats in defeat acquired much more of a reputation for internal quarrels. Whether it was the infighting or the liberal-left reputation of their former Democratic associations, the dissatisfied Reagan Democrats for the most part appeared to stay put with Perot for as long as he maintained his campaign. It was this reason, as much as his political inclinations, that caused Bill Clinton to assume an unexpectedly pseudoconservative tinge in his opening appeals for broader support after his victory in the primaries. Evidently, he wasn't too worried about losing substantial additional numbers of Democrats to Perot. He did realize that he needed the support of the Reagan Democrats, which was reason enough for his movement toward the middle-of-the-road part of the electorate—often the deciding factor in other recent presidential elections.

By contrast, when Bush also moved farther to the right to broaden his appeal to the arch conservatives of his party, he discouraged an important group of Republican women who had been among his most fervent supporters in his 1988 presidential campaign. This time, they were upset mainly because of his voluble assault on legalized abortion, which had led him to support the proposed Republican platform plank calling for a constitutional amendment to bar abortions under all conditions. Although the exodus from their party was not marked at once, the threat of a formation of Clinton Republicans, based on the abortion issue alone, was very real and the Republican leadership could not ignore it.

.   .   .

At the end of the primaries, President Bush's approval rating in June had slumped to only 30 percent in a *Time* magazine poll, 58 points below his fantastic high after the Persian Gulf War. Clinton's position was improving just then despite the Democrats' well-deserved reputation for shooting themselves in the foot.

As for Perot, he seemed to have mesmerized a substantial part of middle-class America, and not only the shifting Reagan Democrats, to support his independent but still undeclared campaign. In so doing, he amply illustrated the irrelevance of four months of primary voting and campaigning beginning at least a month before the February 18 New Hampshire primary.

Some may have laughed at him. Others may have moaned or groaned at the susceptibility of the average American voter to put trust in an untested figure who had been popularized mainly by televised talk and call-in shows. Perot had amply proved, however, that it would be a colossal error to underrate him and his promises to re-create the American dream in unspecified ways.

If the electorate as a whole hadn't realized it before, the Texan had demonstrated how easily a well-planned, amply financed TV blitz could promote the presidential ambitions of a wealthy businessman. Even a used care salesman would have been impressed with his know-how in selling himself.

Still more impressive, Perot was ahead in some of the early June polls although not by much and the undecided vote was large, indeed. June polls, as many were quick to point out, weren't necessarily a foretaste of November results. Still, the ghosts of many an old-time political boss must have been choking in their smoke-filled Valhalla at the way this utterly unconventional man had talked himself into being an undeclared presidential contender.

What had happened to both major parties was that large numbers of voters in both organizations, dismayed by continuing uncertainty over the economy, no longer were motivated by what once had been an almost passionate loyalty to their parties' candidates and their principles. This allegiance had been withering for many years, apparently reaching its climax with Ronald Reagan's second-term victory in 1984 over a hapless Democratic candidate, Walter Mondale, by forty-nine states to one.

Now all the available evidence indicated that a profound reshaping of the American political process was under way, motivated mainly by the Perot candidacy. The decline of party loyalties faced with the growing appeal of his projected independent run for the presidency, however, was not the only factor in the realignment of the electorate. Serious sectional differences, especially in the former Confederate states of the South, also were important because some already were weakening on their well-nigh habitual Republican voting record toward century's end. Here, race nearly always was an unmentioned but vitally important issue on which any politician was bound to capitalize in due course.

The Democrats, having lost the once Solid South in the liberal era during which President Kennedy's civil rights campaign brought more force to the cause of black equality, now could scarcely be any more hurt than they already had been in the previous Reagan/Bush campaigns. This time, however, for as long as Perot remained in the presidential contest, declared or undeclared, he seemed more likely to inherit some of the dissident Southern states than the Democrats under Clinton. Clinton, as a result, appeared to have a more difficult road ahead of him in the coming fall campaign than he did in the primaries. He was given little chance in the polls, therefore, of making much of a dent in Perot's support no matter how much progress he made against Bush.

In June, it was that kind of unpredictable, upside-down campaign.

7

The President at Bay

Something had to be done, people in the White House concluded. Despite President Bush's fifty-state sweep of the Republican primaries and caucuses that guaranteed his renomination at the forthcoming national convention, his reelection now was definitely endangered.

It was bad enough for him to be one–two with Ross Perot in the opinion polls. Now the Clinton candidacy was also moving up in the polls and the Democrats were uniting behind him instead of fighting among themselves.

The president came up with a new approach. It seemed that he had been trying, in his more recent stump speeches, to sound a cheery note of optimism by pointing to signs, clearly visible to him, that the economy was improving. The way he put it, times were better than the public had been led to believe but the media weren't telling the story.

Suiting action to fit circumstance, the president held a full-dress news conference in the White House's East Room two days after the end of the primaries to spread the glad tidings to the nation. The slight improvement he noted in the government's figures was just a temporary blip.

The president's premature announcement of economic recovery, therefore, took a bad hit in an unsympathetic press. Faith in the president's judgment waned to such an extent that he complained to a June rally of his campaign contributors that he wasn't being given proper credit for his achievements, something that made him "sick and tired" after his four-year effort in the White House.

The president's strategists then tried to come up with a sounder approach on the campaign trail. Some pointed out that the Bush record on foreign policy had been consistently excellent: the Cold War triumph over the Soviets, the Gulf War victory, and so on. The Democrats' insistence on hammering away at the economy and the needs of the home front, however, caused Bush's people reluctantly to agree that they, too, would have to look homeward.

There was a lingering feeling among the smart money in the White House that what the Bush campaign really needed was another Willie Horton case—the convicted murderer hypothetically linked to the failed Democratic campaign for Michael Dukakis in 1988. Somebody even suggested that maybe Hillary Rodham Clinton would make a better Willie Horton issue for 1992.

The reasoning here is difficult for an outsider to follow but apparently the notion of the political strategists was to contend that Mrs. Clinton, as a working wife whose place wasn't in the kitchen, symbolized what was wrong with the American family today. However, since working wives sometimes made up a majority of the women voters who went to the polls, the suggestion on the face of it made no sense. Mrs. Clinton was spared, but only temporarily.

Finally, that led to a decision to use an old-time, surefire campaign issue: the restoration of family life in America, despite all the diversions threatening the American home. Once before, that issue had been used to boost President Bush's standing, but once again, the president failed to take the lead. As always, the economy was the number-one issue.

And no wonder! The June figures showed there still were about 10 million people without jobs, another 30 million on federal food stamps, and millions more facing a loss of employment. Business bankruptcies were up. Foreign trade was down. The once mighty dollar now was trailing the German mark and the Japanese yen on the financial markets.

Still, what the president wanted to do was to get government off the backs of the people. To the contrary, Governor Clinton was proposing bigger and better government to help those who no longer could help themselves and make the top one percent in the income tax bracket pay higher taxes. As for Ross Perot, he had a book written for him and still made the circuit of the nighttime TV talk shows.

Understandably, the Bush White House became inordinately sensitive to anything that might have affected movement in the stock market. When the Congressional Budget Office issued a report that the Reagan boom had benefited only 1 percent of American families with major gains, it touched off one of the worst rows in the early stages of the presidential campaign. Governor Clinton at once accused the president of pauperizing the middle class. In return, Bush's people charged Clinton with using Stalinist methods.

That in turn brought up, for the umpteenth time, the president's admitted error in violating his pledge against raising taxes. Even then, however, with an anxious eye on the stock market's performance, the White House still tried to fight back. This time, President Bush blamed Congress for much of the failures that had been attributed to the executive office, but without any significant alteration in his standing in the polls.

The president's economic adviser, Michael Boskin, also tried his luck. He announced that the economy was in "structural imbalance" (whatever that may have meant) over which he contended that the president could not possibly exercise any control. Nor could he explain why. Treasury Secretary Nicholas Brady then linked the Federal Reserve to Congress as jointly responsible for the country's economic failures. Congress, Brady explained, was responsible because it kept Bush's economic program (of a cut in excess profit taxes) on the back burner. The Fed, the treasury secretary added, also had goofed by not moving fast enough to cut interest rates.

What the president finally did to try to end this unprofitable argument was to claim credit for stalling the growth of inflation, which was one of the by-products of the recession. It was scarcely the economic triumph that the Oval Office believed it to be. Actually, it was a product of the times.

．　　　．　　　．

President Bush's championship of the embattled portions of the business community, too, created difficulties for him as he headed for the most important part of his campaign for reelection. The Democrats in Congress now were criticizing his proposed reduction in the excess profit tax as a favor for the wealthy and refused to approve it. Governor Clinton centered his attack on the president for what was described as the "trickle-down theory of economic recovery," meaning that if the people who control business could be enriched, they would let some of their gains extend to the less fortunate dependent on them.

Like much campaign rhetoric, the criticism was overly simplified both in Congress and on the campaign trail. During the economic downturn, however, the average American families most affected by bad times did not worry too much about the niceties of language.

The position of the presidency in a lengthening economic downturn was put differently by the American economist John Kenneth

Galbraith in his small but still useful history of the 1929 stock market crash: "A bubble can easily be punctured. But to incise it with a needle so that it subsides gradually is a task of no small delicacy."

If President Bush and his advisers were hunting for the right needle in the White House's economic haystacks, they either hadn't found it or didn't have the faintest idea of how to go about using it. But then, the opposition was in pretty much the same fix with Clinton's as yet untried efforts to center on reduction of the national debt.

As for Perot, it seemed enough for him to tell the nation, as he so often did when reporters asked him about his economic plan, that bringing back prosperity to America would be so very, very simple. He often remarked airily, on and off TV, that he could do it "without even working up a sweat."

It did appear to many of those who worked for him that he believed it enough for people in general to know that he had proved his competence in making money for himself and now was offering these golden talents to the nation to resolve this nagging economic crisis. However, trust in the tycoons of Wall Street—not necessarily including Perot—was very low at that time. During the Bush administration alone, once the recession hit, efforts to punish wrongdoers in the nation's financial exchanges had produced evidence of some of the most monumental frauds on record in the application of insider trading and other illegal ways of making big money.

Although most presidential administrations show great zeal in pushing federal prosecutions of big-buck piracy in an election year, the sins of such larcenous operations uncovered in the Bush years shocked even hardheaded Wall Street.

The worst of the lot for fraudulent dealings was the "junk bond" king, Michael R. Milken, who was convicted in 1990, fined $900 million, and sentenced to ten years in prison (but was set free in about two years). His company, Drexel Burnham Lambert, which had helped merchandise his high-risk, high-yield securities, was fined $650 million and went out of business for good.

In another case, this one a state prosecution, a companion ten-year prison sentence was given to a sharp savings-and-loan operator, Charles H. Keating, Jr. His conviction came as the presidential campaign was getting under way as a prelude to an even stiffer federal case against him in the postelection period. In the state's case, he was found guilty of fraud by peddling "junk bonds" to depositors of his failed Lincoln Savings and Loan Association, with a $250,000 fine added to his prison term.

The two verdicts were evidence of the correctness of the Congressional Budget Office's warning that people least able to afford losses were usually the principal victims of fraud. Even with the imposing record of federal prosecutions of white collar crime in the Bush years, it was clear enough that gambling with other people's money and running up losses high in the billions was scarcely a part of the American dream.

With the economy showing no sign of recovery and stock and bank fraud increasing both in number and total losses, President Bush obviously could expect little help in that area for his chances for reelection. Somewhere, somehow, he needed a better break in this altogether difficult reelection campaign.

. . .

When all else failed, the president usually could count on his skill in foreign affairs to swing a fickle public opinion in his favor. At this stage in his reelection effort, however, he had to give up much of his foreign travel. If foreign leaders wanted to see him, they had to come to the White House.

Among the first to show up was the formidable President Boris Yeltsin of the reinvented Russia, now a shaky republic. His mission was to complete a treaty with the United States for a drastic reduction in their joint nuclear armaments. The deal was to allow Russia only 3,000 nuclear warheads as against 3,500 for the United States out of the current total for both of 22,500 warheads.

The visit came off a lot better than expected. The big Russian so stirred a joint session of Congress with his fervent promises of no more wars and no more lying from Moscow that he won thirteen standing ovations from the enthusiastic members.

True, there was grumbling on the home front as it became known that Yeltsin also would be going back with some extra American favors when there was such demonstrable need among large sections of the American people. What the visitor received were assurances of favorable American tariff treatment of imports from Russia (which amounted to very little), expansion of export credits for American companies willing to do business with Russia, and a modest package of loans and credits.

However, when President Bush tried arm-twisting the Japanese into accepting more American products for sale in the home islands, the familiar answer from Prime Minister Kiichi Miyazawa was the equivalent of "Sorry, no deal." The virtual Japanese blockade against American imports still was ironclad despite the vastly increased flood of Japanese exports to the United States. Besides, the Japanese leader reminded the president, Japan too was suffering from recession.

The position tempted a few American politicians to exploit what they believed to be a rising anti-Japanese feeling in the United States. The way the attitude was tested independently of the two parties' presidential campaigns was to take opinion polls to determine whether a substantial part of the American public believed Japanese exploitation of the American market had been at least partly responsible for the American recession.

Various opinion surveys, for a time, seemed to indicate support for this tentative effort to make Japan the goat for the American economic decline. That in turn may have relieved many an American industrial board room where the responsibility of indifferent American management to compete effectively with Japanese imports was being given serious study.

In a 1992 *Los Angeles Times* poll during the presidential primary season, for example, 31 percent of the respondents blamed the Japanese for America's economic troubles as against 13 percent for the Soviet's successor states. That led to some mild Japan-bashing by Senators Bob Kerrey of Nebraska and Tom Harkin of Iowa as well as former Governor Jerry Brown of California. However, the public response was dismal; people were too preoccupied with their own troubles to waste time looking for foreign villains.

As Senator Kerrey withdrew some anti-Japanese commercials made on his responsibility for television ads, he concluded, "It didn't work."

Governor Clinton's response registered the greatest change of all in American attitudes toward Japan during the presidential campaign: "It would not be in Japan's interest for America to continually struggle economically. It's not in Japan's interest for America to have ten more years in which most Americans work harder for lower pay. . . . I think we ought to begin by saying this is an important bilateral relationship, perhaps our most important one. And we want it to work."

Prime Minister Miyazawa at the time was much more worried about developing attacks at home on a whole series of bribery and influence-peddling scandals shaking his Liberal Democratic party to its roots and threatening to shorten his career at the head of government. Wisely, neither President Bush nor Governor Clinton pressed the Japanese to loosen their import quotas during the campaign after that. The LDP and Miyazawa were in enough trouble without giving them a chance to set up an anti-American diversion in Tokyo—if they dared.

Germany, the other major enemy of World War II, was treated differently by the American government. As the dominant European economic power, the Germans were leading a concerted effort to put together a twelve-nation European union with a common currency and common economic aims to take effect before the coming of the next century.

If the European union came to pass, it would be a tremendous trading bloc and a strong rival to America's foreign trading interests. But the United States, despite that, could do nothing in a practical way for or against the coming into force of the Maastricht Treaty (named after the Dutch city where it was negotiated), so President Bush, always the capable diplomat in such circumstances, repeatedly welcomed the German initiative.

It is just as well that he did, for Chancellor Helmut Kohl soon had to face up to a Nazi-style insurrection in impoverished East Germany, now a part of the West German union, against the influx of sixty thousand refugees who had fled from Romania. It was something that turned off American opinion completely once Germany asked the Romanian government to repatriate its people. Both in the foreign and domestic aspects of these German problems, Governor Clinton took little part and the Germans, like the Japanese, remained nonissues in the presidential campaign.

Even so, for the balance of 1992, the United States did not back off completely from European affairs. President Bush, at the request of the United Nations, intervened in the Serb war of "ethnic cleansing" against the Muslims in Bosnia by sending an aircraft carrier to the Adriatic to try to enforce one of the many UN Security Council cease-fires in the area and to try to insure the delivery of relief supplies, something in which Governor Clinton concurred. What Clinton also sought was to use force against the Serbs if necessary to bring food and medical aid to besieged Sarajevo, which Bush decided not to do.

In the Americas, the candidates were in greater disagreement over the treatment of thousands of refugees from military rule in Haiti who put to sea in leaky sailboats to reach American shores. When President Bush ordered the Coast Guard to turn back the refugees to save lives that would otherwise be placed at grave risk, Clinton criticized the White House. Eventually, he had to concede that Bush had been right at the time.*

---

*As president, Clinton also ordered the Coast Guard to turn back Haitian refugees. In his first year, he had no success, either, in returning President Aristide to power in Haiti.

On another problem in the Americas, the proposed Canada–Mexico–United States free trade agreement (NAFTA), President Bush ran into difficulty almost immediately when the cry was raised in the Democratic-controlled Congress that American jobs would be lost to the cheaper labor south of the border. Governor Clinton, after some hesitation, had endorsed the proposal but his House majority leader, Richard Gephardt of Missouri, didn't agree with either of the presidential candidates. What Gephardt wanted before anything else was done amounted to a renegotiation of the relatively weak labor and environmental provisions of the draft treaty. With that, the NAFTA pact was shelved in Congress for the duration of the campaign, which seemed to get everybody off the hook for the time being.

The president then came up with a more saleable proposal, this one involving peace in the always turbulent Middle East—something his strategists believed would help him in New York and California. With a dramatic flourish, he issued a call from the White House for still another attempt at a peace conference between Israel and its Arab neighbors. It was something that often had been tried from the time Israel was established as a state in 1948 without any sign that either the Arab states or the Palestine Liberation Organization would change their hostile position.

This time, to win Israel's approval, Bush pledged the United States would issue a $10 billion loan guarantee to the new government of Prime Minister Yitzhak Rabin if it would agree to listen to the Arabs and refrain from using the money to build settlements for the massive influx of Russian refugees. What the Israelis had to settle for was a freeze on Jewish resettlement in its occupied territories, won from the Arabs in the 1967 Six Day War.

It helped, too, that Governor Clinton, after thinking over the arrangement between the White House and Israel, announced that he would try to avoid "politicizing" foreign policy. He explained, "I think the American people want a president who will play it straight in foreign policy and tell them the truth. They desperately want this election to be about them and their future."

Noble words, but a resurgent Saddam Hussein in Iraq was making it very difficult for President Bush—and Governor Clinton, too—to drop all differences over foreign policy at the water's edge.

.   .   .

The president's problems with Iraq were twofold: First of all, through the UN, he was trying to find and destroy Saddam's supposed facilities for the development of atomic, chemical, and biological weapons of mass destruction. At the same time, again through the UN, he had the authority, which he used at once, to send American aircraft on overflights of northern and southern Iraq to bar the skies to Saddam's planes and end his persecution of his minority peoples: the Kurds in the north and the Muslims in the south.

Although the Iraqi aircraft didn't try to challenge the U.S. overflights, Saddam's ground forces continued their attacks on minority peoples north and south without letup—an embarrassment to the United States and especially to President Bush's reelection campaign. In reprisal the United States and associated powers in the UN agreed to send teams of UN inspectors into Iraq to look for Saddam's weapons factories, both nuclear and conventional.

The first teams assigned to visit Iraq already had been denied entry into Iraq's government buildings, which stalled the inspectors. It took a while longer, therefore, to win Saddam's compliance for such hostile visits but eventually he had to give in. The search then was conducted in earnest, with some suspected sites being set afire.

Meanwhile, in a congressional inquiry into the president's efforts to "bring Iraq into the family of nations," a State Department official testified before the House Judiciary Committee that a $5 billion American loan guarantee had been used by Saddam for his arms buildup including an attempt to make atomic weapons. These loans, so the witness said, had been intended for use in Iraq's purchases of American wheat, corn, and other grains but were used instead for Saddam's arms development.

What also hurt in this recital was that when Saddam defaulted on $1.8 billion of these guaranteed loans, the U.S. Treasury had to make up the losses to the lenders. Secretary Baker, too, was accused before the House committee of authorizing an additional $1 billion of Iraqi loan guarantees even after warnings were received that Saddam was bent on war, not peace. Of the added amount, it was testified, the American government was further embarrassed because it became responsible for $400 million of Saddam's weapons purchases. In effect, if these statements were correct, American taxpayers had been used to subsidize Iraqi rearming including attempts to develop nuclear, chemical, and biological weapons.

All this was upsetting to the White House, but it didn't develop into a campaign issue immediately as the investigators began casting about for supporting evidence. Meanwhile, just before the two national party conventions, the congressional Democrats accused President Bush of using American current overflights in Iraq to try to induce an armed response from Saddam and thereby give the Pentagon a chance for a new attack on Baghdad during the electoral campaign. Bush denied it.

Even so, the confrontation with the Democrats at home and the Iraqi leader in the Middle East continually responded to Bush's disadvantage in the latest polls. He had to fend off still more criticism when he took additional measures to defend Saudi Arabia and Kuwait if Saddam tried once again to invade one or the other. The White House continued to reject charges that these were specious measures intended to whip up the public.

At any rate, the only part of the American peace effort in the Middle East that remained unchallenged was the Arab-Israeli peace conference, which had been deadlocked from the start and soon ended.

Manifestly, it was a difficult position for the Bush White House. Yet although disturbing reports continued about Iraqi intentions and supposed atomic plotting, the American public remained relatively calm during the national convention period. In fact, more TV time was devoted to the navy Tailhook scandal—sexual harassment of women during a navy convention—than was used to report a new Middle East war scare.

As far as the national conventions were concerned, the electorate remained more anxious over the depressed state of the economy and the slow pace of attempted recovery than anything else.

That was the greatest problem of all for President Bush.

8

Southern Strategy

Governor Clinton picked Senator Al Gore of Tennessee as his vice presidential candidate just before the Democratic National Convention in mid-July. The Arkansan's decision signaled another turning point in the presidential struggle. This time the Democrats were counting heavily on retaking the South, in whole or in part.

It was a challenge that George Bush could hardly match for as long as Ross Perot remained in the race and took more votes from the Republicans than he did the Democrats. For that reason mainly, the adoption of a Southern strategy gave the Democratic faithful new hope for a long-deferred return to presidential power.

The Georgian, Jimmy Carter, had been the last Democrat to break the Republican grip on the South by taking all except Virginia of the fourteen old Confederacy and border states in 1976. Now the Clinton-Gore team, from their neighboring states bordering the Mississippi River, seemed to have a good chance to retake a substantial part of the Southern bloc with its 144 electoral votes, more than half the number needed to win the presidency.

What the Democrats were aiming at in particular were Texas, with its thirty-two votes, and Florida, with twenty-five, the third and fourth largest in electors next to California's fifty-four and New York's thirty-three. Of them all only New York seemed likely at that point in the campaign to land in the Democratic column.

Florida, with its huge population of retired people from the Midwest and New England, had been Republican territory since the Eisenhower election of 1952, Lyndon Johnson in 1964 and Carter in 1976 being the only exceptions. As for Texas, there was a little more hope because it had given its vote to four Democrats in the same period: John Kennedy, Johnson, Hubert Humphrey, and Carter.

The rest of the Southern bloc, however, had been consistently

Republican in every presidential contest since Richard Nixon's second run in 1972, except for the Carter election.

In the long and bruising campaign against President Bush that seemed likely for the fall, beginning with Labor Day in early September, therefore, the success of the Clinton-Gore Southern strategy could scarcely be taken for granted. Much would depend on what happened to the undeclared Perot candidacy, the tragic unexpected events such as the Los Angeles riots, and even the vagaries of the economy.

There were no sure things in any presidential election that spread itself over almost a year and involved so many ever-shifting issues of public importance and so large and easily confused an electorate.

. . .

The Southern strategy adopted by the Clinton-Gore ticket amounted to something more than the surface argument that Southern candidates for the highest offices in the land should represent Southern interests and therefore command the loyalty of Southern voters. For this was by no means the sentimental old South of song and story, nor even the Solid South of assured faith in FDR and his New Deal. Some Republicans hoped that the sweep they had made beginning with the Reagan era meant that the South automatically belonged to them but President Bush already knew, by early summer of 1992, that this, also, was wishful thinking.

As a relative newcomer to the South, a sketchy acquaintance of a little more than fifteen years as a roving resident of Tennessee, I was already well aware that the southeastern United States no longer could be considered anybody's exclusive political territory either in this year of decision or later. Certainly not, surely, in the twenty-first century when the force of industrial change would affect all elements of Southern life from the Atlantic Ocean to the Rio Grande.

Even today, it would have been difficult for the most casual visitor to expect to find some mythical bond of interest between the highly industrialized Atlanta region, the heart of a different new South, and the rural backwoods of Louisiana. The great cities of the Texas plains and their rivals farther east beside the Mississippi River stood out in stark contrast as well against the remnants of the old agricultural South where cotton was king.

To be sure, there were strains of varying degree here as well as elsewhere in the United States, but this had long since become a national problem. Moreover, in many parts of the southeastern

United States, the troubles of neglected Hispanics also created concern because they were by far the fastest-growing minority in the region, especially along the coastal areas facing Latin America.

Rapid growth in the urban United States, here as elsewhere, inevitably left a devastating mark on the face of society as inner city decay and a withdrawn mostly white suburbia. However, in my Southern travels I never found anything to compare with the shock and the misery of Harlem and Bedford-Stuyvesant in my native New York City. So far, at least, the delayed onset of industrial growth in the South had spared a hard-working people these extremes of social disaster.

It followed that the Clinton-Gore strategy of appealing to the electorate of the southeastern United States for special consideration in this presidential election had to be based on something more than a pumped-up band playing "Dixie" with wild, supporting rebel yells and the waving of faded Confederate flags.

At bottom, the Democratic team wanted to sharpen their economic appeal to the less fortunate and neglected potential voters in the region at a low point in the slump through which the country was passing. In the fourteen states, many blacks and Hispanics already had been shown in a series of polls to be heavily disposed to vote against the established order. What Clinton and Gore now had to do was to convince the rest who had been adversely affected by the recession, most of them the so-called Reagan Democrats in largely white suburbia, that it was in their best interest to return to their old party allegiance.

This was no mean task in a region that at last was beginning to live down a long history of racial antagonisms. However, there was risk in the plans of the ambitious Democratic team well before election day. They realized it, without doubt, but pushed ahead with an elaborate show of confidence that couldn't by any means disguise the uncertainties facing their campaign.

.   .   .

Many of the conflicting attitudes in the southeastern United States were grounded in the civil rights struggle of a previous generation. Despite the gains that had been made at the time, it was perfectly apparent that much remained to be done before most of the underprivileged minorities could be brought abreast of the white majority. That, mainly, was what accounted for the shaky mixture of hope and apprehension that the Clinton-Gore ticket aroused south of the mythical Mason-Dixon line.

The groundwork for the conflict had been laid in the decisions of the Supreme Court headed by Chief Justice Earl Warren in 1954 and 1955 outlawing segregation in public schools and, by extension, in all other facilities operated by the states. The Civil Rights Act of 1957 had followed but, except for President Eisenhower's path-breaking decision to send federal troops into Little Rock to enforce the law in the schools there, comparatively scanty federal moves ensued to back up the high court's demand for "all deliberate speed."

It was left to President Kennedy to do that. He increased black registration in public schools from a disgraceful total of less than 1 percent from the time he took office in 1961. He also appointed a record number of blacks to federal offices—a 36.6 percent increase in the middle civil service grades and a whopping 88.2 percent in the top grades.

In the attorney general's office, the president's brother, Robert, stepped up the prosecution of violators of laws forbidding discrimination in employment and, even more important, attempts in the Southern states to deny the vote to eligible black citizens.

Then came the fatal struggle to register James Meredith as the first black student at the University of Mississippi over the objections of the state's governor, Ross Barnett, and jeering crowds of white students at Oxford, seat of the university. When federal troops were called this time to enforce the law, Kennedy wasn't as lucky as Eisenhower had been before him. This time, two people were killed and scores of others injured in the fighting, teargassing, and shooting that followed, but Meredith at last broke the color ban at Ole Miss, federal marshals guarding him for much of the year until his graduation.

From 1961 to 1963, with the president's encouragement, the Reverend Dr. Martin Luther King, Jr., and his associates led sit-ins, pray-ins, sing-ins, freedom marchers, and freedom riders throughout the South as black protests reached epic proportions. In Alabama, Bull Connor, the Birmingham police chief, set loose police dogs to break up a black freedom parade while a white mob pelted the marchers with bricks and bottles. Once again, the president dispatched federal troops to the scene.

At Vanderbilt University, as a result, the president ranged himself with the blacks, saying their struggle for civil rights was "in the highest traditions of American freedom." The fighting raged from Birmingham to Selma in Alabama, and from Nashville in Tennessee to Greensboro in North Carolina and beyond.

Then came the climax of the struggle. Governor George Wallace of Alabama personally turned away two black students as they sought to enter the university under a federal enabling court order. Again, it took federal troops to enforce the law despite the governor's resistance.

Much worse was yet to come. After the murder of Medgar Evers, another black leader, the president gave the bereaved family his support by brining Evers's widow, children, and brother-in-law to the White House while the president's brother, Robert, attended the funeral.

Despite that and the president's signal victory in the 1962 missile crisis by forcing the withdrawal of the Soviet Union's Cuban-based missiles, he still could not bring the civil rights battle to a successful end in his time. Early in November 1963, Adlai E. Stevenson, the twice-defeated Democratic presidential candidate in the Eisenhower years, was mussed up, jeered, and spat upon by violent opponents in Dallas.

That, however, did not deter the president from going to Dallas on a previously scheduled visit. There, on November 22, 1963, in the back seat of an open car, he was assassinated by two shots from a telescopic rifleman, Lee Harvey Oswald. Two days later, Oswald was slain by Jack Ruby, a Dallas nightclub owner.

The first indications of a swing away from the South's well-nigh traditional Democratic loyalty followed in the 1964 presidential vote. At the time, Lyndon Johnson, who had succeeded to the White House as Kennedy's vice president, won the election from Barry Goldwater, but five Southern states went Republican: Alabama, Georgia, Louisiana, Mississippi, and South Carolina.

Although Johnson did not let his Texas background deter him from winning better social conditions with his Great Society program, which helped him relax racial tensions, he could not surmount public opposition to his policy of widening the Vietnam War and did not seek reelection. Richard Nixon thereupon led the Republican comeback in 1968, allowing the Democrats only Texas and Louisiana helped by a fragmented third-party vote. He, too, ran into trouble after his reelection when his newly disclosed role in the Watergate scandal forced his resignation in 1974. His successor, Gerald Ford, lost out two years later to Jimmy Carter in a close election, leading to a brief Democratic revival.

After so much turbulence, the nation fairly reveled in the prosperity of the Reagan years. Although racial tensions persisted, it was a sign of new times and slowly changing attitudes as both white and minority leaders did their best to maintain public calm. They had been through the fire in the brutal 1960s. In the 1990s, they seemed to realize a renewal of so devastating a struggle would harm them all beyond repair.

.   .   .

Under these conditions, Governor Clinton and Senator Gore sought somehow to indicate that the party was turning to the right in the 1992 campaign. Under the lash of Republican criticism of "tax-and-spend liberals" in that presidential election year, the Democrats also began forming a conservative front. The liberal heritage of the FDR-Truman era seemed to have been placed in cold storage together with the gallantry of the Kennedy years. The risk, however, was a potential split in the Democratic party.

What the country now was offered appeared to be an ill-assorted collection of political organizations ranging from the familiar American middle-class center, at one end of the political spectrum, to the hard-line conservatism of the religious fundamentalists on the far right. The far left had been wiped out during the Cold War. A badly mauled, sharply reduced labor movement seemed to be just about the only remaining source that admitted to a left-liberal leaning. What other liberal sentiment there was across the land seemed to be confined to disadvantaged peoples in the big cities, the limousine liberals of the arts, and the more combative university campuses.

So restricted a political atmosphere hadn't existed in America since the boom-time 1920s. In keeping with the up-and-down nature of the 1990s, a different breed of career elective officeholder was emerging: well-educated, practical in the extreme, but touched at times with a glint of idealism. Among those on the national scene who fitted that description, Bill Clinton's choice for vice president, Senator Gore, was outstanding. Together, they sought through the Democratic party to lead the country out of the economic morass that was closing in on President Bush.

.   .   .

Albert Arnold Gore, Jr., had the makeup of a twenty-first-century man. Like Bill Clinton, whom he complemented in many ways, he was born after World War II and thereby escaped much of the strain generated by that conflict and the Cold War with the Soviet Union that followed.

To his father, who had preceded him in the House and Senate from Tennessee, he was born to be president. The first time he tried it in 1988, he fell far short of the Democratic nomination, although he didn't do too badly in the primaries until he hit New York. After that, he dropped out of the contest for high office and didn't re-emerge until he received the call as Clinton's running mate just before the 1992 Democratic National Convention.

For most of Gore's forty-four years, the nation's capital had been home for him along with the family farm at Carthage, Tennessee, some forty miles from Nashville. He was born in Washington in 1948 and attended prep school there. Then, like Clinton, he qualified for an Ivy League education, being graduated from Harvard cum laude with a degree in government in 1969.

Although Gore wasn't any more enthusiastic about the Vietnam War than many others of his generation, he enlisted in the army directly after graduation. In the following year, he was married to his high school sweetheart, Mary Elizabeth Aitcheson, known as Tipper to her friends.

Then came service in Vietnam with an engineering battalion, to which he was assigned as a journalist. To those who never were there, a noncombat role may have seemed like a soft touch but, if my experience as an over-age World War II type in Vietnam was typical, the Viet Cong didn't differentiate between Americans in or out of uniform. In a hotel in the center of Saigon where I was staying during the war as a journalist, the lobby was blown up by a Viet Cong bomb ten minutes before I returned there from an interview with Gen. William C. Westmoreland.

Gore's luck was good, too. He came home after a year in the field and joined the staff of the *Nashville Tennessean* in 1971 as a reporter, later an editorial writer, where he remained until 1976. Meanwhile, he took a graduate year of religious studies at Vanderbilt University, then two more years at law school there but in 1976 decided instead to run for Congress. He made it at age twenty-eight.

From then on, national politics was Gore's prime interest, which included service in the House until 1985 when he was elected at thirty-six to the Senate seat from Tennessee previously held by Howard H. Baker, Jr., the old pro who had bailed the Republicans out of so many scrapes in the past. Baker's former Democratic colleague in the Senate, the elder Gore, had lost his seat in 1970 but now, in his eighties, he was inordinately proud to see his son moving from the Senate into a presidential campaign.

Tipper Gore, too, had a special role in this new family dispensation. Having a master's degree in psychology, she also knew something about the way to project family values before the public. In a response to Republican concern about the subject, Mrs. Gore and three of their four children often took to the campaign trail with the Senator and Governor Clinton. With them, usually, were Hillary Clinton and the Clinton's twelve-year-old daughter, Chelsea, making a colorful showing of family values on the Democratic side. The Gores' oldest daughter, Karenna, was away at Harvard during most of the campaign.

To match such a show of virility and enthusiasm, the Bushes were obliged to enlist the help of their grandchildren as well as the younger Vice President and Mrs. Quayle. The president also announced that the Democratic campaign platform had omitted three important letters, "G - O - D," as he put it. That didn't work any better than the supposition that family values were inherently a Republican blessing.

All in all, nothing seemed to divert public attention from the economy as a dominant campaign issue, not even the antics of Ross Perot. This ultimately was the goal of the Clinton-Gore Southern strategy.

9

The Democratic Convention

The presidential nominating conventions of the major parties seldom explode with surprised nowadays. Because of the growth of the presidential primary elections and the decline of the old-time political bosses, the most the assembled delegates can do is to ratify the decision of the voters with few exceptions.

Behind all the hoopla, the marching bands, the press agentry, and the speech making, there is often little more than a yawning vacuum of political posturing and empty promises to a cynical citizenry of better times to come and miracles to be performed. In such a society, trust in the average politician rates just about as low as confidence in the irresponsible element of the press and television.

Yet, as H. L. Mencken wrote earlier in the century about his boredom with national conventions, "One sits through long sessions wishing heartily that all the delegates and alternates were in hell. And then suddenly there comes a show so gaudy and hilarious, so melodramatic and obscene, so unimaginably exhilarating and preposterous that one lives a gorgeous year in an hour."

This, however, was far from the expectations of the gallery gods who packed themselves high under the rafters of Madison Square Garden in New York City for the Democratic National Convention of 1992, a three-day affair that began on July 14. Everybody knew long in advance that the Clinton-Gore team would be nominated, that a platform few people bothered to read would be adopted, and a lot of sentimental speeches would be made by old-line Democratic favorites.

But between President Bush's scheduled renomination by the Republicans a month hence and Ross Perot's still undeclared but well-financed independent drive, even the most hopeful of Democrats were far from certain of victory. As late as June, one influential poll had shown the president and Perot virtually tied at 32 and 30 percent of respondents respectively, and Clinton winding up in the rear with 24 percent. Another, concluded three days before the Democratic convention began, had Clinton moving up to second place with 30 percent to Bush's 33 percent, and Perot dropping back to 25 percent.

It was far from an augury of Democratic success after 24 years in the presidential wilderness except for Jimmy Carter's unfortunate four years. If the polls were any indication of the probable outcome of a three-way race in November, the delegates had to conclude that none of the three would command a majority and the House of Representatives, heavily Democratic, might make the final decision early in 1993.

Altogether, that wasn't a very exciting outlook for a July surprise at the Madison Square Garden convention, certainly not something like the Mencken prospect of a show so "exhilarating and preposterous that one lives a gorgeous year in an hour." It was, however, the best the delegates and their prospective nominees could expect.

. . .

Mario Matthew Cuomo, three-time governor of New York and the party's favorite orator, performed his duty admirably as the convention keynoter who sounded a political high C—"a new voice for a new America." The delegates dutifully applauded although some would have gladly settled for an old voice, a reminder of the glory days of Franklin Roosevelt or Harry Truman, but that line had long since run out. The voters had picked the oncoming Bill Clinton—and that was that.

In a prayerful climax that impressed the party faithful, Governor Cuomo cautioned: "This time, we cannot afford to fail to deliver the message, not just to Democrats, but to the whole nation."

That, indeed, was the thrust of the keynote address, which made it far more somber than jubilant in tone. Listening to Cuomo respectfully, many a delegate must have reflected that this eminent Democrat might easily have been the convention's choice for the presidential nomination had he decided to contest the Bush reelection drive. However, like the Democratic leaders of the Washington Establishment, he had backed off when the president seemed a shoo-in, thereby clearing the way for Clinton's bold challenge.

All that was now history. Cuomo, as the good soldier despite all the might-have-beens, kept laying it on the Republicans with vigor and pulling out all the stops for Clinton in a fancy peroration that brought cheers from the delegates: "So step aside, Mr. Bush. You've had your parade. It's time for a change—someone smart enough to know, strong enough to do, sure enough to lead. The comeback kid. . . ."

The problem, however, was indicated in the polls. The comeback kid, so the figures pointed out, had yet to convince enough Reagan Democrats to return home from their political wanderings as voters for that president and George Bush as his successor. It was all very well for the original comeback kid, Harry Truman, to have scorned all the unfavorable political polls when he was trailing Tom Dewey, the Republican nominee in 1948, and still won. Could Truman have done it against two major opponents such as a sitting president and an independent, which was Clinton's task?

Doubts like that may well have influenced the latest Democratic standard-bearer later that night when he was interviewed on television and asked about his encouraging rise in the polls at convention time. His response, modest by Truman's standard, was both reflective and careful: "The polls will change a hundred times between now and then [election day]. We live in a time when the fragile confidence of people in their political leaders can be easily frayed."

There were few within Madison Square Garden that night who would have flaunted bold predictions of victory for Clinton and Gore. One who hoped for a victory, but muted his forecast before the delegates, was the dean of the Senate's liberal Democrats, Edward M. Kennedy. Like the presidential nominee, Kennedy stressed the changing nature of the times but added: "The ideals are the same. We will never give up. We will never give in. . . ."

That, too, wasn't much of a glowing foretaste of forthcoming triumph at the polls for the governor of Arkansas, for on that opening night of the Democratic convention, Clinton was still pretty much of a long shot for the White House against a fighting president and a hot-tempered independent.

In short, if there were any in Madison Square Garden that night who looked for a sudden change in the Menckenian scene—"gaudy and hilarious . . . melodramatic and obscene"—they maintained a discreet silence. And with good reason. To realists, even at that stage in the campaign, Bush could scarcely have been shunted aside through wishful thinking when he still could exercise the enormous powers of the presidency and was capable of doing so for his advantage.

· · ·

The White House was curiously quiet with the onset of the Democratic convention. It was known that some of the president's nervous campaign officials had been telling him that Vice President

Quayle was bound to be a handicap for the fall drive, but no move had been made to replace him. There was disquiet, too, that the president had been refusing point-blank to start campaigning actively before the August convention of the Republican nominating delegates. Still, as the titular head of the party, he was bound to have his way.

Leading Democrats could read apprehension into such responses as these from the White House, but few believed them to be caused by anything more than the usual campaign jitters over a stubbornly disappointing economy. Nobody of importance, certainly, took such political atmospherics seriously as a sign that the president, all at once, had become fearful of reelection. From the record heights of the New York Stock Exchange averages in early summer to the steady flow of respectably sized campaign contributions to presidential coffers, the Republican high command seemed to be little worried by Bush's fluctuations in the polls. His lead may have been narrowing, but most polls still put him ahead.

The news from the Perot camp, however, pointed to mounting internal troubles between the undeclared candidate and his advisers including the two he had only recently hired as codirectors based on their reputations as leaders respectively of previous Democratic and Republican presidential campaigns.

There already had been published reports on the very day of the opening of Clinton's nominating convention that Hamilton Jordan, the Democratic expert, had warned that he would quit unless Perot, still the undeclared candidate, began taking some of his advice. It was said, too, that the Republican cochairman, Ed Rollins, was also unhappy with the way the campaign was being run.

Had there been no substance to these stories, they could easily have been dismissed as campaign stuff planted with an agreeable reporter by insiders to embarrass the opposition. It was known, though, that Perot, in a typically sudden move to show who really was in charge in his Dallas headquarters, had fired a television advertising firm, Hal Riney & Partners, which had been commissioned to prepare some commercials. That made credible the current rumors of worse to come.

Just what the undeclared candidate's objection was to the Riney firm did not become common knowledge at once, but insiders assumed that he still didn't want to announce specifics on his cure for the economy or anything else. This was the flaw that any seasoned professional political organizer spotted at once in the independent campaign.

Perot's flip-flops in his public pronouncements, too, had become embarrassing to both Jordon and Rollins. In one instance, representatives of homosexual voters, scarcely a pressure group to be feared, had persuaded Perot to announce he would no longer oppose the appointment of homosexuals to cabinet posts if elected, a reversal of a previous position he had taken. As for another ban, his stated opposition to homosexuals in the armed forces, he weakened that by leaving the decision to the secretary of defense he would appoint it elected.

The independent candidate didn't help himself, either, with a poorly written, badly delivered speech that was patronizing, even derisive, in tone. Between his failures in dealing with blacks and homosexuals, it seemed to some that he had little patience with the aspirations of any of the nation's minorities.

Such problems, coming with a slide of twelve to fifteen points in the polls to a low of 25 percent, meant that Perot's proposed run for the presidency could be seriously damaged if he continued to reject the advice of the professionals he had hired to reinforce his own intuition.

The unpalatable truth was that Perot's concept of a nonpolitical campaign for the presidency simply wasn't working. Yet, he was too stubborn to admit it and accept the guidance of the old pros who could have been of help to him as he was headed for rock bottom.

Even after the lively opening of the Democratic convention that put so much heart and spirit behind the Clinton-Gore team, Perot still insisted on spending lavishly on his volunteer help across the country but begrudged the cost of political advertising on television, wouldn't approve the Hal Riney commercials, and didn't even want to hire pollsters to do private surveys for him. Such things as these were the nuts and bolts of political campaigning as it was conducted in the United States, but the candidate didn't believe in them and thought he could do without them.

So it developed that Perot and his professional staff were poles apart, each thoroughly frustrated with the other. In such a situation, something had to give way sooner rather than later in a campaign for the presidency for which the candidate hesitated to make a formal commitment. In the memory of the oldest of political writers, nothing like this had ever happened before and, as events were shaping up, it couldn't last much longer.

Perot would have to decide either to get into the campaign as a declared candidate for the presidency or get out. That, at least, was the professional view of the position in which the Texan had placed himself.

.   .   .

Ed Rollins quit the Perot campaign the next day, the second of the Democratic convention, while the delegates were bumbling through the adoption of their platform. Rollins was good-natured about his separation form Perot, said little of consequence beyond admitting that he and the undeclared candidate couldn't agree on very much, and quietly went his way.

Except at Perot's headquarters, and in a few leading newspapers here and there, the seriousness of the position of his campaign was not emphasized. Among the Democratic delegates at Madison Square Garden, to be sure, there was speculation on how much longer Perot's drive would last and what would happen to his volunteer organization and the millions of people who had wanted to vote for him if he did give up.

At the White House, however, there seemed to be a greater awareness that a break in Perot's campaign was imminent. Perhaps the ill feeling between the president and Perot had something to do with the close watch the Republican campaign maintained on every move of consequence by the independent candidate. Perhaps the Rollins pullout, taken together with Mrs. Rollins's former position on the president's personal staff, sharpened the anticipation of the Republican high command for a drastic development.

No matter. When Perot announced he was quitting on July 16, the last day of the Democratic National Convention, this was the kind of surprise that thrilled the delegates because it was, in Mencken's words, "so unimaginably exhilarating and preposterous." It is to be doubted, however, that anybody at Madison Square Garden was catapulted, as the crochety old journalist from Baltimore had imagined, into living "a gorgeous year in an hour."

Instead, almost as soon as Perot's decision was flashed by the wire services and the broadcasters, both the Republicans and the Democrats began scrambling for Perot's followers. Also, any pollster who wasn't at work at that moment started taking the pulse of the nation to determine what could happen in a two-way presidential race. It was assumed thereby that Perot was through, which didn't fully take into account the whimsical nature of his moods.

Still, this was the interpretation some of Perot's closest advisers put on his announcement. One of them, Thomas D. Barr, a New York lawyer, went so far as to proclaim that Perot had been discouraged in his presidential quest because the process had been "wretched and onerous and appalling." Barr also concluded that only a few people, and he named Bill Clinton for one, were prepared to go through such an ordeal.

As the lawyer put it, Perot had expected rock throwing but wasn't prepared to be ridiculed. That seemed to slam the door on his candidacy for good although, as matters turned out, he still kept his options open for a return to the campaign trail at a later date. Only that was by no means a part of the record of that startlingly dramatic finish of the Democratic National Convention in which Governor Clinton and Senator Gore were telling the delegates how they planned to carry the fight to the Republican enemy.

. . .

For Clinton, in his speech accepting the Democratic presidential nomination, there was only one issue of major importance before the country during the fall campaign: President Bush's mismanagement of the economy. The Democratic nominee wasted no time in attacking the president's "failed economic theory."

"People want change, but government is in the way," Clinton said before the newly confident delegates, primed for success through the Perot pullout. "It has been hijacked by privileged private interests. It has forgotten who really pays the bills around here. It's taking more of your money and giving you less in service."

It was the nominee's concept that the middle class, not very well defined by either social or economic status, had been "forgotten" and "victimized" by a long line of Republican administrations. As president, he pledged, "you will be forgotten no more." As for family values, another ill-defined concept on the Republican side, the new Democratic standard-bearer ridiculed the president and his followers once again saying, "I'm fed up with politicians in Washington lecturing Americans on family values. Our families have values. Our government doesn't."

There was much in the acceptance speech that was reminiscent of old-fashioned Rooseveltian rhetoric but Clinton was careful to avoid the usual Republican label attached to any Democratic challenger as a "tax and spend liberal." He came perilously close to disavowing his own liberalism by assuring the nation at large: "The choice we offer is not conservative or liberal, Democratic or Republican. It is different. It is new. And it will work."

That, of course, was his bid to the independents, the mugwumps, the Reagan Democrats, and the dissident Republicans who

72

had flocked to Perot's standard and now were left to go either to the president or the Democratic nominee—or sit on their hands in disgust and stay home. To them, he appealed: "Join us. Together, we will revitalize America."

Had that been the crux of the acceptance speech, Clinton might have won a much better press than he received. The excerpts that were heard over network television and emphasized in the morning newspapers, together with the news of Perot's pullout, did make a favorable impression on a decent proportion of wavering voters, judged by the swing in the polls almost overnight. In succeeding days the press accounts of the speech became far more critical mainly because of its extraordinary length, fifty-four minutes. If anything, the network people were far more critical than most of the newspaper and news magazine commentators.

This was the way the Clinton candidacy began, once the Democratic nomination was voted to him and he became the titular head of the opposition party. He couldn't seem to control his eagerness to make a good impression on the undecided vote, especially after he learned within forty-eight hours after the convention's end that he had taken a twenty-four-point lead over the president in the important *New York Times*–CBS poll, the greatest margin in fifty years at that point in a presidential campaign.

The figures gave Clinton 55 percent, Bush 31 percent, and 13 percent undecided.

The poll also showed that its respondents, Perot's ex-supporters, split 45 to 26 percent in favor of Clinton over Bush at that early stage in the campaign but that obviously was subject to change. In any event, Clinton wasted no time to hit the road with Senator Gore, their wives, and sometimes their children as well for the first of a series of bus tours across America. Being unable to match the television schedules of the better-financed Bush campaign, the bus operation was the best the Democratic ticket could devise then to take their appeal to America.

The first trip, a six-day, 1,240-mile expedition through eight states from New York City to St. Louis, was aimed at the American heartland—places such as Carlisle, Pennsylvania; Vandalia, Illinois; and Muscatine, Iowa. The bus caravan pulled up at a lot more places and even halted for crowds strung out along highways and smaller groups gathered along country roads.

These were plain folk—women in shorts or house dresses, men in overalls for the most part, with kids tagging along sometimes. All of them had a lot of questions for the political tourists in the middle of America and not many could be easily answered. As one network reporter said to Al Gore, "The fact that people are out there is amazing, that they are gathering on the side of the road to watch you guys is amazing."

The network people noticed, too, that some of the hard-boiled big city reporters also were working the crowds. After that, the bus tours were regularly reported to many millions of Americans on the almighty tube.

That kind of campaigning, however, turned out to be exhausting. More often than not, the principals were up at 6:00 A.M., on the road by 7:00 A.M., and off and away until midnight or later. In return, the candidates and their wives learned a lot at first hand about what Americans were saying and thinking, the cost of the recession, and its effect on average American families. These were not lessons that would be soon forgotten.

That first tour was such an unqualified success that more than twenty-five thousand people cheered the caravan as it wound up in St. Louis before the city's main public library. Clinton proclaimed to rockets of applause: "If you're tired of being heartbroken when you go home at night and you want a spring in your step and a song in your heart, give Al Gore and me a chance to bring America back. . . . It's time for them to go, time for us to come on."

Next, Clinton bused to New Orleans and backwater Louisiana while Gore campaigned in his native Tennessee. Then both joined forces for another bus tour through five states from St. Louis to Minneapolis and St. Paul, often on winding roads along the Mississippi. In response to Republican attempts to ridicule them as "boy wonders" and "whiz kids," the Democratic team kept emphasizing the nation's need for change. As Clinton put the case at LaCrosse, Wisconsin, "Let's have the courage to change. The thing that has kept this country forever young is that at critical junctures in our history we have had the courage to change and embark on a new course. We represent that new course."

Far beyond the people who saw the two couples on these and later bus tours, the cumulative effect of the reporting in local, statewide, and national media swelled the audiences to many millions both in the American heartland and beyond. This, truly, was what made the Democrats' campaign by bus unique in modern American politics toward century's end. There would be tens of thousands of miles yet to go in every part of America before this presidential campaign finally halted on election day.

No one could remember when a presidential candidate had stopped off before to address a few hundred people at Coatesville, Pennsylvania, or stay overnight at a small hotel in York, Pennsylvania, as Clinton once did. The child held aloft by his father to see somebody running for president by candlelight wasn't likely to forget the scene. I wasn't much older when my father held me up high one night in the Pacific Northwest to see my first presidential candidate, Woodrow Wilson. I still remember how impressed I was because he wore a shiny tall silk hat.

10

Perot Lingers On

Almost everybody in American public life is treated with brutal disregard of the amenities of social discourse and Ross Perot was no exception.

During the Texan's undeclared independent presidential campaign, which lasted only five months, he was methodically subjected to monumental abuse both on the air and in print. His detractors called him a snoop, a spoiler, a bumbler, a poseur, and a traitor to his privileged class.

After he suddenly dropped out, he was called a quitter.

Perot was no political knight in shining armor and he didn't fit very well into the political process as it is practiced nationally in America. But the way he was pounced upon with ridicule and epithet could not have seemed to the outside world to be a very pretty exhibit of the workings of American democracy.

The Republicans, perhaps, were more vehement than the Democrats in trying to knock Perot out of contention because he represented a greater threat to President Bush than Governor Clinton. Neither major party nor their presidential candidates and most of the supposedly impartial reporters assigned to Perot, however, ever seemed to care whether he received a fair hearing or not. On the contrary, for the most part, these actors in the political process seemed to take a savage satisfaction in knocking him around.

Maybe this was the way the century of the common man was supposed to work in America. Still, it would have been nice if one of the principals in this benighted campaign had stood up for the First Amendment in Perot's behalf and said, "Let the man talk," but no one did.

So the public never knew during his brief campaign, because of all the hubbub created by his prospective third party presidential candidacy, whether he made sense or not. He was kept too busy answering his detractors to be able to devote much time to anything else. His detailed economic program, being developed from his ideas by a capable staff, didn't appear until almost two weeks after he ended his campaign.

The doubts raised about Perot, personally and politically, finally overwhelmed him and his prospective candidacy. It probably gave him a little satisfaction to announce, within twenty-four hours after he dropped out, that he would leave his name on the ballot anyway so that people could still vote for him if they wished to do so.

At a reported cost of about $500,000 a month thereafter, he maintained a reduced staff of volunteers to continue work to put him on the ballot in all fifty states. One again, his motives were questioned, particularly from the White House, for he was viewed there as a continued threat to President Bush in big states where the major party candidates were closely matched. A few thousand votes given to Perot by disaffected Republicans on election day, so it was said at the time, might make the difference in whether such a state's electors would be for or against the president.

Some even argued that Perot might be vindictive enough to renew his candidacy, a suggestion to which he responded primly by saying he was keeping all options open. That, in a way, could have been his revenge against the mean character of much of the American body politic.

* * *

There were excuses aplenty for how Perot became a noncandidate rather than an undeclared candidate for the presidency.

Some of his intimates at his Dallas headquarters said he had been discouraged with his prospective run when both President Bush and Governor Clinton passed him in the polls. That, in substance, continued to leave him with only a 25 percent share of the respondents in most polls, something that surely would have indicated to him that he had no hope of becoming the master of the White House.

Others at the Texan's headquarters, who also shared in the guessing game about his motives, suggested alternatively that he might have been fed up with the abuse he had been taking from all sides. And this also could have led to his decision to call off his campaign once Ed Rollins had left him.

For a while, some of Perot's intimates let it be known to a few insiders that he may well have been worried about the effect of all the criticism he received on his family, whose privacy he guarded with intense devotion. Rumors were floated, too, that threats had been made against his family, but there never was any direct confirmation of that. However, because the gun has been an all-too-recognizable evil influence in American presidential politics in this century, the possibility could not reasonably be disregarded.

James Squires, a former *Chicago Tribune* political analyst who became Perot's communications director, suggested that the candidate had delayed his commitment to a full-scale presidential effort and eventually pulled out because he realized it would be difficult for him to "tell the truth" to the American people about what it would cost them to restore prosperity.

Squires elaborated on television by saying, "I think the prospect for that, though there were many other factors involved, had a lot to do with Mr. Perot's decision."

The communications director was not alone in reaching so sensitive a conclusion. Barry Bosworth of the Brookings Institution commented after he saw a digest of a Perot recovery plan calling for much higher taxes and much larger cuts in entitlements, "I bet it [the plan] wouldn't have seen the light of day if he had stayed in the race."

As for Perot's response to the question of motivation for his abrupt withdrawal, he told a reporter directly after his announcement that he believed the Democrats were on "the right track" to bring the country out of recession, the issue that seemed more important to him than anything else. In considering the position of the major parties in the presidential race, he called the Democrats "revitalized." He had no rating for the Republicans in sponsoring Bush's campaign for re-election, however, although he invariably proclaimed his neutrality under questioning.

．　．　．

The Republicans were the first to try to persuade some of the uprooted Perot supporters to shift to the president for the fall election. Soon after the undeclared candidate's withdrawal, Vice President Quayle was in Louisville, Kentucky, meeting with Perot's local backers to try to win their allegiance. They weren't ready to respond, but the vice president maintained his sales talk anyway and added to it an appeal to vote for Republican senatorial candidates as well.

All in all, the Perot volunteers felt betrayed when their man left them stranded. Some determined to travel to Dallas to plead with him to reconsider, something he refused to do. Others issued bitter comments in interviews with television or newspaper reporters. Most of them simply faded away, the main exceptions being those few loyalists who had been in charge of substantial statewide operations for Perot and hoped that somehow they might be kept on.

The professionals—the few who had remained—didn't dally very long before they, too, went on about their business. It was, in sum, a movement that collapsed even faster than it had been put together.

In a late *New York Times*–CBS poll, 70 percent of the volunteers who could be reached regretted that Perot had not remained in the presidential campaign, 58 percent felt he had accomplished relatively little, and 41 percent blamed him for leaving them in the lurch.

The same poll showed that those who described themselves as conservatives outnumbered self-described liberals 2-1. It was no surprise, therefore, to find that the poll takers had found in their sample that Republicans working for Perot substantially outnumbered Democrats or independents. Yet, the poll indicated that twice as many Perot backers had decided to switch to Clinton over the conservatives who settled on Bush.

In fact, the poll reported that Perot's former supporters by an unspecified majority expected President Bush to lose the election regardless of how they themselves voted.

Nevertheless, the Republican high command refused to concede that any part of the Perot contingent was permanently lost to the president. Instead, the expectation at the White House was that people who had followed Perot, whatever their purposes, were likely to shift their allegiance several times during the succeeding fall campaign and could well wind up casting their ballots for Bush.

Loyalists at the White House, possibly to keep up appearances, argued that never before had a third party aspirant for the presidency dropped out during a major party convention, and polling conclusions, therefore, might be exaggerated for the Democrats. However, in the month that remained until the Republican National Convention, the margin between the major party candidates did not narrow sufficiently to indicate that Democratic poll support had been hyped up.

On the contrary, the twenty-four-point polling "bounce" for Clinton, coming off the Democratic convention, held up a lot better than, say, Walter Mondale's 1984 double-digit lead over President Reagan that dissolved almost at once. Governor Dukakis's seventeen-point advantage over then Vice President Bush in 1988 seemed to melt overnight.

No, Clinton may have lost some points once his nominating convention ended but he still was in good shape despite all the Republican attacks on the "character" issue through which the White House sought to gloss over Bush's economic failures. However, with more than three months before election day, the Democratic team could not take anything for granted and dispatched Governor Clinton and Senator Gore, with their families, on their first bus tour of disputed territory before the cheering at Madison Square Garden could be forgotten.

President Bush had the last word for the wandering Perot supporters when he appealed to them: "Don't run away from the system. I hear you and you come through loud and clear."

The president was still hoping.

.   .   .

Perot sought to reassure his former backers that he had not forgotten them by making public his plan for economic recovery ten days after the end of the Democratic National Convention. It was his reminder that, even though he had withdrawn as an active if undeclared presidential candidate, he still was determined to remain on the ballot in all the states. At the very least, he let it be known that he wanted to influence the Democratic and Republican campaigns by putting his ideas for economic recovery before them and the nation as well.

In essence, what his complicated formula was intended to do, if it worked, was to wipe out a current $350 billion deficit and produce a balanced budget and an $8 billion surplus as early as 1998. It was an ambitious undertaking for only five years, far from the usual explanation he had given audiences and the press during his undeclared campaign: "See, it's simple!"

Considered as a whole, it was breathtaking in the immensity of the effort it forecast for the nation in achieving solvency once again. Instead of being limited to soaking the rich and cutting military appropriations, as many had expected, this proposal spared no class in American society. Even the elderly were listed to give up some of the money the federal government had allotted to them.

Although the plan had been prepared by Perot's erstwhile director of campaign issues, John P. White, it bore the stamp of many of Perot's pet ideas from bucking special interests and rebuilding public confidence without indicating precisely how such operations could be conducted.

Prominently displayed in the Perot recovery program was his plan to boost income taxes on people in the highest bracket from 31 to 33 percent—an estimated gain of $7.6 billion for the federal government. The biggest contribution by far came from his proposed reduction of Medicare and Medicaid benefits, estimated at $52.8 billion. Almost as much, $50 billion, was estimated to be added income from a fifty-cent-a-gallon increase in the gasoline tax over five years and an additional $3.8 billion from doubling taxes on cigarettes and other tobacco products.

Another levy on the elderly was proposed in Perot's program to tax 85 percent of Social Security benefits for any single person with an income of $25,000 or more and for couples with a joint income of $32,000 or more. That, the Perot plan estimated, would bring in an additional $7.9 billion.

Perot's plan also limited deductions of mortgage interest from taxation to the first $250,000 of mortgage value. He also proposed to tax 50 percent of business entertainment expenses. The farmers didn't escape unscathed, either, for Perot proposed to slash farm subsidies by $17 billion over five years, From employer-paid health insurance, he expected to derive $15.9 billion from taxes on such policies in some form with another $23 billion coming from a 10 percent cut in most federal discretionary programs.

To be sure, there were Perot's suggested cuts in the military, which would yield $17.1 billion, and other economies in government operations. Large chunks, however, were taken out of that by tax credits for worker training, a $40 billion investment in public facilities such as roads and telecommunications to create jobs, and $70 billion invested in public education, civic improvement, and various types of research and development.

A little later, Perot elaborated on these and other ideas in a book published under his name. He also remained active in other public affairs by advocating the formation of a pressure group called "United We Stand America" to continue to plug his ideas for economic recovery. Over the long run, as most economists agreed, there was little chance of an enactment of the Perot financial plan as a whole or even in substantial part.

As a former director of the Congressional Budget Office, Rudolph Penner, politely observed, "Candidates usually don't issue such plans because of the enormous turmoil and complaints they would bring, especially from the elderly."

That, however, didn't bother Perot. He seemed to be revitalized himself, along with the Democratic party, as he continued to strike out with seeming impartiality against both Democrats and Republicans in the most extravagant fashion. In an article that appeared in the *New York Times* under his name, he said, "Both parties act is if they bear no responsibility for the $4 trillion national debt that burdens our country. . . . Unfortunately, the parties have lost touch with the American people. . . ." He concluded, "Five and a half million people who feel they have no voice in the country they own joined together in a petition signing process to put me on the ballot. . . . Their goal is to influence every Congressional race, as well as the presidential race, and they are active in every state. At their request, I am actively supporting them."

Whether he was an undeclared candidate for president or a non-candidate, Ross Perot would be heard from again. Had it not been for him, there is a very good chance that the 1992 presidential campaign might have turned out differently.

11

On Women's Rights

Just before the Republican National Convention, so much criticism came Hillary Clinton's way from the Republican leadership that her outraged husband asked plaintively if President Bush was running for first lady.

As the Democratic presidential nominee, Bill Clinton had good reason for his protest against the attack on his outspoken lawyer-wife. Rich Bond, the Republican national chairman, already had led off with a warning to the nation that Clinton, if elected, would be taking advice from a wife who compared "marriage and the family to slavery."

To add to this unsavory image, Barbara Bush, the first lady, had announced that she believed the Clintons were planning a "co-presidency." Just what that was, nobody could be quite sure but, coming from a White House under siege, it sounded decidedly sinister.

At any rate, Clinton retorted with a barnyard epithet. "A load of bull," he said, but the Republican fusillade continued. Nothing quite like this battering of a woman prominent in presidential campaigning had taken place since malicious foes of Franklin Roosevelt had decided to get at him by ridiculing his wife, Eleanor, who was politically active in so many worthy causes of benefit to underprivileged people during the Great Depression.

Long afterward, Mrs. Roosevelt recalled that the head of the American Red Cross had feared to accept a donation from her on the supposition that her participation would drive away other contributions. She wrote of that experience:

"It is startling to realize that one is so deeply, fanatically disliked by a number of people. And yet, while I weigh as honestly as I can the grounds for disapproval, when I feel that I am right in what I do, it seems to me that I cannot refuse to do a thing merely because it will make me disliked. . . . As a result, when I believe, after weighing the evidence, that what I am doing is right I go ahead and try as hard as I can to dismiss from my mind the attitude of those who are hostile. I don't see how else one can live."*

There has been a considerable change in the position of women in America since Eleanor Roosevelt's time, and that is especially true of working women. Moreover, women today make up 51 percent of the nation's quarter-billion population. Yet, when a presidential candidate for the first time had a wife who was among the leaders of her profession and a graduate of Yale Law School, she still had to undergo the same prejudiced treatment that lesser members of the male species practiced on Eleanor Roosevelt.

However, Mrs. Clinton, no less than Mrs. Roosevelt, showed the strength and the courage to face down her detractors. For that performance, regardless of whether her husband won or lost the presidency, she was able through her example to stimulate still more principled and accomplished women to enter a field that once had been an almost all-male preserve and not always one that was a credit to the world's largest practicing democracy. The newcomers, regardless of their political faith, hoped to do better for the nation than their detractors. They couldn't possibly do much worse.

.   .   .

Before the emergence of women who were both willing and capable of competing with men on the often shameful terms so characteristic of public life in America, most first ladies were obliged to muffle their feelings as best they could. Whatever provocations they suffered because they were thrust in a position of outstanding prominence through the status of their husbands, they managed with few exceptions to remain outside the kind of political brawling, ranging from personal insult to blatant untruth, that we dignify as public life in America.

This is not to say that first ladies let themselves be shoved into a subordinate role as White House wives, sweet little old ladies who tried to be amiable and socially proper over their teacups. Far from it.

Mamie Eisenhower, a tough-minded army wife and mother, saw her husband collapsed and near death by a sudden illness in the White House, which caused her to oppose his run for a second term as vigorously as she could. Only when she realized that Ike had made a remarkable recovery and was ready to carry on as an old soldier did

*The Autobiography of Eleanor Roosevelt (1961), p. 416.

she give in. She never was very happy about being confined to the White House and made no secret of it.

Pat Nixon was less venturesome and far less visible for obvious reasons while President Nixon was so deeply involved in the Watergate scandal that became his undoing. At one time, she was so timid that she confessed to a governor's wife, while drinking a second martini, that she never would have had more than one cocktail if the president's personal watchdog, Bob Haldeman, had been around. Mrs. Nixon's attitude was understandable under the circumstances: a time of troubles for the White House such as no other first lady had ever been obliged to endure.

By contrast, Nancy Reagan, still not forgotten, retained a different image among political gossips, especially those in the news business. She, too, was quite unfairly depicted at times to be what amounted to a "co-president," Barbara Bush's term, with Ronald Reagan. The more malicious gossips spread the story that Nancy Reagan frequently consulted astrological charts to advise the president properly. This was of a piece with popular mythology at the time that her husband, one of the most successful chief executives in the nation's history during this century, didn't know what was going on around him at the White House sometimes.

What it amounts to is that gossips, regardless of political orientation, can be both inconsiderate and cruel, especially when there is such a juicy target as a woman directly involved with the presidency as first lady or challenger. Unless American politics undergoes an enormous change both in principle and manner in the next century, the lot of the first woman candidate for president of the United States will be something to behold.

And to endure.

. . .

What Hillary Clinton did during her husband's presidential campaign was to create at least one role model for the combative women of the future who aspire to lead the nation. Although she matched first ladies such as Eleanor Roosevelt and Mamie Eisenhower in vigor, she was far less tolerant than they were of opposition.

What Mrs. Clinton seemed to enjoy in her professional life was to support the aspirations of other women who were less able to stand up to their detractors in asserting their rights. A case in point was her leadership of the American Bar Association's commission on women from 1987 to 1991 when she did her part in fighting the kind of abuse, discrimination, and even sexual harassment that some women in legal practice had to endure.

Less than a month after the Democratic National Convention formally gave her husband its presidential nomination, she celebrated by appearing before the American Bar Association Convention in San Francisco arm in arm with Professor Anita F. Hill. Of the black lawyer who had testified against Supreme Court Justice Clarence Thomas at his Senate confirmation hearing, Mrs. Clinton said: "All women who care about equality of opportunity, about integrity and morality in the workplace are in Professor Hill's debt, and I am pleased to share this platform with her today."

Both the University of Oklahoma law professor and her champion won applause that day from the twelve hundred lawyers and their guests at that usually reserved gathering. The burden of their message consisted of a challenge to all other women lawyers to join them in an effort to improve the lives of disadvantaged American women and their families.

There was no mistaking the earnestness of Mrs. Clinton's appeal and the support for it that Professor Hill offered her. This is the way the Democratic nominee's wife put her case: "It is time that we as women and as lawyers commit ourselves to the idea that we will not rest until public policy recognizes and accommodates women's needs and priorities. . . .

"The law, the lawyers and the judges protecting our families deserve at least the respect now given to the law, the lawyers and judges protecting our corporate boardrooms."

The nation's women, she concluded, "need a helping hand, and they need respect for what they are going through."

The basis of Chairman Bond's attack on Mrs. Clinton apparently was a legal discussion some twenty years previous, when she was just out of Yale Law School, in which she wrote about legal precedents in which a person's rights may be involved, marriage being one of them. To Governor Clinton, Chairman Bond's comments were a "gross distortion" of the views of his wife, whose annual earnings in recent years have been several times his pay as the first citizen of Arkansas.

Clinton also recalled that before he became President Bush's opponent for reelection, the president "always expressed his personal admiration for Hillary and her outstanding achievements and her commitment to children." As for the other Republican opponents of his wife, he said, "They ought at least to try to be fair."

.　　.　　.

There was an unrealistic air about the Republican argument against Hillary Clinton as the working wife of a presidential candidate, certainly the first woman lawyer to be an aspiring first lady. The 1990 census demonstrated that more than 53 million women, almost half the nation's work force, are gainfully employed, many of them being in labor unions and most of them earning considerably less than men doing the same work.

The working wife, therefore, has long since become a fact of life in America where two-income families in a wavering economy are the rule rather than the exception. Yet, when Hillary Clinton struck back at her detractors by arguing against "staying home, baking cookies, and having teas," she stirred up scathing opposition comment once again.

Some in Governor Clintons' confidence as campaign advisers urged him to ask Mrs. Clinton to lower her visibility for the balance of the presidential campaign after that. Even if she tried, choosing sometimes not to respond to criticism, that didn't make her any less controversial a figure. After all, as mild a personality as Rosalynn Carter touched off a heated argument when she joined her husband, President Jimmy Carter, at cabinet meetings. This, so his Republican critics said, was an outrage.

Mrs. Clinton's comment was: "So what?"

What it amounted to was a hangover from the long struggle of women for equality in America that finally won them at least the right to vote in 1920, but still delayed general public acceptance of many another right exercised by men. The 1992 presidential campaign issue of abortion, legalized since 1973 and more recently emaciated by more conservative Supreme Court decisions, was also a part of the deeper involvement of women in the political arena.

All kinds of epithets were coined by Mrs. Clinton's public detractors to hurt both her and her husband in the political campaign, one being a "liberal wonk." It was all too reminiscent of the way Eleanor Roosevelt had been treated even though she was a four-time first lady. However, Hillary Clinton was by no means as forgiving of her enemies as Mrs. Roosevelt had been, all of which made her good copy for journalists and an almost continual target for her husband's opposition.

Little by little, she did manage to learn to hold her temper against the kinds of barbs even reporters use to make a story sometimes where no story seems to exist. A television reporter once asked her, for example, how she would describe herself in response to some who think of her as an "overbearing yuppie wife from hell." Instead of rising to the televised bait, Mrs. Clinton restrained her temper and remarked mildly that she was too old to be a yuppie, which disposed of at least one provocation. There were others. It took a while for Mrs. Clinton to realize that not all her detractors were politicians. It was a rough game that some journalists play, too, women not excepted.

.　　.　　.

What made Barbara Bush as first lady less vulnerable than Hillary Clinton, Nancy Reagan, and Rosalynn Carter? Mrs. Bush's explanation for her popularity, usually described as twice that of her husband's, was that she seldom spoke publicly on policy matters. Perhaps so, but as a white-haired gentle grandmother type in her sixty-eighth year and her forty-eighth married to George Bush, her background and usually retiring personality had something to do with her favored status, too.

Still, Mrs. Bush could be tough when she wanted to be, as witness her description in 1988 of Geraldine Ferraro, the Democratic vice presidential candidate, as "a word I can't say but it rhymes with rich." And then, too, there was her estimate of Mrs. Clinton as an ambitious prospective "co-president."

Somehow, the 1992 campaign brought out a more combative streak in the first lady, possibly because her husband was having so difficult a time of it in his reelection campaign. Yet, on the abortion issue, in which the president favored outright repeal of the law legalizing the practice, his wife told a news conference that abortion was "a personal thing" and should not be in party platforms or conventions. As for allegations about the president's personal life that Mrs. Clinton once made obliquely but withdrew, Mrs. Bush's response was: "Disgusting."

However, the first lady defended Mrs. Clinton from attacks because of her views on marriage, saying, "She's not running for office." She also was a lot gentler on Governor Clinton than her husband and others in his administration, confessing that she hadn't particularly cared for the persistent questions about his personal life but apparently couldn't resist adding, "He never denied he had a fling, did he?" She also insisted that the persistent questions raised about his position in the Vietnam War draft were fair and deserved to be answered.

It was such an apparently balanced assessment of the president's challenger and his wife that added to, rather than detracted from, Mrs. Bush's personal popularity. It also led the Republican high command to press her into action as a convention speaker, something she didn't seem to be wildly excited about doing, even though she was being billed as the star of a "Family Values Night" at the convention. To the people at her news conference, she said, "Don't expect anything. It's not going to be a great speech."

In this manner, Mrs. Bush broke with her sense of family values that had led her for so many years, with few exceptions, to avoid political controversy and partisan issues. On one of her personal attitudes, however, she was unshakable. Her husband, she proudly proclaimed, was the greatest man in the world.

.   .   .

The contrast between Mrs. Bush and Mrs. Clinton was, at bottom, symbolic of the changing nature of the status of women in the closing years of the twentieth century. The Republican first lady, like Bess Truman and Mamie Eisenhower, was satisfied until the 1992 Republican convention to maintain a safe distance between herself and the practical politics of life in the public goldfish bowl that is the White House. Mrs. Clinton, who aspired to succeed her, deeply believed in liberty of thought and action in a professional sense on any issue of concern to women in public life.

Their attitudes were poles apart. Mrs. Bush had made a great name for herself because she involved herself in anything of importance to the improvement of homemaking and family life. Mrs. Clinton's interests went far beyond these basics as a woman active in her profession, something her husband encouraged. As he remarked after Vice President Quayle charged that Mrs. Clinton's activities constituted evidence that the Clinton campaign was "in the pocket of the American Bar Association leadership," "It's amazing that he thinks he has to take her on. But I think she can take care of herself."

In a sense, attitudes toward the presidency itself were changing, too, which was also an important part of the story of the election of 1992.

12

The Republican Convention

President Bush sympathized with a suffering nation in mid-August on his way to the Republican nominating convention in Houston.

He realized people were "hurting," he said in a televised interview. He added with emphasis, "I know it. I feel it. We pray about it."

However, once the four-day convention ended on August 20 with his renomination and the adoption of a stern platform emphasizing family values and forbidding abortion, even the best-informed delegate couldn't be sure what the president and the party intended to do about ending the long and damaging recession.

That, after all, was the issue on which the upstart Democrat, Bill Clinton, had built a lead in the opinion polls. Despite the convention oratory about depraved "tax and spend" liberals, the objectionably professional Hillary Clinton, and all the other targets in the Democratic party, President Bush still was far from closing the gap in the polls.

The most the president had been able to do in his acceptance speech to demonstrate he had an economic recovery plan was to promise voters an across-the-board tax cut, provided the Democratic-controlled Congress would oblige him by finding enough reductions in the cost of government to make up for the expense of his promised tax cut.

Even that conditional promise was hedged, in a different way, with the president's apologetic remarks about the tax increase he had fastened on the nation, causing him to break his well-advertised 1988 campaign pledge, "Read My Lips, 'No New Taxes.'" With that, the homebound delegates and a wondering public had to be content.

All in all, it hadn't been a very inspired convention. The White House had been in turmoil with the removal of Samuel K. Skinner as chief of staff, but his replacement, the talented secretary of state,

James A. Baker, wasn't scheduled to take over as combined White House and campaign director until August 23. Into that vacuum, the leaders of the extreme conservative wing of the party had leaped with abandon and had taken the president with them to the dismay of the solid, middle-of-the-road delegates.

To the fainthearted at the convention, that had seemed to be a formula for disaster. The president and his upbeat conservative vice president, Dan Quayle, did not then sense anything was wrong. Quayle, on his part, was entrusted as a loyal conservative with the mission of converting the electorate to the theme he had sounded as a convention speaker. He had come out strongly for strictly conservative family values, against one-parent family life-styles such as that featured in the television program "Murphy Brown," and, by all means, no abortion under any circumstances for any woman, even those violated through rape and incest.

.   .   .

The extent and duration of the split in the Republican party weren't realized at first by the public at large even though the party's orators, for the most part, faithfully followed the party's stridently voiced position on family values. Nevertheless, there were some delegates, homebound to face a lot of angry voters, who were upset over the "us vs. them" approach. As one delegate and elected official put it, "I think a tone was set that seems to imply that only Republicans have family values, but I represent a lot of Democrats who hold family values and who exemplify family values very well."

Another, who feared a backlash might set in because the party had placed so much emphasis on a nonissue rather than the economy, put the position frankly: "I came down here [to Houston] thinking about the economy." To which a fellow delegate chimed in: "This talk about family values could lead to a backlash."

The reply from the Bush campaign team was comforting, however, assuring the unsettled delegates that, as one official put it, "Women are tired of hearing they have to have careers," a thrust at Mrs. Clinton as a practicing lawyer.

In retrospect, what apparently happened at the convention, with no strong direction from the White House, was that the extreme conservatives, such as Pat Robertson and his associates, filled the gap with denunciations of the faults, real and imagined, of the opposition Democrats. This, at least, was the tone of ferocious condemnation that came through to the public in televised convention segments and the longer press reports (except for the live CNN and C-Span gavel-to-gavel coverage).

Anxious citizens, hurt by the lack of economic growth and the resultant rise in unemployment, looked and listened in vain for any clue to operative Republican proposals to ease the nation's ills. All they received for their pains was President Bush's insistent effort to blame the Democratic-controlled Congress for all faults, theirs and his. He contended that if Congress had passed his key proposals to restore economic growth, all would have been well. Still, the only part of the program he sponsored that came through to the public clearly was his campaign for a cut in the excess profits tax.

That, however, did not stop Rich Bond, the Republican National Chairman, from proclaiming what he called a "cultural war" against the Democrats. This was elaborated on by Vice President Quayle in his convention speech as follows: "The gap between us and our opponents is a cultural divide. It is not just a difference between conservative and liberal. It is a difference between fighting for what is right and refusing to see what is wrong."

The basis for this seeming decree of excommunication appeared to rest in the platform and the conservative ideas of women's rights, expounded among others by Marilyn Quayle, a former practicing lawyer and the vice president's wife. As Mrs. Quayle put the case: liberals are "disappointed because most women do not wish to be liberated from their essential nature as women."

Whatever Mrs. Quayle's concept of women's wishes may have been, well over half the liberated women who vote in most national elections are in today's work force (or at least, they work for as long as jobs for them are maintained in a wavering economy).

That was one of the difficulties with the entire Republican concept of family values. It seemed to Democrats as a whole to apply less to women who work and try at the same time to maintain a family of growing children, with or without a husband, than to people in less straitened circumstances.

At least one Republican, Senator Richard Lugar of Indiana, worried about the continual conservative message in which liberals and feminists were invariably linked with homosexuals and lesbians. While the convention was under way, he told a group of news people at breakfast: "You don't build majorities by excluding whole groups of people and you don't have to be nasty to be conservative. I wish they'd cut it out, especially the attack on Hillary. I'm not comfortable with that at all."

President Bush apparently was undisturbed by the way the convention was going, and his new chief of staff and campaign director, Baker, hadn't taken charge yet. Nobody was looking over any of the speeches at the convention before they were delivered so the extremists did as they pleased.

For a few days at least, they were in effect running the party of Abraham Lincoln and Theodore Roosevelt, and the polls showed the result all too soon.

. . .

There was at least a pause in the negative jamboree in which the extreme conservatives spread their beliefs throughout the country. That was when the still-popular former President Ronald Reagan appeared before the delegates and provided a pleasant interlude in the form of a speech that didn't damn anybody to perdition, not even a liberal-minded Democrat. There wasn't anything memorable about Reagan's remarks, consisting as they did of the commonplaces of American politics. Mainly, he supported his crowd and swatted the opposition in a general way except for a good-humored thrust at a president he had defeated, Jimmy Carter.

However, because he had remained a strict conservative, Reagan's remarks to the far right are worth repeating: "We are all equal in the eyes of God—whether we come from poverty or wealth, whether we are Afro-American, Christian or Jewish, from the big cities or small towns and we must all be equal in the eyes of one another."

One of his adherents commented later that the ex-president once had saved the Republican party from "the perils of negativism" and maybe he could do it again at this convention. Not even the old movie cowpoke could perform that added feat. Another speaker, the broadcaster and columnist, Patrick J. Buchanan, forecast that a Democrat in the White House would bring about "abortion on demand, a litmus test for the Supreme Court, homosexual rights, discrimination against religious schools, and women in combat units."

However, at least two speakers did follow the Reagan line, and with relish. Although a current poll had shown 63 percent of the Republican convention delegates were conservatives, only 45 percent of Republican voters and 29 percent of all voters so described themselves.

The first to endorse the Reagan approach, Housing Secretary Jack Kemp, appealed to the delegates "not to denounce the past but to inspire the nation to a better future." Senator Phil Gramm of Texas contented himself with a forecast that America's next century would be its greatest and offered relatively moderate opposition to Democratic policies.

However, neither made much of an impression on the delegates as a whole. Most of them seemed to welcome Chairman Bond's declaration of a "cultural war" on the Democrats, evidently assuming that only one side would be hurt in such a conflict. He was wrong. His own people already had suffered far more than he realized.

If President Bush was sensitive to the damaging split in his party while he was amid a bogged-down reelection campaign, he did not show it.

.   .   .

An embattled Secretary of State Baker took over the faltering Bush campaign the week after the 2,210 convention delegates went home, wondering what was to become of their divided party as well as their president. Despite all the histrionics at the convention, it had failed to give Bush anything more than a small temporary reduction in Governor Clinton's lead in the opinion polls. The president, in fact, had made no gain in the polls and soon lost whatever advantage he had been able to achieve.

Much of what happened to the Bush campaign beginning that first Monday after the Republican convention, August 24, might have been ascribed to bad luck. Without doubt, there also had been a lot of bad management of the resources of government in an emergency.

The morning began well with the president campaigning in Connecticut in calm, sunny weather. He seemed to radiate confidence as he worked the crowds in what had formerly been his home state. His speeches seemed more incisive, his gestures stronger. Somehow, even the crowds seemed to be more responsive to him with cheers and chants of "Four more years."

Then, in a few moments, everything changed. There had been a phone call to the president from a panicky White House. A killer hurricane had struck Florida and he was needed there at once, as Secretary Baker urgently recommended. To his well-wishers, it seemed as if the very elements were conspiring against him in this most difficult presidential election year.

As the president and his party headed south on *Air Force One,* the preliminary reports of the tragedy of Hurricane Andrew were being broadcast and he listened with growing concern. Even now, first reports said many were dead, hundreds were injured, and perhaps as many as a quarter of a million Floridians were homeless. There was no way of immediately assessing property damage but it was certain to run into the billions of dollars. At the center of the storm, Homestead Air Force Base had been devastated by winds that had reached 160 miles an hour. There was no word of any activity by federal relief agencies.

Rain was still pelting Florida in torrents as the president descended from *Air Force One* to do what he could, which was very little. After a relatively short stay, in the mistaken belief that he had done whatever he believed possible, he returned to his campaign schedule that same day.

Two days later, the determined Secretary Baker insisted that the president must visit Louisiana because much-promised federal help for the victims of the disaster in both Florida and Louisiana still hadn't put in an appearance. (It was, in fact, two days more before the Federal Emergency Relief Administration began operating in Florida.)

That August 26, the presidential party didn't fly in the comfort of *Air Force One*. The president had to use a far less luxurious aircraft for his trip to devastated areas in Louisiana, which ended in a stiff wind and another downpour.

In Florida meanwhile, thousands of survivors and their children were without enough food, shelter, or even medical assistance. Florida's Governor Lawton Chiles by then had to almost beg for federal aid for the essentials of life for his devastated people and added police and troops to halt looting.

Hordes of families had given way to frustration amid the wreckage of their homes. They had heard TV reports that the president was dispatching fighter aircraft and standby troops to the Middle East, after which at least one radio station manager commented while being swamped with complaints, "How can we send a half-million troops halfway around the world and yet we can't get food and water to our own people?"

The anger and the helplessness among the hurricane's refugees were overwhelming, as the president discovered all too soon. Even now, two days after the hurricane had passed, many still did not even have a crust of bread or a cup of drinkable water.

The avalanche of complaints finally did break through the president's preoccupation with his reelection campaign, to which he had returned after his second visit to a disaster area. From a campaign stop at Findlay, Ohio, he gave hasty assurance on the night of August 27 that food, water, temporary shelter, and troops would begin arriving in the devastated areas to end the four-day delay.

Next day, at last, twenty thousand federal troops began arriving at the stricken areas. With them they brought mobile electric generators, electric food kitchens, large tents and cots, and—most needed of all—food, water, and ice. Gasoline, too, was shipped in by the army in huge drums.

Amid scenes of devastation resembling war-torn land, the storm's victims waited in long lines with their children to be fed and given shelter and medical assistance where needed. It would be weeks before electric power and telephone service could be restored, years before the area could be rebuilt.

Some notion of the confusion and haste with which the emergency had been handled remains in a comment from a weary, harassed, and utterly frustrated Governor Chiles as help began arriving: "Right now, a truckload of food arrives, 200 people show up and 50 people get food and 150 people are angry. We've got to find a way to solve that."

Tent cities now were being set up in large Florida fields that had been cleared of ruins to provide temporary shelter for many of the displaced families. Attention was paid to the construction of many more facilities for public sanitation because of the ever-present threat of disease. Several emergency grants of millions of dollars in assistance also were authorized by the White House and more money was appropriated by Congress with the president's approval. Such furious activity had not been seen in Washington for years.

As the fourth largest state in the union, Florida's twenty-five electoral votes were up for grabs. The ill will toward the president, caused by the delayed federal response to the emergency, had so encouraged Governor Clinton that he, too, added Florida to the list of big states in which he would challenge the president in the fall campaign.

It was scarcely the best way for the federal government to conduct disaster relief but this was what happened in Florida and Louisiana in the presidential election year of 1992.

. . .

President Bush's second visit to south Florida on September 1 featured the most lavish promises for the future. Among the assurances he gave was that the federal government would pick up all the bills for rebuilding Florida's public property and services and that grants of $11,500 would be made to families whose homes had been destroyed and who had no insurance. Private insurance companies meanwhile put the storm's cost to them at about $7 billion; to the taxpayers, it may have been more more.

Besides the thirty lives lost in Florida during Hurricane Andrew, at least 85,000 homes were destroyed or badly damaged and an estimated 250,000 people were homeless. The estimates of total storm damage in that state alone ran as high as $20 billion. It was, all in all, the costliest storm in the nation's history.

The president did his best to enable the federal government to recover from its blundering relief effort. Upon returning to Washington after his second visit to the devastated areas in Florida and Louisiana, he addressed the nation by TV to announce that the Florida relief effort was unprecedented in scope. He added praise for self-help among the storm victims of Louisiana and thereby tried to smooth over the rising attacks on the failure of the federal relief effort and its delayed response to the emergency.

The victims of Hurricane Hugo, which had wrecked part of South Carolina's picturesque coastline in 1989, knew all too well how arduous the task of reconstruction was after a great natural disaster. Many homes of less fortunate people, insured or not, had never been rebuilt there and their owners had left with their families to start life anew elsewhere. As for businesses and factories, they took much more of a hit than they expected, especially when the federal government's aid effort totaled somewhat less than $1 billion. According to local estimates the storm's damage had been triple that sum.

With such wide publicity now being given to federal funding of the Florida storm's damage in an election year, it was understandable that South Carolinians may have been envious, but as one official insisted in that state, "I think our recovery has been little short of marvelous."

In Florida, as the fall presidential campaign approached, the mood was different. Instead of gratitude being shown for federal assistance, there still were scenes of desperation and mourning from Miami to Homestead in south Florida, in the bayous of storm-ravaged Louisiana, and elsewhere in the path of Hurricane Andrew.

No poll then could possibly have reflected the feelings of the tens of thousands of Florida refugees who could be thankful mainly that they still were alive and much less interested in forecasting what effect the disaster would have at the ballot box in the presidential election. That, principally, was President Bush's problem and he fully realized it.

To win, much more than his campaign style would have to be changed from how he had conducted himself at the Republican National Convention and immediately thereafter.

PART TWO
THE FALL CAMPAIGN

13

The State of the Presidency

President Bush was less than a commanding figure as he approached the home stretch of his race for reelection in the last days of what had been an unproductive summer for him.

On Labor Day, traditionally the take-off point for the final phase of the electoral process, he was trailing his Democratic rival, Governor Clinton, by from nine to fifteen points in the opinion polls. However, instead of urging his supporters to make greater efforts during the climactic drive ending with election day, the president was still belaboring Clinton with personal attacks—and falling still farther behind.

This time, the conventional political campaign of name-calling, half-truths, and other forms of negativism simply wasn't working and the president had no one to blame but himself. Instead of facing up to the damaged condition of the nation's economy that had begun midway during his term in the White House, the principal issue Clinton was stressing, the president was trying to assert that Clinton's failure to fight in the Vietnam War of almost a quarter of a century ago was much more important.

Bush couldn't seem to understand that he was trying to dodge his responsibility for near-record unemployment and despair among millions of people by stressing instead character and family values, as measured to the disadvantage of his opponent. At length, when he finally was forced to face the economic issue, what he often did was to complain that the press was misrepresenting the progress the government had made in overcoming the long recession.

That approach also failed to reverse the president's continuing decline in the polls.

Already, with two months to go before election day, the two biggest states in the union, California and New York, with about 40 percent of the electoral vote needed for victory, appeared to be lost to the Bush/Quayle ticket. Much of the Republican southern base also had eroded and even once-solid Republican states, such as Michigan and Ohio, were wavering.

Regardless of how much more forthcoming Governor Clinton had been on such dominant issues as turning the economy around and getting people back to work, this election still was mainly President Bush's to win or lose. As the nation's chief executive, in control of all the formidable powers of his high office, he had the authority to divert federal money and patronage to benefit key states that might be decisive in a close race.

Although that condition did not now exist throughout the land, as measured by nearly all the opinion polls, the president could not be ignored. The cautious Democrats, having been out of power in the White House for the better part of a generation, did not make the error of letting their current advantage cause them to believe that Clinton's lead was irreversible. Because American armed forces were once again deployed in the Middle East to safeguard the nation's supply line to that region's oil deposits, a new test of strength was possible at any time if Saddam Hussein became bold enough to challenge American-led overflights of his country or showered his Chinese-built missiles on Saudi Arabia or Israel. The prudent Israelis already were holding gas mask drills for their people.

Such were the circumstances in which the last weeks of this presidential election dragged by. Nobody, neither candidates nor campaign staffs nor the public at large, could feel sure about the outcome—or even mildly optimistic that some untoward event might not mar the tense interval before election day.

.   .   .

To add to President Bush's problems, Ross Perot began hinting that he, too, might renew his independent bid for the presidency, this time as a declared candidate in the fifty states. About Labor Day a few speculative newscasts and published articles, most of them seemingly inspired by Perot or his people, discussed the possibility of a renewed three-way contest. To all inquiries that resulted, neither Perot nor his representatives gave an unequivocal response.

It became evident soon enough, therefore, that Perot was considering some move in connection with the campaign, but it was difficult for experienced practical politicians in both major parties to believe that he would want to become a full-fledged third candidate after a six-week layoff. True, he had now qualified for listing on the presidential ballot in all fifty states through signed petitions gathered by the relatively few volunteers who had stayed on in his service. He also had kept most of the volunteer directors in the fifty states on his payroll and maintained offices for them and their skeleton staffs. In Dallas, he had kept his headquarters people busy but most of his former directorate had left him. It seemed reasonably clear, as a result, that the Texan couldn't hope to defeat both President Bush and Governor Clinton in a three-way race no matter how much television time he could buy with money out of his deep pockets.

From initial outside estimates that Perot was budgeting a half-million dollars a month to keep his campaign going on a stand-by basis, if nothing else, the speculative reports in print and on the air began guessing that he was likely to spend about $10 million in this interim if he planned to reenter the race.

There was a steady stream of conflicting accounts dealing with Perot's intentions. The air of mystery and expectation he could create proved to be intriguing enough to cause his book, *United We Stand, America*, to lead the best-seller lists. In an article under his name in the *New York Times* on August 30, he added to his promotional effort by challenging both major parties, asking, "How stupid do they think we are?"

Perot's position was that neither the Democrats nor the Republicans had tried to solve the country's most pressing problems, which he identified mainly as economic with a specific warning about the nation's $4 trillion debt. As a result, he wrote, the volunteers who had supported his abortive candidacy now had formed a new political organization, "United We Stand America," which he asked all his readers to join to try to deal with the issues the major parties had failed to resolve. "It is time to clean out the barn," he concluded. "Join us—pick up a shovel. Get to work!"

However, after noting how he had dropped his campaign in mid-July, people evidently weren't breaking down the doors of his headquarters or other volunteer offices to join his organization. Whereas he had been at or near the top of the polls in a three-way race in June, even though he was not then a declared candidate, the first test polls after his book was published gave him a washout single digit response. Many of the volunteers who had flocked to his standard no longer trusted him.

Most polling organizations indicated that about two thirds of the volunteers, most of them broadly identified as Reagan Democrats, had returned to their original party base and supported Governor Clinton. The rest had either gone with President Bush or remained on the sidelines except a few who had stayed on the job as Perot volunteers.

How many would return to Perot's standard if he chose to become a full-fledged independent presidential candidate for the "United We Stand America" organization, whatever it turned out to be? The first guesses of those attuned to the political process, the reporters and the pollsters, were that President Bush would be more affected than Governor Clinton, whose lead by that time was in double digits on a national basis. It followed, too, that even if the Perot movement remained relatively small in support of his resumed candidacy, he could well cause President Bush to lose a large state like Texas, home to both of them, in a very tight race.

This was the line of reasoning that led most of the ever-suspicious journalists to conclude that Perot's aim, if he did reenter the campaign, would be an effort to insure a crushing defeat for President Bush. When the question was posed to Perot, however, he still took no position on the possibility of his renewed candidacy, testified to his admiration for the president and his family, but explained that they differed widely on the issues, meaning a cure for the stagnant economy.

Perot wasn't ready to come out of his self-imposed isolation but he proceeded, nevertheless, with his war of nerves against both major party presidential candidates from his protected position. As to which one ranked higher in the Texan's hit list, there was little doubt that it was President Bush.

.   .   .

Coming up to Labor Day, the Democratic campaigners for Governor Clinton picked up Ronald Reagan's salient question to voters in his first presidential campaign in 1980: "Are you any better off today than you were four years ago?" The answer then was a loud and oft-repeated "No!" In 1992, Clinton and his vice presidential candidate, Al Gore, repeatedly used the same question.

Just before Labor Day, the Census Bureau, in its annual report on income and poverty, announced that 35.7 million Americans were living in poverty at the end of 1991, more than at any time since 1964 when President Lyndon Johnson started his "war on poverty." Specifically, the census report said 2.1 million Americans within the first year of the recession during the Bush years 1990–91 had fallen below the poverty level to increase the total to 35.7 million. That, the report continued, put the poverty rate at 14.2 percent for the nation, an increase for a second consecutive year. As for the purchasing power of a typical American household, the estimate was that it decreased in 1991 by nearly $1,100.

The poverty level for a family of four was identified by the Census Bureau as a unit with a cash income of less than $13,924 in 1991. The total of impoverished Americans was roughly the number of unemployed people plus others who were eligible for food stamps and used them.

There was no doubt that the Census Report didn't help President Bush's cause. On the contrary, Governor Clinton seized upon it quickly after it was issued, saying: "This administration has compiled the worst economic record in fifty years—since Herbert Hoover was president—and at Houston we saw what they promise for the next four years is more of the same."

A White House spokesman seemed almost resigned, saying that the increase in poverty was understandable even though the administration had tried to relieve national distress, "knowing that the recession would have a deleterious effect."

The Commerce Department, in another report about the same time, elaborated on the effect of the recession by saying that average earnings in the private sector had fallen 3.2 percent in hourly earnings since the outset of President Bush's term in 1989. In a companion study, the Congressional Joint Economic Committee reported that a thirty-year-old male with a high school education earned $3,500 less annually in 1991 than a comparable worker did in 1979.

One of the most damaging economic reports followed when the Labor Department announced 167,000 jobs had been lost to the private sector in the single month of August. Although the unemployment rate dropped one-tenth of a point to 7.6 percent at the same time, this was not a source of encouragement because labor specialists acknowledged the lower figure was due to the discouragement of many jobless people who had given up looking for work and no longer were counted.

Lane Kirkland, president of the AFL-CIO, argued that if the long-time unemployed and the part-time job holders had been included in the unemployment count, the total would have been nearly 18 million unemployed, or about 14 percent of the work force. Even so, separate government figures for some of the large states showed that their unemployment rates were above the national average, notably California's 9.8 percent and New York's 8.5 percent.

.   .   .

While campaigning in New Jersey a few days later, President Bush admitted the economy was in "lousy" shape but repeated his 1988 "Read My Lips" campaign pledge against no new taxes, which he had violated. Again, he blamed it all on the Democratic Congress saying, "I went along with one Democratic Congress and I'm not going to do it again. Ever! Ever!"

The president made more specific proposals to ease the pain of joblessness in other states he visited. In Texas, for example, he announced the sale of up to 160 F-16 fighter aircraft to Taiwan, and in Missouri a bit later he proposed to sell 72 F-15 fighters to Saudi Arabia, operations that were expected to preserve thousands of jobs in arms factories in those states and California among others. To ease the fears of the Israelis over the largesse to the oil-rich Arabs, he later promised the Jewish state a number of American helicopter gunships.

In the farm belt, the president also tried to boost his lagging reelection campaign once again, this time by promising $1 billion in government subsidies to promote larger wheat sales abroad. However, upon inquiry, government officials admitted that the supposed gains for farmers were largely illusory because larger foreign wheat sales tended to increase domestic wheat prices and thereby cut domestic government subsidies.

At the White House the general attitude seemed to be that the president couldn't be blamed for trying to help the farmers and at the same time giving his chances for reelection an upward nudge. Almost anything that helped his declining political fortunes, some of his supporters said privately, was better than nothing. It was an attitude the president seemed to share, especially when it developed that Perot and his people were seriously considering resumption of his independent campaign.

.   .   .

In his long and distinguished career as a public servant, George Bush had often won public approval for his management of difficult situations. In the first two years of his presidency, he also had accumulated some personal popularity, although by no means as much as the first lady, Barbara Bush. By hesitating to attack the long recession frontally by using the powers of government to relieve growing public hardship and distress, his popularity had vanished during his reelection campaign and even his credibility in the conduct of his high office had come into question.

Regardless of the outcome of this election of 1992, accordingly, there was no doubt that the preponderant share of public opinion wanted the full powers of the presidency to be invoked, together with the support of Congress, to end the recession within a reasonable time and restore the effectiveness of the nation's economy. It had been attempted at much worse times in the nation during this century, both in war and peace. It could be done again without the kind of disgraceful civil strife that was talked of so irresponsibly by some of the president's supporters.

Through their desperation and their threats, they were causing the public to believe that the condition of the country was much worse than it appeared to be. This may have mainly been the philosophy of the extreme conservative wing of the Republican party but the president went along with it. And eventually he and the party itself paid heavily for his temerity.

14

Hard Times

The nation had gone through other tough recessions in the latter part of the century, notably in 1974–75 and 1981–82, without the virtual panic that seized the Bush White House over the longer slump of the 1990s even though it was not as severe.

Partly this had to do with the latter-day American political tradition that linked presidential reelection campaigns, such as Bush's, to the state of the economy. In a bad economic election year, so the belief decreed, the sitting president was doomed no matter what he had or hadn't done to merit defeat.

Partly, too, this president seemed so put off by this syllogism that he often swung to extremes of emotion in his reelection campaign. Early on, he had seemed listless, even apathetic on the campaign trail. Toward the windup, he was making so many rash statements that he undermined his credibility with some of the voters.

The way he handled an unfortunate forecast that he would create 30 million jobs, given an eight-year term in the White House, illustrated his state of mind. In the last report of his Labor Department before election day, almost 10 million still jobless, he had to admit that his vision of three times as many new jobs had been an illusion.

Moreover, most economists saw little hope of any immediate improvement in the job market even if the president, by a miracle, could win reelection at the last hour.

All he could do at the White House, for the time being, was to talk earnestly about reemployment and hope for better things yet to come.

The president then was reduced to a lame form of political apology for his failure. He blamed the Democratic Congress for not approving a plan he had put before the honorable members, which, he said, would have provided 500,000 of his promised 30 million jobs.

It was of a piece with his explanation for breaking his other important campaign pledge, "Read My Lips, No New Taxes."

That, too, he moaned, had been the fault of the opposition. However, he went into the last weeks before election day with another loss of 57,000 jobs in the month of September. As his Bureau of Labor Statistics reported: "The unemployment rate was little changed from August but, at 7.5 percent, was down .3 percent from the June high of 7.8 percent."

Governor Clinton repeatedly called it the worst economic record of any president for fifty years. The president, still hoping for a turnaround by election day, argued that the .3 percent cut in the jobless rate was evidence of "slightly improving job markets."

The Labor Department suggested instead that the lower unemployment rate could be accounted for by the 1.1 million unemployed who had given up hope of finding work, had dropped out of the job market, and weren't counted. This administration spoke in different tongues.

It had been a tough year for everybody, the president included, and only slightly better for Governor Clinton, who had to take a lot of heat because of the president's examination of his rival's personal life. It was turning into that kind of a campaign.

. . .

President Bush centered some of his campaign on a denunciation of his opponent's sex life, his conduct as governor of Arkansas, and even his patriotism. The president was so heated up that he attacked a few hecklers as "draft dodgers" even though some hadn't even been born at the time of the Vietnam War. It wasn't an impressive display.

As for the unemployment problem, Bush told the Detroit Economic Club on September 10: "I want to stimulate entreprenurial capitalism, not punish it. I want to empower people to make their own choices, not yoke them to new bureaucracies. I want a government that spends less, regulates less, taxes less."

The president repackaged all his previous economic proposals in his Detroit speech. He emphasized that he wanted another four-year term on the basis of planned spending and tax reduction, more free trade agreements with foreign countries, and money-saving changes in some government social service operations.

The proposed tax cuts, however, weren't specific. He also hedged on his familiar proposal to reduce the capital gains tax by linking it to a proposed cut of $132 million in the federal budget. He seemed to be on firmer ground by promising cuts in a small business tax by one-third. As for income taxes, he evidently now planned to reduce them by just one point, only no sensible person believed any income tax reduction was then possible.

The president's package was compromised still further by a White House caveat to an antitax speech he had made the day before saying, "We do not need to raise taxes in this country." Marlin Fitzwater, the press secretary, announced just before the president's Detroit speech that this was no renewed promise of "Read my lips, no new taxes."

The Republican tax program was full of loopholes. First, the president proposed to cut his budget by one-third but only if Congress did the same for its operating budget. He also said he would reduce and merge or abolish various federal agencies but mentioned only one, the Arms Control and Disarmament Agency. Even these savings were compromised, however, by other provisions for boosts for job training and education programs.

Governor Clinton commented, "This is more of the same. More tax cuts for upper-income people and more deficits and less growth. We've had this for twelve years." Then he gave the President a final jab, saying, "It is a wrong-headed notion that prosperity will trickle down if we just make the rich even richer and get the government out of the way."

．　　．　　．

The Clinton program was more specific, having been put into a twenty-two-page economic plan and made public in June, but it had since undergone changes in degree. On August 22, the day after the end of the Republican Convention in Houston, the Arkansas governor, too, had outlined the main thrust of his ideas about the economy before the Detroit Economic Club. He also elaborated on them from time to time in the fall campaign.

What he began with was a tax increase for people with total incomes of more than $200,000 a year. He proposed to raise the top rate for such incomes from the current 31 percent to 36 percent.

Knowing quite well that some of these people may also have many deductions to offset large tax bites at the federal level, the Democratic plan also proposed to raise the minimum tax to be paid by such wealthy people and slap a 10 percent surtax on incomes of more than $1 million.

For middle-class taxpayers, he suggested either a 10 percent tax cut or a tax credit for families with children.

Besides such revenue-raising measures and reductions in the cost of government, Clinton's public works programs were his chief reliance for guaranteeing his promises to resolve the nation's problem of unemployment. What he suggested in his June economic paper was a $220,000,000 program for creating jobs in public works, improving education, and retraining the unemployed as well as those just coming into the work force without the necessary skills to handle advanced technology.

This was the heart of what the Democratic nominee called a "national economic strategy," explaining, "Our economy is struggling and the American dream is in trouble." He then predicted rashly that his economic plan would cut the national deficit in half within four years, but it was by no means clear how he expected to do it when the country was in industrial stagnation. There are limits to how much can be taken out of the nation's defense budget and both candidates were well aware of it, just as they were cautious about even hinting at cutting entitlements, such as Social Security, Medicare, and Medicaid.

The president, in commenting on Clinton's economic program, was just as savage assessing it as the Democratic candidate had been about Bush's objectives. As the president put it at one point, in a thrust at his rival, "He says he wants to tax the rich but, folks, he defines rich as anybody who has a job." At a little greater length: "Our nation has never been seduced by the mirage my opponent offers of a government that accumulates capital by taxing it, borrowing it from the people, and then redistributing it according to some industrial policy. We know that the clumsy hand of government is no match for the uplifting hand of the marketplace."

.   .   .

All this conflicting rhetoric about an economic program to create new jobs, as encouraged by both Democrats and Republicans, had other shortcomings. Neither side was willing to address the more serious problem of the numbers of jobs that might be lost through the adoption of such free trade programs as the United States–Mexico–Canada treaty, if finally approved by all concerned, through the massive cuts in Pentagon spending; and in the abolition of a number of federal agencies.

Here the noncandidate, Ross Perot, figured in the debate on the economy with proposals he had published in his book, *United We Stand, America*. Having dropped out of the race abruptly in mid-July, he was only hinting at coming back beginning a month later.

In a summary of previously announced plans, Perot again called for tax increases on individuals and businesses and reductions in benefits for the elderly and the poor. He also was all for making people who could afford it pay higher premiums for Medicare and taxes on Social Security benefits. He wanted to soak everybody an additional fifty cents a gallon gasoline tax and put a cap on health care costs. Even the military was hit under the Perot program by reducing cost-of-living increases over five years for military and federal pensions. On top of all else, he proposed further eliminations of federal departments and jobs.

As a result of figures attached to each of these programs, Perot contended his plan would eliminate the deficit and make possible balanced federal budgets within a reasonable time. The Bush and Clinton programs, he charged, would not.

Both President Bush and Governor Clinton appeared to be counting on cutting military jobs to provide more civilian employment, but nobody liked that very much, least of all those who would have been affected. Clinton, for example, at one point proposed the elimination of 2.6 million jobs in the armed forces. a million of them in the uniformed services. The Bush score sheet, based on Republican plans for armed forces reductions, was smaller but the projected savings were almost as large as the Clinton total.

In such situations as these, both major party nominees were trying to reassure adverse public sentiment with talk about tax breaks and other savings in an effort to compensate those who might be affected. As for overly large reductions in the uniformed forces themselves, anybody who ever had been associated with the Pentagon and its problems knew perfectly well that there was a limit to such economies at the expense of national security. The pell-mell rush to cut the heart out of the armed forces after World War II had left the country unprepared to stave off the first attacks on South Korea from Communist North Korea only five years later.

No matter who was elected in 1992, it would have been the sheerest folly once again "to scuttle the nation's military might," as President Truman called it in his era, on the theory that international peace and security could be assured merely by wishing for it at the UN.

The latter-day collapse of the Soviet Union did not eliminate America's last enemies by any means. Nor could the nation's security be assured by trying to squeeze excessive savings out of national defense to create the illusion that this, by itself, would put the fifty states back on the high road to economic recovery.

If the presidential campaign of 1992 had done nothing else, it had exposed the executive, legislative, and judicial branches of the government to the extent of public frustration, and even rage at times, over the workings of the political process. Not since the most desperate stages of the Great Depression in the early 1930s had there been such widespread mistrust and suspicion over the way the public's business was being conducted by a government that seemed, all too often, to have forfeited the respect of its constituents.

More than anything else, this glowering mood among so many angry and dispirited people demonstrated the depths to which public trust in democratic self-government had fallen in the United States. If those in the White House and the Treasury Department wondered why so few people dared make any kind of major investment or assume other and greater obligations for the future, the answer was clear for all to see. Few sensible people hoped for any improvement in the nation's economy for as long as the political process was dominated by an outrageous degree of political irresponsibility—by Democrats and Republicans alike.

This was the heritage of ill-will toward government that the victor would inherit on election day. The only way it could be diminished, let alone dispelled, was to put forward a sensible and realistic effort toward economic recovery as the first priority of a new presidential administration.

15

Panorama

On a sunny day in early autumn, President Bush appeared on national television at the controls of his little cigarette boat while cruising along Maine's coastal waters.

Within a short time, he would be back on the road trying as best he could to catch up with his challenger, Governor Clinton, who had been ahead of him in the opinion polls for weeks. For the few minutes the American public saw him piloting his cigarette boat that crisp fall afternoon, he appeared to be a very superior figure.

Neither the president nor his political advisers seemed aware at the time how his altogether brief period of relaxation would appear to a segment of the television audience that viewed him only as a far too comfortable president at a time of great hardship for millions of his fellow Americans.

I remember the despairing comment of an elderly black man who caught the speedboat scene on television at a convenience store: "Well, the president's having a good time and that's okay for him. But there's been many a day when I didn't have enough to eat this year and no money to buy food and so I had to go hungry. Only the president, he wouldn't know about that. He don't care about people like me, I guess."

It was a part of the president's problem during his faltering re-election campaign that he was so often depicted as a public official insensitive to the plight of the elderly, the jobless, the homeless. Yet, as the cigarette boat incident on television demonstrated, he sometimes wasn't aware of the extent to which he prejudiced himself among less fortunate people.

At a time of deepening recession across the land, it was the president's misfortune that he came across to a considerable part of the electorate as someone so far removed from ordinary folk that few could think of him as a sympathetic character, much less a savior. Under such circumstances, it followed that the closing stages of the presidential campaign that fall turned it into one of the ugliest in this century.

Regardless of what political considerations the two major parties presented to the electorate, the real issue for many a voter—not all— was the choice between a government that cared and a government that didn't. Truly, the need throughout the land was great, so much so that the private relief agencies among religious and charitable organizations were overwhelmed. Yet, by arguing for less government with particular reference to taxing and regulating big business and industry, the president was leaving the impression, rightly or wrongly, that he sought to limit what government could do in public assistance.

At a time when so many were being deprived of the bare means of existence, such economies at the expense of life itself were unthinkable. And yet, there was rising concern among the elderly, the handicapped, the indigent, homeless and unemployed that the very means of their own survival might in some circumstances be sharply reduced. This turned out to be the most frightening part of the campaign.

.   .   .

Because of a steady increase in the national debt beyond $4 trillion and the annual budgetary imbalance in the federal government's operations running into the billions, it was only reasonable to expect that the major party candidates would agree that tighter management was a priority. If, however, President Bush was calling for lower taxes and Governor Clinton was limiting his tax increases to those earning more than $200,000 annually, it was evident that sharp reductions in government operations would be necessary no matter who was elected.

Here Ross Perot, still flirting with a reentry into the presidential race, stressed his position about a reduction in entitlements. By quoting from his book, which was widely read, he increased public apprehension for the future in his insistence on major economies in social services as well as higher taxes to bring income and outgo for the government into balance over a period of years.

This continued to be one of the primary sources for the increased apprehension among some segments of the public that Social Security, Medicare, and Medicaid faced remorseless reductions. To be sure, President Bush was voluble with his reassurances against the kind of "tax and spend" policies he attributed to his Democratic opponent. However, no one among those who could least afford to lose government benefits was likely to feel safe with a president who already had violated one antitax pledge. Further, his warnings that Governor Clinton could not be trusted scarcely were calculated to increase public confidence in the front-runner. The politics of fear can sometimes react against those who advocate it.

This is precisely what happened during the closing stages of the presidential campaign. Owing to so much discussion among the candidates of the limitations of government, it was inevitable that the victims of the great hurricanes that leveled parts of south Florida and Louisiana would become restive over the delays in the president's promised assistance in rebuilding devastated areas.

For a long time after the storms ceased, thousands of helpless families still had no roof over their heads. They also remained dependent on the uncertainties of government assistance for the necessities of life. Protests from mayors and even governors over delayed assistance seemed unavailing. When there were displays of relief supplies being shipped abroad to the destitute people torn by civil wars in Bosnia-Herzegovina and Somalia, one of the staples of television news for a time, feelings of discontent among the refugees here at home boiled over into mild demonstrations of protest.

·   ·   ·

One of the most critical areas of social policy throughout the nation, the presence of almost five million families on government welfare rolls, became a part of the presidential campaign almost by indirection.

During his first three years in office, President Bush seemed to take little note of the astronomic growth of people on welfare—almost 14 million in all. Mainly because Governor Clinton had been trying to find a solution to the problem in his own state, and was proposing drastic changes in the system, the president finally realized that something had to be done about welfare.

Mainly, he asked the states to come up with experimental plans to cut the welfare rolls. Then, toward the climax of the presidential campaign, he put on a tough show for the voters by demanding that people try to "get off the dole." Even some Republicans—to some extent—regretted the president's approach, especially as they applied to mothers of dependent children. For how could they possibly "get off the dole" without the ability to find and hold a job at a time when jobs were so scarce?

The Clinton program was much more detailed and at least presented the electorate with several propositions worth discussing even if there was considerable doubt that the new Congress would find them practical, even palatable. There were no easy answers in the Clinton plan.

Basically, what Clinton proposed was to require the able-bodied people on welfare, especially welfare mothers, to perform community work or find a paying job after two years on the welfare rolls, provided they were capable of working. To help welfare mothers, what he suggested was to spend $6 billion a year for training and tax credits.

The basis for the proposal was the passage by Congress in 1988 of the Family Support Act, which requires states to put able-bodied welfare mothers to work or provide them with training and education to hold a job.

The problem dealt in particular with the fate of the children affected either by the current state programs or Clinton's proposed extension of it to federal law. It developed that one in five American children in the early 1990s was dependent on welfare for at least a year before before age eighteen. For black children, the total was close to 75 percent who were supported by at least a year on welfare before they turned eighteen.

Presumably, what Clinton wanted to try to do under a federal law, Aid to Families with Dependent Children, was to provide better education and training for the children to get them off the welfare rolls. It was an ambitious outlook, but there was little certainty that it could get past Congress without major changes. Even then, no one could be certain that it would appreciably reduce the country's welfare obligations.

The only thing on which everybody of influence was agreed, including the two major party presidential candidates, was that it would serve the interests neither of the federal government, the states, nor the millions of welfare clients to permit the system to degenerate into a dole from which people rarely could free themselves.

So the millions on welfare, like so many of the others who were dependent in whole or in part on Social Security, Medicare, and Medicaid, became virtual hostages to political fortune as the presidential campaign entered its climactic stage. Until the newly elected

president and Congress took over at the onset of 1993, none of the
dependents could be certain what would happen to them. Nor would
it be something that the new administration could shove into the
background and try to ignore.

.   .   .

Regardless of how the government discharged its responsibilities
to the least able among its people to survive, the support of both
private agencies and individual volunteers was remarkable. This was
particularly true during the presidential campaign, when so much
doubt was raised about the willingness of the American people to
support the least fortunate among them who needed help.

This, at least, was in the warmhearted American tradition. If the
great ones at the seat of government, and some of the aspirants to
high office were hesitant and fearful of the nation's ability to solve its
societal problems, there was scant evidence of such despairing attitudes among the citizenry as a whole.

Among the individual volunteers who came unbidden to Florida
after the hurricane that devastated the southern part of the state, Marilyn Quayle was discovered hard at work among distressed families
with children. As long as she could pass unnoticed, the vice president's wife was satisfied to play a small role, along with thousands of
others, in providing whatever help she could to the victims of the
storm. Only after her identity became known generally did she feel
her usefulness was lessened.

Although the response of the volunteers was notable in these
devastated areas, it wasn't as clear in the other great metropolitan
centers of the land that private relief agencies and individuals could
make a difference among the millions of ghetto dwellers who also
needed help. There were few signs of progress in cities like New
York City and Chicago, for example, that deplorable living conditions for some of the population were yielding to improvement. Or
even that children had milk and enough food.

States and cities and private agencies had struggled throughout
the recession to relieve want and distress in such areas without making much headway. The scale of the effort at rebuilding was so great
that only the federal government was likely, over years, to undertake
what amounted to a revival of inner cities.

In smaller communities workaday citizens could make a discern-
ible difference. So could the religious and charitable relief organizations with which they were affiliated. Indeed, a few people here and

there who had businesses to attend to by day were known to devote their money and their efforts to relieving distress, especially in places where government money was in short supply.

One such volunteer widely known for her work among the poor and the homeless was Anna Mae Denton, who fed 150 to 200 people on many an evening in and near her home in Knoxville, Tennessee. As a tax accountant with an excellent reputation, she was usually busy taking care of her regular clients, but all her spare time and even her earnings, beyond a minimum for her own needs, went for the relief of hunger and want among destitute people.

A widening circle of acquaintances and friends were drawn into Ms. Denton's work as the community's own relief efforts expanded. Often she received food from owners and managers of markets who donated their leftovers and sometimes fresh produce as well. With the passage of time and a greater appreciation of her work in the east Tennessee area, larger business concerns also came to admire and support her efforts.

What such examples of merciful human conduct provided was a communitywide awareness of the value of self-help to supplement and perhaps increase the extent of government participation in nationwide relief at a difficult time in the country's history. This is what had been done in so many cities during the Great Depression, while the New Deal concentrated on large-scale efforts to revive the economy. If what Ms. Denton was doing in Knoxville could have been widely duplicated in larger communities, given sufficient safeguards, some of the distress in the inner cores of the nation's largest cities might have been alleviated. As her work demonstrated, there still was need for individual endeavor to feed, clothe, and house distressed people in America at a time when government relief agencies were overburdened.

16

A Question of Trust

Still trailing in the polls, with Ross Perot poised to reenter the presidential race in the fall campaign, President Bush had to do something to rally his shocked supporters. What he did was to redefine his closing campaign strategy around the issue he called "trust."

By that he meant faith in him, in his ability to lead the nation, in his promises and in the people who worked so closely with him, notably the new director of his campaign, Secretary of State Baker. As for the lamentable state of the economy, and his responsibility for it, which was Governor Clinton's main issue, the president kept blaming Congress for all the ills in his administration.

The president hoped to convince the voters that his Democratic rival wasn't to be trusted inside the White House. The problem with this approach was that Clinton at once jibed that the president couldn't even be trusted to keep his own promises, notably the "read my lips" pledge against raising taxes. Moreover, the president also found it difficult to convince the public that Clinton was a shady character, and damn the economy—the verdict of the polls. For that, Bush and Baker had nobody to blame but themselves.

The other major problem the president and his White House strategist had to face was the virtual certainty that Perot would be making a three-way race out of the fall campaign sooner rather than later. Perot, to be sure, still hadn't committed himself, remaining coy about his plans and grabbing off as much publicity as possible by sponsoring a "Will He–Won't He?" debate.

All the signs, though, now pointed to Perot's reentry into the presidential contest, this time as a declared candidate, regardless of the abrupt manner in which he had dropped out in July. Certainly no friend of the President's, Perot was letting rumors spread about how much of his money he would invest this time in a campaign he couldn't possibly win. From the original proposal of $10 million, these stories now were suggesting that the total Perot investment in advertising, headquarters, and paid campaign staffers could run as high as $60 million or more.

And why not? It was *his* money and he was accountable to nobody for how he chose to spend it. At Bush headquarters, it was argued that Perot was being very foolish, that he couldn't expect anybody to believe he could win against two major party presidential candidates and therefore he was just going to be a spoiler.

A spoiler? Against which candidate? Without evidence to the contrary, the Bush people had to assume Perot's candidacy was aimed directly at the president—a threatened split in the Republican vote that would be to Clinton's advantage. The White House decided, therefore, to put a spin on that entirely logical conclusion and try, if at all possible, to split the anti-Bush vote between Clinton and Perot.

It was evident at Democratic headquarters that all this was bound in the end to benefit Clinton's candidacy. The mood there became cautiously upbeat. Although the Republicans put out pejoratives about a renewed Perot campaign as "kooky," "irrelevant," and "disruptive," nothing like that could be attributed to the Democrats.

The center of attention, Perot, fairly beamed in his occasional public appearances but he still remained noncommittal. However, there was no doubt that he was enjoying himself as the potential source of more bad news for a president who already had more than he could handle.

. . .

President Bush's "trust" issue developed into a lot beyond a rehash of Clinton's bout with the draft in the Vietnam War and the tabloid tale of an adulterous adventure that his wife had already knocked down. Now the president took out the brass knuckles to try to make Clinton's character questionable among the voters mainly because it was the only option that remained to the White House. Ordinarily, the president had left such questionable tactics to surrogates, a precaution warranted in view of what had happened to President Nixon's involvement in the Watergate plot. This time, however, Bush took on the tasteless assignment himself.

In the cold-blooded mood in which most old-time politicians approach such objectionable operations, some observed hopefully that these tactics had wrecked the Dukakis candidacy in 1988 when he had been seventeen points ahead. With nothing else at hand to use against Clinton, it might help the president's cause if he could tear down Clinton's image of competence and determination and show him to be untrustworthy, so the White House crowd argued.

What the president and Secretary Baker hadn't figured on, it soon became evident, was a counterattack from Clinton. Once the White House assault began on his character, he slammed back sometimes with two blows for one.

The governor and his hard-working staff had perfected a system of prompt responses to anything that came out of Republican headquarters or the White House. If the president called Clinton "weak-kneed," a "know-nothing" and "not to be trusted," the name-calling also mounted on the Democratic side that the president was "irresponsible," "pitiful," and "afraid to debate the issues."

It wasn't a particularly edifying spectacle for the rivals for leadership of the world's sole remaining superpower, but this was what the president and the secretary of state had planned and that was the first response. The rest was just as bad.

Now the president shifted tactics. He turned to Clinton's admitted single experience with smoking marijuana as a student—the occasion during which he drew laughter from late night TV comics when he insisted he hadn't inhaled. The president implied that his Democratic rival had had a much more sinister experience with the drug habit. He also contended that his opponent, if elected, would raise taxes on the middle class and would cut Social Security, Medicare, and Medicaid for the elderly.

This drew prompt and indignant denials from the Democrats and Clinton.

.   .   .

The president's assault on Clinton's character also included suppositions that had been broadcast for some time over a cable network, C-span, to the general effect that there was something suspicious about Clinton's trip to Moscow in the late 1960s as a Rhodes scholar at Oxford University. This was the kind of thing right-wing Republicans had used in the heyday of the McCarthy era to discredit their opposition, as the Democrats were quick to point out.

However, the president had not been a party to these broadcasts at first. They had been undertaken by four conservative congressmen. According to published reports, all four had talked to the president at the White House about using the Clinton student trip to Moscow to show that there may have been a link between the Communists and the Vietnam War protest in which thousands of young Americans participated in the late 1960s.

By implication, so the congressmen's theory went, this could raise doubts about Clinton's part in the anti-Vietnam protests in which he participated in England while an Oxford student. It may have been an index of the president's desperation that he seized upon the notion and used it at the first possible opportunity.

It took place in the president's second appearance on the "Larry King Live" show on CNN. King himself raised the issue by asking what the president now thought of Clinton's trip to Moscow as a student twenty-three years ago. The president responded: "Larry, I don't want to tell you what I really think because I don't have all the facts. But to go to Moscow one year after Russia crushed Czechoslovakia and not remember who you saw—I think, I really think, the answer is to level with the American people."

It followed that the story hit the top spot in the news media at once because it had become the president's responsibility, not that of conservative congressmen on a cable network station. Clinton now had to respond and he did so by accusing the president of using McCarthy's tactics to besmirch a rival's patriotism.

After some hesitation, the president announced he would accept Clinton's explanation of his student trip. Still, Bush renewed the attack on the governor by charging it was wrong for him to have demonstrated against the Vietnam War in a foreign country, England. This time, Clinton responded with more spirit, pointing out that the president's father, Senator Prescott Bush of Connecticut, had been right in opposing Senator McCarthy but the president himself had been wrong in using McCarthy's methods in trying to discredit an opponent.

Nevertheless, Bush maintained his effort to make Clinton seem unpatriotic as a protestor against the Vietnam War on foreign soil. Between that and a continued emphasis on how Clinton had tried to escape the draft, what the Republicans hoped to do was to convince the public that Clinton could not be trusted to be elected as president and commander-in-chief.

It was the president's response to Clinton's continued use of the Bush administration's alleged failure to resolve the country's economic problems as the major argument against the president's effort to seek reelection.

What the Democratic campaign managers did to blunt the president's attack was to obtain an endorsement of Clinton's presidential candidacy from retired Adm. William J. Crowe, Jr., who had served as chairman of the Joint Chiefs of Staff under Reagan and Bush.

The sixty-seven-year-old admiral defended Clinton's deferred status in the Vietnam War draft by saying that the issue had been overblown. It was an example, he went on, of how the political process "has a tendency to take flimsy evidence and reach grand conclusions." Other military veterans agreed with the admiral, and the opinion polls showed little difference in the lagging position of the Bush/Quayle ticket, which remained far behind the Clinton/Gore team.

For the time being, at least, the public seemed to have continued to accept Clinton's position that the condition of the economy was the major issue in the campaign and Bush's performance to date had been ineffective. As for the draft issue, Clinton continued to base his own defense on his eventual receipt of a draft lottery number so high that he was unlikely to have been called up for military duty. He also denied having received favored treatment from federal, state, and local officials in 1969 while his status was being determined.

There is little doubt, however, that the governor increased his difficulties by tending to speak at length on almost any subject. In the case of the draft, the confusion surrounding the issue was twice confounded. Nor did Clinton do much better in philosophizing on the subject as follows: "The problem is when people ask you about special treatment, they mean did you leverage money or power or something to get something that other people wouldn't have gotten. And the answer is no."

The main trouble with the Vietnam draft, he added, was that the system itself favored well-educated people. In any future draft, he said he believed fewer exceptions should be allowed for healthy men within the range of ages specified for military duty.

Despite all the back and forth, Clinton still could not seem to shake off a continued Republican buildup of the issue of "trust" against him. Vice President Quayle also was criticized when his enlistment in a National Guard unit in Indiana at the time of the Vietnam War was said to have saved him from the draft and possible exposure to enemy bullets in Vietnam.

One of the few times that Quayle had to take the heat for his experience with outmaneuvering draft boards came in mid-September at a rally in Ravenna, Ohio. At the time, his detractors hooted down his appeal for President Bush's reelection. When he asked the unruly crowd, "Who do you want as president?" most yelled, "Clinton!"

The best the vice president could do then was to shout in an effort to make himself heard over the booing: "We'll never give Bill Clinton a chance to be president of the United States."

It was not the finest hour either for the vice president or the Republican campaign.

.   .   .

Another major issue Governor Clinton had to face was President Bush's charge that Arkansas state taxes had been raised 128 times during Clinton's dozen years as governor. It may have been an exaggeration but, under the general political theory that most people are willing to believe ill of candidates for public office, this was the line the president kept repeating in his stump speeches.

What the Democrats came back with was an accounting that the nation's taxes under Bush had been raised 178 times. These statistics, based on every boost in fees as well as taxes, were published at length in as respected a newspaper as the *New York Times*—which indicated how seriously such outrageous statistics were taken.

This, in short, was the level at which the respective campaigns of President Bush and Governor Clinton were conducted in the presidential election of 1992.

To the mythical Man from Mars, it surely would have seemed strange that a large country on planet Earth should be selecting its leadership in such a manner. And yet, this is what the American people were asked to believe of the respective presidential candidates of their two major parties. So far as is known, the electorate, having been trained to expect the worst rather than the best of their chosen representatives, remained perfectly calm faced with the misrepresentations about their presidential candidates.

Actually, on the basis of the latest statistics from the Department of Commerce—those of the census year of 1990—the average state and local taxes for Arkansas were the fourth lowest among the fifty states, $9.60 for each $100 of personal income earned in the state. The three with lower taxes still were Alabama, $9.47; Tennessee, $9.36, and New Hampshire, $8.36. The highest were New York, $15.65, and Alaska, $19.87.

It was not at all a bad showing for one of the poorest states in the union at the time of Governor Clinton's dozen years in office. Even so, the state's sales taxes had been boosted twice, others had also been increased, but the total gain from the time Clinton was first elected in 1979 was exactly forty-three cents through 1990. It should be noted, however, that this kind of rigid economy at the state level was also true of a number of other states. In reality, there had been relatively little increase in state and local taxes anywhere since the late 1970s. In 1979, Commerce Department figures showed that the average state and local tax rate for all fifty states was $11.37 per $100 and in 1990 it was only seven cents more.

Nevertheless, even if Governor Clinton had turned out to be the big "tax and spend" liberal that the Bush people tried to make him out to be, he would have had a hard time jacking up many Arkansas state levies. There is a provision in the Arkansas Constitution that requires three-quarters of the state's legislators to approve any tax boost they or the governor propose. The law in Arkansas also provides for an automatic cut in spending in any fiscal year if there is a decline in expected revenues.

But, quite naturally, it would have been tiresome for Clinton or his campaign people to have elaborated on all this in response to the charges of the opposition. The American electorate, never very long in its attention span, would have turned off the truth, mainly because the lies were more interesting. And anyway, who wants to listen to figures?

.   .   .

There was a price to be paid for all the negative campaigning during this presidential race. It may not have been the worst, but it was close enough so that it created public doubt in the nation's immediate future. That in turn, as rising business and industrial bankruptcies showed, caused a drop in consumer confidence. As a result, spending by the nation's consumers—normally accounting for two-thirds of the country's production—remained low through 1992.

Under the circumstances, it was unlikely that the rubber bands would be taken off people's wallets at least until after all the bad-mouthing ended and the election was settled. Even then, as repeated polls of public opinion demonstrated, few people were willing to speculate with their savings under the dreadful conditions each presidential candidate accused the other of being likely to create if elected.

There had been a suspicion throughout the land for many years that something was wrong with the way we, the people, elect our presidents. Probably the sheer length of the campaigns and how even the most distinguished candidates belabor each other and the nation's prospects, as well, may have had something to do with the negative attitudes so prominent a part of the election of 1992.

If so, an exceedingly simple solution was readily at hand: Shorten the presidential campaigns.

17

Trust and the White House

For inspirational effect, President Bush was fond of talking about a "new world order" during his reelection campaign. It was his way of seeking to uplift a doubting populace beyond mundane considerations of the shortcomings of government in order to concentrate on America as a force for freedom in the world.

The president fairly glowed sometimes in describing how many nations had thrown off the totalitarian yoke during his presidency, mainly through the collapse of the Soviet Union. The "new world order" aspect of the campaign, however, all too soon ran afoul of the ongoing congressional inquiry into the Bush administration's admitted help for Saddam Hussein's Iraq with loans and credit just before the dictator invaded Kuwait.

This was when the president made his defense, much in the spirit of his "new world order," by saying his effort "to bring Saddam into the family of nations" had been well intentioned even if it did fail. However, Senate investigators kept probing for suspicion of wrongdoing and a snooping press quickly christened the revived inquiry "Iraqgate" after added disclosures that American aid to Iraq had been used by Saddam for his arms buildup.

As Senate investigators delved deeper into the case, Senator Al Gore, Clinton's vice presidential candidate, took center stage with a bitter attack on what he called the president's duplicitous policy toward Iraq. As Gore stated the issue, he accused the president of "poor judgment, moral blindness and bungling policies" that had led to a war "that should never have taken place." Moreover, the senator continued, the president's decision had put the lives of members of the American armed forces at risk when they were sent into battle against the marauding Iraqis in the Gulf War.

Directly on the issue of trust, the Tennessean charged the president had not been truthful about his dealings with Iraq and therefore did not deserve reelection. This was how Gore put the position: "Bush deserves heavy blame for intentionally concealing from the American people the clear nature of Saddam Hussein, for convincing himself that friendly relations with such a monster were possible and for persisting in this effort far beyond the point of folly."

The White House shot back that Gore's accusations were untrue, that he was trying to "rewrite history" for the sake of personal advantage in the presidential campaign. As the Senate's inquiry proceeded and others were launched both inside and outside government, some believed that there was substance to Gore's challenges to the good faith of the White House.

In any event, the senator's attack took a lot of the steam out of the president's criticism of Clinton's character as unworthy of public trust. The Senate's inquiry into Iraqgate pushed ahead.

. . .

Aside from testimony that the Iraqi dictator misused the American-guaranteed loans and credits by diverting them to military uses against Kuwait, the various inquiries finally produced an indictment against the American manager of a small branch in Atlanta of a major Italian bank as the conduit for Saddam's illegal use of the American-guaranteed loans.

The manager, Christopher P. Drogoul, pleaded guilty in Atlanta's Federal Court to a specification in the indictment that he had participated in the illegal loans. His alleged crime was that he had acted without the knowledge of his main office in Italy of the Banca Nazionale del Lavoro (B.N.L.), almost wholly owned by the Italian government.

Still, when a House inquiry, parallel to the Senate's, showed that the CIA had withheld documents indicating that the B.N.L. had known of the actual uses of the American loan guarantees, Dragoul changed his plea from guilty to innocent with the permission of both the federal judge and prosecutor in his case. The Democrats in Congress then charged the White House with a cover-up.

As a result, the presiding judge, Marvin H. Shoob, removed himself from the case, set down trial for Drogoul after the election, and stated for the record that he was acting on the basis of classified CIA documents offered by the prosecution that showed the B.N.L.'s knowledge of the deal with Saddam was not limited to the small Atlantic branch. It was Drogoul's contention that if his home office knew of his activities, he had violated no rule or statute and therefore wanted a court trial to prove his innocence.

Judge Shoob, in entering the classified documents in the court record, explained: "They definitely support the defendant's position that B.N.L. in Rome was aware of what he was doing and they also undermine the government's position that this was a 'lone wolf' type operation."

The judge thereupon rejected a government prosecutor's plea to keep the incriminating CIA documents a secret, explaining, "I have concluded that the failure of the U.S. investigators to conduct an investigation in Rome and Iraq and to question knowledgeable persons available to them indicates an effort to absolve B.N.L.–Rome of complicity in the Atlanta branch bank loans."

The issue at that juncture was a CIA letter dated September 17 in which the agency had said that all available information at its command already had been given to government prosecutors. This turned out upon later examination not to be true. The agency had in its files more than enough evidence to indicate that at least some members of the Atlanta branch's home bank in Rome knew what was going on when billions of dollars in loans to Saddam Hussein were flowing unquestioned through the Atlanta branch.

These, so the government charged in line with Drogoul's prosecution, were the loans for which the United States had assumed responsibility and which Saddam was accused of misusing to arm his forces. In President Bush's words once the deception was exposed, the Iraqi military machine had become the fourth largest in the world at the time of the Gulf War.

The role of the Italian government, if any, was not further clarified at the Drogoul hearing on his change of plea except that both the CIA and the federal prosecutor denied they had tried to cover up the Rome bank's involvement. This did not square with other information given congressional investigators in tracing the growth of a national scandal and determining who would ultimately be held responsible.

However, on the fundamental moral issue of public trust in government, it would appear that the White House had some questions to answer about its relations with Iraq before the beginning of the Gulf War.

.   .   .

This much was known about the problem of dealing with Saddam Hussein in the Middle East that President Bush had inherited from the preceding Reagan administration when he entered the White House in 1989: some time in the middle 1980s, while Bush had been Reagan's vice president, Iraq had arranged through the U.S. Department of Agriculture to take advantage of a system of American loan guarantees for customers for American farm products. The Iran-Iraq War, which had begun in 1980, still was being fought at the time and the United States was using arms sales to Iran as part of a deal to free American hostages being held in Lebanon by a pro-Iranian group. (This developed into the Iran-contra scandal when profits from these arms sales were channeled by the United States to support the anti-Communist forces that were fighting for control of Nicaragua, the contras.)

Once the hostages were released and the Iran-Iraq War ended in 1988 with Iran's defeat, the Bush administration evidently decided to shift its main attention to Iraq and Saddam Hussein as a potential threat to American access to the rich Middle East oil supplies in Saudi Arabia and Kuwait. It is unclear at what point American intelligence discovered that Saddam had been using the American loan guarantees to buy arms instead of the supplies of American grain for which he supposedly had contracted. That remained to be determined from the closely guarded CIA reports about the complicated scheme through which Iraq got the money to buy guns instead of grain. The key reports were classified and restricted to a very small group in government.

However, the Federal Bureau of Investigation during the summer of 1989 received a tip that something peculiar was involved in certain loans to Iraq, guaranteed by the United States, that were passing in large volume through the small branch bank in Atlanta that belonged to the B.N.L., which in turn was largely owned by the Italian government.

Despite all the niceties of diplomatic relations, the FBI soon raided the Italian bank branch in Atlanta—the date was August 4, 1989—The branch was closed, its records were seized, and its manager, Drogoul, was closely questioned about the bank's dealings with Iraq.

Not long afterward, an argument developed between Iraq and Kuwait over their border. Being well aware that Saddam had picked a fight with Iran in the previous decade in an argument over control of the Shatt-al-Arab waterway leading to the Persian Gulf, the State Department at once became concerned about the border dispute with Kuwait.

Some time in July 1990, Foreign Minister Tariq Aziz of Iraq reported to the Arab League that Kuwait was a threat to Iraq because it refused to yield in the border dispute. Still acting in low key, the Bush administration sent a midlevel State Department official to complain to the Iraqi ambassador to the United States against the belligerent tone Iraq had adopted against Kuwait. By this time, too, it is apparent (with the wisdom of hindsight) that the FBI and the CIA had accumulated evidence from the seized Atlanta branch bank files as to the large sums of money passing through that conduit—a lot more, certainly, than normally would have been used to buy wheat and other farm products. Much of it was being guaranteed by the United States for payment if Saddam defaulted.

On July 17, 1990, Saddam Hussein warned Kuwait of military action if his demands were not satisfied, and Iraqi troops massed on the Kuwaiti border. Now Secretary of State Baker cabled the American ambassador to Iraq, April Glaspie, to try to determine Iraq's intention. After Ambassador Glaspie talked with Saddam on July 25 and cabled the White House, there was enough concern for President Bush to caution Saddam against a military attack.

(Later in the Presidential campaign, Ross Perot was to accuse the Bush administration of withholding the text of Glaspie's messages because, so he alleged, the ambassador had given Hussein what amounted to a go-ahead with his projected attack—something President Bush denied with a show of outrage.)

The text of the president's message to Glaspie, as it was made public long afterward, was exceedingly mild in tone in keeping with his policy of trying to bring Saddam into the family of nations. Once Glaspie delivered the message, she was summoned home by Secretary Baker on July 30. On August 2, 1990, Saddam's Iraqi forces launched an all-out attack on Kuwait.

President Bush then finally took off the kid gloves and used his acknowledged skill in international affairs to form a coalition of forces under American leadership to fight Saddam and made a first-rate record for himself as a commander-in-chief by smashing Saddam's invasion force within a short time in the Gulf War.

.   .   .

Once the United States persuaded the United Nations to investigate Saddam's arsenal and destroy his weapons of mass destruction, the Bush administration proceeded to deal with the source of Saddam's money for his Kuwait attack. This was when Drogoul, the

Atlanta branch bank manager, was induced to plead guilty to an indictment for fraud handed up on February 28, 1991, in Federal Court, Atlanta. The guilty plea, however, did not come to public attention until June 2, 1992, and even then it did not make much an impression in the middle of the presidential campaign because the plea was on a technicality—that Drogoul had violated his parent bank's rules by not informing its management (the Italian government) of what he had done to help Saddam launch the Gulf attack on Kuwait.

In the final weeks of the presidential campaign on September 17, when Drogoul asked the Federal Court in Atlanta to let him change his plea to innocent, another story came to public attention. About the same time, Rep. Henry Gonzales, a Texas Democrat, read aloud on the House floor from a classified document received from the CIA in which it was indicated that Drogoul's home office in Rome had known of his work in channeling billions of dollars of American-guaranteed loans to Iraq before the Gulf War.

This was the basis for both the change of plea and the criticism of the Bush administration by Judge Shoob. A CIA argument with both the Justice Department and the FBI followed thereafter, but Senator Gore kept pushing his charges against the president and others.

Before election day, it finally became known that about $5 billion in illegal loans to Iraq has passed through the Atlanta branch bank, according to prosecutors' charges. Of that total, nearly $2 billion were immediately subject to restitution to lending agencies under the terms of the American guarantees. The Bush administration contended, however, that Iraqi monies frozen in the United States with the beginning of the Gulf War would be used to imdemnify lenders' losses.

Still in advance of election day, there was one more twist to an exceedingly puzzling story. In pursuing his charges that Governor Clinton was not to be trusted, President Bush tried to involve his Democratic rival in the government's pre-Gulf war effort to keep Saddam Hussein's Iraqi regime in line.

In one of his appearances on CNN's "Larry King Live," the president first denied that he'd known of the illegal sales of military equipment to Iraq, adding that it was a mistake to accuse him of participating in the buildup of Saddam's military power, and then remarked: "Do you know who wanted to make loans, grain credit loans, and get hold of [Nizar] Hamdoon, the Iraqi ambassador, on grain credits?" A pregnant pause, then: "Governor Clinton."

Clinton brushed aside the president's attempt to make him a part of a scheme to help Saddam. The governor explained briefly that Arkansas farmers sold a lot of rice in the Middle East, and it was his routine, as their representative, to call on the Iraqi ambassador when he visited Little Rock. As for supporting the covert program of arms sales to Iraq before the Gulf War, the governor called the implied accusation incredible. That was the last that was heard of it. President Bush did not refer to it again during the rest of the campaign.

.   .   .

On trust within the White House, two other cases embarrassed the Bush-Quayle ticket that fall in its run for reelection.

The more important one involved another inquiry into a bank fraud, that one in the Middle East, and it had to do with an institution that had been closed, the Bank of Credit and Commerce International (B.C.C.I.). A Senate report connected it with such crimes as terrorism and the laundering of drug money running into the billions of dollars.

The American government was charged with laxity in the case.

As the allegations were described by Senator John F. Kerrey, a Massachusetts Democrat whose committee issued the report, lobbyists for the B.C.C.I. succeeded in blocking a detailed investigation of the bank and even concealed criminal acts. As in the case of the Italian bank that dealt with Saddam Hussein, Kerrey's report accused the CIA of knowledge of the way the B.C.C.I. had operated.

Paralleling several other ongoing inquiries into bribery and associated crimes, the Kerrey committee urged severe punishment for banks that do business in the United States while also dealing with banks in other countries where there is little or no regulation of banks on the international level. Much stricter American laws also were advocated within the United States to punish former American government officials caught in illegal lobbying.

A second Senate report dealt with what was called a politically motivated punishment for a convict who claimed to have sold marijuana to Dan Quayle before he became President Bush's vice president. The prisoner, Brett C. Kimberlin, charged that he had arranged for a 1988 news conference on the subject while still in prison but had been put in solitary confinement over election day that year. The news conference was never held.

The Senate report on the matter concluded that the primary purpose of the actions against the prisoner had been to keep his allegations out of the 1988 presidential campaign. It had no effect on the 1992 reelection drive.

All in all, the Bush administration's handling of the issue of trust appeared to have undergone some strain on the Republican side in the 1992 presidential contest. It was not an atmosphere in which truth was easy to come by and the electorate was well aware of it. The president's vision of a "new world order" under America's inspirational leadership offered a much prettier picture to the average American voter but it could not fairly be said to approximate reality.*

*Two postelection developments in the cases pf the B.N.L. and the B.C.C.I. should be noted here for the record. Drogoul, the B.N.L. branch manager who successively pleaded guilty, then innocent to federal charges, again changed his plea to guilty on September 2, 1993, in connection with charges growing out of the secret arming of Iraq. In the trial of a defendant in the B.C.C.I. case, the jury verdict was innocent. A second figure in the case was never tried.

18

Government in Distress

W hen Ross Perot announced his reentry in the presidential race after an eleven-week absence, he found it awkward to explain why he had dropped out.

In one of his subsequent talk show appearances, he explained, with good humor, that he had come back as a "cleanup man." Before a national audience, on NBC's "Today," he elaborated, "I'm just a guy showing up after the party with a shovel and a broom trying to clean it up."

Although that scarcely accounted for Perot's dropout and return to the hustings, it was in character with the insultingly personal nature of most American presidential campaigns toward century's end. Threats and insults, in practice if not in theory, seemed necessary to most politicians to catch the attention of the electorate.

Moreover, at that point in the contest for the presidency, just a bit more than four weeks before election day, the government of President Bush did show distressing signs of breakdown. If it wasn't a mess, in Perot's folksy definition, it was at least a study in confusion among the nation's top-level leadership.

At this inconvenient period in President Bush's reelection drive, some of his chief law enforcement officers were accusing one another of lawless conduct in the Iraqgate scandal. And the finger pointing seemed to spread despite the White House's efforts to stop the infighting.

And no wonder! Besides the mutual accusations of improper conduct between the Central Intelligence Agency and the Justice Department, it turned out that the chief investigator in the scandal, the director of the Federal Bureau of Investigation, himself was being investigated.

As far as the public was concerned amid a dirty presidential campaign, the whole sorry business was a puzzlement. Nobody in authority seemed to be sure who would be involved next.

While accusations and denials piled up routinely, the president seemed so vague that some suspected he was being victimized by his own bureaucrats. If he knew the answers to this scarcely responsible performance of his law enforcers, he didn't display his knowledge for the public's benefit.

Instead, apparently in the hope of blanketing the confusion, what he did do was to reassure the electorate about his plans for economic recovery. His proposal was quite simple. If reelected, he would fire his entire economic team and install replacements.

This is not to say that the president had quit fighting Governor Clinton and the resurgent Perot. On the contrary, he kept attacking Clinton as untrustworthy while appealing to Perot's followers not to waste their votes on Perot.

Despite that, as Perot zoomed upward in the polls almost immediately after rejoining the presidential contest and Clinton's leading position in the polls dropped below 50 percent, Bush's candidacy was being squeezed. Perot took advantage of the president by accusing him of being out of touch with events and, by implication, unable to control his own chief bureaucrats.

Allowing for bad feeling between the president and Perot, it did appear that there was some validity to Perot's criticism for as long as the White House merely watched the president's leading law enforcement agencies squabble over blame for the Iraqgate scandal.

During the interim, Perot's explanation for leaving and reentering the presidential campaign remained a mystery.

·　　·　　·

The bureaucratic explosion over American-Iraq relations before the Gulf War was touched off by Senator David L. Boren, an Oklahoma Democrat who was chairman of the Senate's Intelligence Committee when he accused the CIA of a cover-up. "I don't like the smell of the whole thing," he said.

Because this happened within a few days of Perot's reentry in the presidential contest, a feeling amounting to near panic seemed to spread from the White House to its chief law enforcement officers. Almost anything that hurt the president so close to election day, given the delicacy of his position, was also bound to reflect on those responsible. This was especially true of the law enforcement agencies.

At once, Robert M. Gates, the CIA chief, ordered his inspector general to investigate. However, the spectacle of the CIA investigating itself was far from reassuring. One reason was that the agency's chief lawyer already had admitted publicly that it had misinformed both the Department of Justice and federal prosecutors in Atlanta about the extent of American assistance to Iraq before the Gulf War. Another was that, regardless of what the public had been told, the CIA at a private session with congressional leaders had accused the Justice Department of a request to mislead Congress.

With the Justice Department's own denial of bad faith, Atty. Gen. William Barr next asked William S. Sessions, director of the Federal Bureau of Investigation, to conduct an immediate inquiry into the confusing tangle of charges. Almost at once, however, it became known that Sessions had been made the subject of an internal ethics review of his income tax claims and expense accounts.

Senator Boren commented: "The timing of the accusations against Judge Sessions makes me wonder if an attempt is being made to pressure him not to conduct an independent investigation."

Attorney General Barr had to wiggle out of this bind as best he could. Although he continued to deny Democratic requests for an independent special prosecutor to investigate who was at fault in the admitted American aid to Iraq before the Gulf War, what he did do was to name his own prosecutor to conduct the inquiry: Frederick B. Lacey, a fellow Republican and a retired federal judge.

Senator Al Gore, as the Democratic vice presidential nominee, led the criticism of the Lacey appointment, charging he would not have the necessary independence to conduct an impartial inquiry and place responsibility for misinforming the courts about the extent of President Bush's pre-Gulf War relations with Iraq. Because the issue had developed in the last month before election day, it was obvious that neither the Democrats in the Senate, the Republicans in the White House, nor the accused agencies could influence a verdict on fault. The way the government worked, the voters would be the first to pass on the issue and later, perhaps, the courts would take over, depending on the political makeup of the next administration.

Regardless of what happened, there was more than enough blame to be spread around among the law officers in the Bush administration and the White House.

·　　·　　·

The role of the CIA, as the most secretive and sensitive agency in the federal government, was the most disturbing of all in the development of the Iraqgate affair. Although it was not the first time the agency's actions had verged on illegality, what the agency had done in this case, intentionally or not, was to hoodwink both the courts and the public.

Since the CIA's establishment under the National Security Act of 1947, some of its freewheeling directors tended to assume they could do whatever they wished in the cause of national security. The actions of the CIA in the Iraq case, therefore, were troublesome not only on the question of legality but also of government control of so powerful and evasive an agency for good or ill.

In the bank fraud case that enabled Saddam Hussein to use American guarantees of big bank loans to create his army before the Gulf War, it turned out that the CIA had two positions, one public and one private.

In its official public admission of error, the agency's chief legal officer asked the electorate to believe that it had not purposely withheld critical information from the courts or tried to frustrate an investigation. At the same time, privately, as it later became known, the agency took the position that it had deliberately withheld information at the request of the Department of Justice.

Meanwhile, in the thick of the president's reelection campaign, the White House pretended to be hearing, seeing, and speaking no evil. It was, all in all, a display of irresponsibility in the conduct of government affairs, regardless of who was at fault. For what the CIA had done was to assure a federal court in Atlanta in mid-September that it had no secret information bearing on the fraud Saddam had helped perpetrate when the opposite was true, as a search of its files later disclosed.

Yet, the agency, posturing injured innocence, still maintained the position, once its misstatements were disclosed, that it had meant no harm, certainly no cover-up. As to the reason for its unusual admission of fault in the case, insiders guessed that it had to do with relations between the American and Italian governments far more than any attempt to protect President Bush from charges that his government participated in Saddam's arms buildup before the Gulf War.

At the very least, it was an embarrassment for the president. At worst, it caused some Democrats in the Senate to accuse the Bush administration of fomenting a criminal conspiracy. However, because the CIA was an agency responsible to the National Security Council, any finding of fault had to be cast in wider terms.

· · ·

The position of the Department of Justice at the outset of the Iraqgate scandal was familiar enough to the public. Its top officials accepted no responsibility for the affair and denied knowledge of the criminal acts. In particular, the department argued it had not asked the CIA to put false statements into the court record in the bank fraud case against Christopher Drogoul.

In both the Iran-contra affair in the Reagan administration and the Iraqgate scandal as it developed in the Bush administration, the department had had a rough time, as did some of its attorneys general. However, despite five years of inquiries by an independent special prosecutor, the department had escaped major damage up to election day in 1992, as had President Bush.

What eventually happened in the continuing 1992 inquiry into the Iraqgate scandal was that the CIA, after its misleading statement to federal court in which it denied having secret information on the Atlanta bank fraud, finally demonstrated that it had wanted to put out a correction that was closer to the truth. However, responsible officials at the Department of Justice admitted they had counseled the CIA against issuing the correction.

In confirming this sequence of events in his continuing investigation, Senator Boren, as chairman of the Senate Intelligence Committee, agreed that the cause of justice would have been better served if the Department of Justice had issued the CIA's correcting statement instead of quashing it. In the Senate, Al Gore attacked the Bush administration's handling of the case saying: "It is not just failed policy or bad judgment in question. It is a seemingly blatant disregard for the law and those responsible for enforcing it."

The upshot of the dispute within the Bush administration was that the main office of the Rome bank was shown by evidence entered into the federal court record to have known of the billions of dollars that were funneled through its Atlanta branch to give Saddam Hussein illegal monies to help him rearm before the Gulf War.

The Bush administration also was charged at a later date with issuing export licenses for sensitive materials with which Saddam Hussein might have been able to construct atomic weapons for use against Israel if UN inspectors had not intervened. Once again, the president denied knowledge of this development, although it remained subject to renewed inquiry after election day. Even before the votes were counted, it was unlikely that Attorney General Barr would be depending on his original choice to investigate the CIA and the Department of Justice, the director of the FBI.

. . .

It remains an open question why Attorney General Barr, knowing that FBI Director Sessions was involved in an internal inquiry before the Office of Professional Responsibility of the Department of

Justice, insisted on naming him to investigate both the department and the CIA in the Iraqgate affair.

First of all, the Sessions inquiry had been under way since June and was unrelated to anything having to do with Iraqgate. Moreover, there had been tensions for some time between the attorneys general in the Reagan and Bush administrations and the FBI, which, though technically a part of the Department of Justice, had usually been fiercely independent of domination by the department.

As for the charges involving Sessions, a judicial figure of long experience in the federal government, they had to do with some long distance telephone calls billed to the director's office without any proof that they had been made by Sessions and an accountability for some family travels on government aircraft. Sessions already had repaid some of these expenses, it was said, and others were not viewed as serious breaches of official conduct. As for the income tax matter, it had to do with Sessions's application for exemption from District of Columbia income taxes on the ground that he was a citizen of Texas. There was no doubt that he was in deep trouble although he still had some time to go in his ten-year appointment as head of the FBI in 1987.*

It was against this background that Attorney General Barr, still fending off Democratic demands for a special prosecutor in the Iraqgate scandal, turned to former Federal Judge Lacey to do the investigating of the CIA and the Department of Justice under Republican rule. For the time being, that also enabled President Bush to fend off the inquiries about what he knew and when he knew it in the Iran-contra affair while he was vice president. The Iraqgate mess, to use Perot's term, also was involved in these inquiries.

All in all, such scandals as these had tainted both the Reagan and Bush administrations despite the denials.

The way these matters were handled at top level, most congressional inquiries had concluded, indicated the extent of the blot on the Bush administration's record during the presidential campaign. Next to the president's positions on the economy and on health care and education, the involvement of some of his cabinet departments in Iraqgate and Iran-contra cover-ups may well have caused continued desertions among disaffected Republicans to the Perot ticket.

To be blunt, there was too much hanky-panky in government for the health of the country—and the public was well aware of it.

*When Sessions refused to resign early in the next administration, President Clinton fired him.

19

Perot and the Polls

Ross Perot had to face an apathetic public when he reentered the presidential campaign.

Far from assuming a special role in shaping the course of events, as he did closer to election day, Perot had trouble at first convincing a skeptical electorate that he was on the level. Yet, before he dropped out on July 16, he had at one point led both major party candidates in the public opinion polls.

However, when Perot resumed his independent candidacy on October 1, his appeal in the polls was rated in single digits. Probably, just a few believed he had come back merely because some of his volunteers had urged him to do so, his first explanation. Probably even fewer took stock in his claim that his sole interest was in the issues.

Perot seemed forthright only when he freely admitted that it had been a mistake for him to quit the race. The polls were the best evidence of that. For now, instead of battling for the lead, he was dead last behind the front-runner, Clinton, who topped President Bush by only a few points.

Worse still, Perot aroused little enthusiasm. Media commentators concluded for the most part that he had come back into the contest mainly to save face because so many people, including some of his original supporters, had called him a quitter. Some also speculated as well that he would merely be a spoiler, a theory based on his well-publicized but unexplained feud with President Bush.

Perot's comparative inactivity after the dramatic buildup for his return did nothing to discourage such assumptions. Instead of hitting the campaign trail and facing up to a lot of tough questions from both the reporters and the electorate, the independent candidate kept his own counsel while limiting himself to an initial round of talk show visits—still his way of campaigning.

In one sally before an NBC "Today" audience, he criticized President Bush, his presumed No. one target, for a listless campaign, saying, "You've got to get out there on the front lines and taste it." However, he showed no inclination to follow his own advice. He didn't like being questioned.

During the first few days of his return engagement in quest of the presidency, the public on the whole seemed to have a ho-hum response. A *New York Times*–CBS survey, for example, concluded that 80 percent of the respondents now mistrusted him and only 1 percent believed he had a chance to win the presidency. Why he bothered to run under such conditions remained a mystery.

This was particularly true of the *Times*-CBS poll, in which only 7 percent of respondents just then were willing to vote for him. As if that hadn't been bad enough, he aroused still more doubts with his argument that he'd come back only because his volunteers had asked him to do so. A comment by his former campaign manager, Edward J. Rollins, reflected on the candidate's rhetoric as "completely void of any substance, commitment or veracity."

Perot shot back at his media critics during an ABC interview with Barbara Walters. "Anybody who's not trying to be politically correct would make it clear that journalism needs to clean up its own act. They've got their own agendas. They've got their own candidates."

He then let it be known that he intended to run an advertising campaign on national television as his principal method for boosting his presidential candidacy. He didn't call these thirty-minute to one-hour features commercials. Instead, he invariably referred to his long features as his *programs,* which is what they turned out to be.

· · ·

When Perot went on the air with his first paid program in early October, what he represented was a thirty-minute talk including a set of graphic illustrations. It was primarily an effort to arouse public interest in his first explanation for the nation's economic plight and to place responsibility mainly on President Bush.

To the more sensation-minded media representatives, this looked like terribly dull stuff: Perot droning with statistics. Yet, the Nielsen ratings for his one-man show attracted an astonishing audience of 16.5 million people.

Despite his reputation as a political operator, the independent candidate was introducing new objectives into the presidential campaign and developing new methods of trying to awaken public interest in them.

He followed up with another thirty-minute program three days later in which his sole purpose appeared to be a televised account of his role as a family man. The entire theme was presented as an introduction to the nation of his undeniably handsome and well-mannered grown children and his gracious wife, Margo.

For this second program, Nielsen put the audience at an additional 10.5 million. It was evident, therefore, that Perot's productions on easily understandable themes—especially when they were competing for interest with the usual TV sitcoms, sometimes a World Series baseball game, or a major college football game—were interesting enough to outdraw some of these popular features on the air.

Instead of the painstaking travel by air (or in the Clinton-Gore campaign, by bus) in search of uncommitted voters to address and try to convince, what Perot was buying with money out of his own pocket was a whole series of mass audiences. What he talked about, however, was not at all what his opponents or even the viewing audience had come to expect of a presidential candidate.

For Perot, in his initial presentations, didn't belabor his opponents with epithets in the Bush manner. Nor did he try to approach the electorate with Clinton's often wearisome detailed discussions of relevant issues. What his productions tried to do was to center interest on himself, his experiences, his efforts to make himself seem expert in business and sympathetic to an audience that, as he already knew, would run into the millions.

Shortly before resuming his presidential campaign, he even argued during an appearance on NBC's "Today" that he was being forced to renew his candidacy to buy time on television to explain his motives. This is how he put it: "Interestingly enough, I'm trapped. They won't sell it to me unless I declare as a candidate, so I may be the first guy in history who will have to declare as a candidate so he could buy TV time. . . . The lawyers are working on it now, but it's a funny world out there, that you're forced to become a candidate so that you can explain to the American people what the problems are."

Yet, once Perot renewed his candidacy in the fifty states, it didn't take him long to announce with a seeming show of confidence that he hoped to win the presidency from his major party rivals. He proposed to spend $60 million or more of his own money to do so. Because only a bit more than a month remained before election day, his television campaign would be costing him about $2 million a day.

There were other inconsistencies in Perot's reappearance. Although he was fighting the two-party system as an independent, he argued that he was trying to preserve it, saying, "I think we can get more done, more quickly and efficiently, that route, if the people who run the parties will listen to the people." He also defended his use of his half-hour to one-hour programs by expressing his lack of confidence in shorter programs. As he put it, "You can't cover much in a minute." Yet, he also bought thirty-second to one-minute spots on network time.

The problems of his candidacy mounted when it came to the heart of his appeal to his constituency: a call for sacrifice in the national interest that would include higher taxes, a fifty-cent-a-gallon boost in the levies on gasoline, higher Medicare premiums, and even a tax on Social Security benefits. "You got to go to fair-shared sacrifice," he said.

His main criticism of President Bush and Governor Clinton was that they had refused to face up to the necessity for immediately tackling a reduction in the $4 trillion national debt. As for the creation of millions of new jobs to cut the unemployment rolls, he pleaded that would logically follow if tighter budgets stimulated industrial growth. He also defended much less spending for military purposes. On the whole, his suggested cuts in spending seemed to be deeper than Bush's proposals but fewer than Clinton's.

Otherwise, the opinion surveys on Perot's reentry continued to show that many of the respondents were disillusioned with him as a presidential candidate because he hadn't stayed the course. One poll demonstrated that only 12 percent believed he could be trusted to bring about significant change in the way the nation's business was conducted. Three out of four respondents also believed he might make a serious mistake.

The confidence level was even lower when respondents were asked if Perot had attracted a favorable opinion as a presidential candidate, for only 7 percent said yes. And 56 percent concluded that he represented a distraction in the presidential campaign.

However, the conclusion was inescapable that Perot might very well represent the difference between victory and defeat for his major party rivals in a close race. If he could take enough votes from either President Bush or Governor Clinton in a state such as Texas or Florida, each having large electoral totals, he might hold the balance of power.

The most difficult question of all, upon Perot's reentry in the race, was which major party candidate he would hurt the most. The Democratic high command, in urging Clinton to refrain from attacks on Perot, assumed at the outset that President Bush would be Perot's ultimate target. In the furious ups and downs of the last month of the presidential campaign, however, it turned out that that wasn't necessarily so.

.   .   .

Despite Perot's energetic television campaign, based on his continual argument that he was in the presidential race to win, the odds favoring his victory remained appallingly low. Among professional politicians, he wasn't given a reasonable chance of throwing the election into the House of Representatives.

What President Bush argued in his speeches and paid television advertising was that a vote for Perot would be wasted. Perot's tangy response, in view of Clinton's lead in the polls, was that a vote for Bush amounted to zero. Clinton also used the "wasted vote" theme, but guardedly, and didn't emphasize it as much as the president did. Consequently, the impression spread as Perot gained his first few points in the polls that he was taking votes away from the president, which was true enough. However, Clinton, too, was yielding more votes than he had expected to lose.

The end was not in sight because Perot seemed determined to vary his commercials with continued visits to network talk shows where he received free time. However, the network commercials that ran thirty to sixty minutes often cost anywhere from $400,000 to $650,000 and up. Even the one-minute spots on prime time cost several hundred thousand dollars.

Among the first short messages was this one, delivered by the candidate, on voting: "The closer we get to the election, the more people will be telling you how to vote. The press. The polls. The parties. They're all counting your vote before you even leave your house on November 3. I'm not going to tell you how to vote. That's wrong. But you ought to vote for what you believe in, and you know that's right.

"If you want to rebuild the job base, let your vote say so. If you want a government that comes *from* the people instead of *at* the people, let your vote say so. If you want to reduce our $4 trillion national debt, let your vote say so. Look at the issues. Look at all three candidates. And then vote your conscience."

Another minute-long pitch—Perot again directly facing the camera and addressing the audience—appealed for votes: "Our great nation is sitting right on top of a ticking time bomb. We have a national debt of $4 trillion. Seventy-five percent of this debt is due and payable in the next five years. This is a bomb that is set to go off and devastate our economy and destroy thousands of jobs. . . .

"This is a critical time. I know you don't want to waste your vote. The fact is, you are wasting your vote this year if you elect a candidate who continues politics as usual. I will not do that. I will deal head-on with these problems. I will fix these problems. Cast your vote for your children."

The Perot campaign generally followed this sober-minded persuasive approach to the kind of argument he wanted his private advertising agency to develop in his shorter commercials. His longer ones, including one of the first for sixty minutes, were shaped to tie in with an attempt to build confidence in him as a cheerful, down-to-earth business leader who fairly radiated confidence in America.

Going with this kind of material were the public-relations themes he developed in his separate talk show appearances from early morning until late at night. Some were stiffly in earnest, others amusing, but all supported the independent candidate's main arguments in his revived presidential campaign.

Summed up, the principal issue he put before the country was the urgency of reducing the national debt. Associated with it was his belief that the American people as a whole should be willing to endure sacrifices for the common good.

How much sacrifice? In a thirty-minute advertising program first broadcast on October 16, he put together the gist of a broader plan he had previously presented in his book, *United We Stand: How We Can Take Back Our Country*. These were his salient points:

1. Proposed tax increases on individuals by $293 billion, on businesses by $49 billion

2. Proposed reductions in federal spending on optional programs of $315 billion plus $268 billion in added cuts of automatic benefits for the elderly, the poor, and other specialized classes

3. Increases in taxes on certain Social Security benefits and higher Medicare premiums to produce an estimated $268 billion in added savings

4. To give the economy a jump start, a proposed reduction in capital gains taxes and others by $62 billion and stepped-up federal spending on several other programs by $109 billion

To criticism that such proposals were far too difficult for people of slender means to absorb, Perot replied briefly, "If common sense and the interest of the American people dictate slowing down, we will slow down. But the thing you can't do is to do nothing."

Regardless of Perot's motives for these and other programs he put forward in support of his independent presidential candidacy, there was no trifling with him during his revived candidacy. He was well aware of the power his money gave him to spread his ideas before the nation on television. He continued to spend money generously to publish and broadcast his proposals in the national interest throughout his renewed run for the presidency.

The result, without doubt, was a puzzling part of the strangest presidential campaign of this century—one that he could not win.

20

The Money Blitz

Long before election day, there was little doubt that the presidential campaign of 1992 was becoming one of the most expensive and disreputable of the century.

Taken together with congressional, state, and local contests, it seemed likely that this election would be remembered mainly for the money blitz it precipitated. All the false charges being made particularly about the presidential nominees, were bad enough. To accuse them as well of seeking to buy the election through heavy spending, another widespread accusation, raised even more serious questions about the effect on the presidency itself.

The way the campaign was conducted, therefore, contributed to a growing public consensus that serious consideration of presidential electoral reforms would be a postcampaign necessity regardless of who won.

At one time, it had been believed possible for public financing to be the answer to big-spending practices of the presidential candidates. However, the grant of more than $100 million to the two major party nominees for president already had been shown to be insufficient, and the Perot independent candidacy, which received no federal financing whatever, already had spent more than the individual federal grants to each major party nominee.

The premise for this legal grant of taxpayers' money to finance presidential campaigns had been that the candidates in turn would cooperate by limiting their acceptance of large gifts from interested corporations. That simply didn't work, especially when corporate donors gave equally to both leading presidential candidates to maintain influence with the ultimate winner.

Independents like Perot, who couldn't be held to any accounting for what they spent, seemed to be accountable mainly to their own consciences. Where practical politics was concerned a winning campaign seemed to be an acceptable excuse for the kind of foul-mouthed operation that had been mainly responsible for the defeat of Michael Dukakis as the Democratic nominee in the 1988 presidential drive.

Under the loopholes in the election laws, other sharp practices also were possible. Large corporate or private donors, for example, could give as much as they wished to party officials with the understanding that such gifts could be used to help a presidential candidate. In addition, the establishment of political action committees (PACs) created an easy source of extra gifts to presidential candidates by trade associations, ideological and religious groups, businesses, industries, and unions.

It was, therefore, comparatively simple to evade the supposedly strict laws for the financing of presidential elections.

The Center for Responsive Politics, a nonpartisan group, already had warned that "huge amounts of money" were being raised for use in presidential campaigns regardless of protective legislation. The group explained, "Today's presidential financing system is so riddled with loopholes that the public can take little comfort in it as a way of eliminating the influence of special interest contributions."

That in itself underlined the suspicion that some public offices up to and perhaps including the presidency were being bought and sold in a money blitz of unparelleled magnitude. What it meant specifically was that Congress, in drafting laws to prevent another Watergate scandal after President Nixon's resignation, had tried and failed to allay public concern that the nation had entered an era of bartered presidencies.

The loopholes in the federal election laws remained wide open. Those who wanted to make presidents beholden to them had no scruples about taking advantage of the laws' weaknesses at the expense of the public interest. Thereby, the presidency itself was cast in the shadow of public doubt.

. . .

It may be unfair to Perot to saddle him with much of the blame for the soaring costs of the 1992 presidential drive but this became the public perception of his activities. As the only billionaire ever to seek the highest office in the land, especially in a time of recession and high unemployment, it was a shock to many among the electorate to witness his reckless display of his wealth to try to swing public opinion in his direction.

No one of consequence, except Perot himself, ever believed he had a chance to win the presidency in either part of his split campaign. Yet, especially in the concluding phase of his first venture into national politics in the fall, he kept spending on television advertising for what really amounted to a salve to his ego.

Perot's description of his motives was pitched on a much higher plane. First of all, he contended he could win if he could rally all the support he needed in the fifty states. To account for his willingness to spend his own money in lavish degree, he pleaded that he knew how to sweep aside the country's $4 trillion debt and the mounting annual budgetary deficits. That, he argued, would be necessary before he or anybody else could restore the nation's economy to good health, create well-paying jobs for the unemployed, and reeducate the large proportion of unskilled labor.

To experienced major party politicians, what Perot was trying to do seemed downright foolish. They pointed out that he had only a sketchy volunteer organization, mostly inexperienced in handling national affairs. Outside his advertising company, composed of Dallas advertising people who called themselves the 270 Group, he had no setup for handling the nuts and bolts of any political campaign—the painstaking travel arrangements, setups for news conferences, his speeches, and the like.

Everything except the televised ads seemed to be handled catch-as-catch-can, apparently the way he operated except when it came to making money, where he was in a class by himself. He seemed to have dispensed with all but a final weekend of travel. Because he disliked news conferences and reporters, he avoided news conferences as much as possible.

It followed, therefore, that his advertising campaign became the centerpiece of his independent candidacy—a venture that set a record for spending by any presidential candidate on displays of commercials of anywhere from ten seconds to an hour on network time plus separate deals with local stations.

He was estimated to have spent more on his televised ads than both his major party rivals combined. Certainly, he contributed the most to total network receipts from presidential ads in the 1992 campaign, which were as follows: ABC, $24 million; NBC, $15 million; CBS, $14 million; and Fox and CNN more than $1 million each.

I wish I could believe the argument of democratic idealists that the American electorate was so independent-minded that it could not be swayed by even the most concentrated advertising campaign. All the evidence would seem to be to the contrary. Advertising does have an effect, both good and bad, and advertising in presidential campaigns can scarcely be considered an exception, especially when responsible experts put many of Perot's audiences in the range of 10 to 13 million and more.

One of the most emotional of Perot's sixty-second spots, for example, featured a closeup of a Purple Heart medal, loaned to him by a Vietnam War veteran with a letter that was read in a televised voice-over as follows: "I was awarded this Purple Heart for wounds received during a Vietnam ambush. . . . Let it remind you of the army of ordinary citizens that has mustered to your call to stop the hemorrhaging of the American spirit. . . ."

Messages such as that *did* have an impact. Moreover, what Perot was spending on television to advance his cause amounted to more than the advertising budgets of some of the nation's most prominent corporations. As a result, he pioneered in broadening the use of the medium in presidential campaigns. He demonstrated that a credible advertising display on television, backed up by the continual presence of a candidate on informal talk shows and call-in shows, can become a powerful influence in a presidential campaign.

Perot's entire appeal, except at the very end of the campaign, was based on television. He never bothered to conduct the extensive travel arrangements and personal appearances that had been the staple of national presidential appeals for much of the century. Nor did he seem worried extensively about another standby of presidential drives, the mass news conference. The only trips he took came at the very end of his effort; as for the news conferences he never did show much trust in the way reporters battered him with questions.

The weakness in Perot's new departures for presidential campaigns seemed to be in the character of the audiences to which he addressed his appeal, which were fundamentally white, middle class, and usually suburban. Plunging into crowds with reckless abandon and shaking (or merely touching) hands in Clinton's style was foreign to Perot's nature.

Although President Bush was well aware that he was one of Perot's main targets, he seldom fought back. The most the president was quoted as saying about the cost and conduct of Perot's campaign was, "Bizarre," to which he quickly added, "Don't worry about him, he's got plenty left." As for Clinton, one of his public relations people said, "We'd be foolish to underestimate Perot's ads."

Certainly, his televised advertising was impressive. Even if it was taken for granted that Perot couldn't win, his impact on the election day vote could not be disregarded. What Perot did without question was to help stimulate voter registration across the land to record highs and insure that the percentage of qualified voters who would go to the polls on election day would exceed the 1988 all-time low of 50.1 percent.

That in itself was a service to the cause of a working democracy in America.

. . .

If anybody among the three candidates had looked like a predestined loser in this presidential campaign as it began in the snows of New Hampshire, it was Governor Clinton. Having finished second to former Senator Tsongas in that first Democratic primary in February, the modest campaign fund he had accumulated soon was exhausted. By April, he and his people had to borrow $4 million from a Little Rock bank to keep going until the primary elections ended in June when he finally clinched the Democratic presidential nomination.

Among the earliest contributors to both the Republican and Democratic presidential campaigns, in equal amounts, were RJR Nabisco, Archer-Daniels-Midland, Philip Morris, and the Tobacco Institute. Each reported giving more than $100,000 to each candidate. For June and two succeeding months, Clinton's fund-raisers also reported receiving more than $7 million in small gifts ($200 or less) plus more than $3 million in additional large contributions.

The treasurer for the Clinton-Gore campaign, Robert A. Farmer, reported that throughout the fall campaign the Democrats continued to pile up additional large contributions, something that seldom happened in the 1988 losing Dukakis effort.

Clinton's continued lead in the presidential polls also appeared to help congressional Democrats raise money in campaigns for the Senate and House, some in record amounts. In the Senate races, for example, Barbara Boxer in California took in contributions of almost $9 million in a race for an open Senate seat. Her colleague, the former San Francisco mayor, Dianne Feinstein, raised more than $7 million in her attempt to unseat a Republican senator, John Seymour.

In a New York contest against Republican Senator Alfonse D'Amato, who raised more than $8 million, the Democratic nominee, Attorney General Robert Abrams, didn't do as well as the two California Democrats, reporting that his fund-raising had barely exceeded $5 million.

For campaigns in the House, nobody exceeded a California Republican, Michael Huffington, who reported raising more than $4 million to win reelection in District 22. The leading House Democrats, Richard A. Gephardt of Missouri and Dan Rostenkowski of Illinois, reported raising $2.6 million and $1.4 million respectively.

In summation, the Federal Election Commission reported all records for congressional spending in 1992 had been smashed, which seemed to guarantee that fund-raising, too, would of necessity reach new highs. Taken together with the contributions and spending on the presidency among all three major candidates, the total cost to the nation on election day was bound to be enormous—scarcely a good sign for the future.

. . .

The most significant imponderable in estimating the cost of the presidential campaign was the calculation of income and outgo for President Bush's drive for reelection. During the summer, when he seemed far ahead of any Democratic rival and well-nigh untouchable, Republican fund-raisers brought in most of the money with which he began his fall campaign. The gifts kept coming in until the large contributors sensed a turning of the tide and began paying more attention to Governor Clinton. Toward the end, what Bush had left were the remaining Republican faithful among the largest contributors, which still enabled him to mount an aggressive campaign with heavy investment in TV advertising.

That, however, was based on the known and above-board gifts to his cause. What was well-nigh impossible to calculate, or even estimate, was the extent to which so many government functionaries in and about the White House and the most important departments of the federal government worked for the Bush campaign while still performing their regularly assigned duties. Secretary of State Baker, who was running the White House as chief of staff and directing the political campaign as well, was the most prominent official with duplicate assignments. There were others of lesser importance.

The division between being presidential and campaigning for reelection also could not be drawn, fairly or not, in such circumstances as the president's work on the Canada–Mexico–United States trade treaty, as completed during the campaign, together with his efforts to insure support for the pact from his electoral rivals and his opponents in Congress. Official receptions such as the one for President Yeltsin of Russia also could scarcely be described even in part as a campaign activity although it contributed to the prestige of the American president running for reelection.

Such matters as these, and relevant activities, were far more than mere symbols of the president's high office. How well he performed these duties was bound to influence the development of American foreign policy whether or not he was campaigning for reelection. The political assumption was that whatever credit the president may have earned with the public in discharging some of his official acts might well be canceled out by other and less favorable official developments.

That at any rate was the approximation of justice to a president who sought reelection. The best that could be said for contributions to President Bush's campaign from all sources was that no sitting president lacks for large gifts from influential sources for as long as he has a reasonable chance for reelection. Even if Ross Perot did manage to outspend him in the final period of his money blitz devoted to television commercials, both his major party rivals more than likely made up for their deficiency in other ways.

21

Spinning the News

Like many American presidents of his era, George Bush tolerated most members of the White House press corps as long as they saw the news his way. Once the long recession set in, however, and his reelection campaign turned into a battle for his political life, the president often seemed to relish attacking the reporters and their news organizations almost as much as the upstart Democrats.

As election day approached, he cried out in delight when he saw signs, bumper stickers, or even painted bedsheets with the legend, "Annoy the Media. Re-elect Bush." Now and then, he observed—indicating the news people with their retinue of still and television photographers—"They wouldn't know good news if it hit them in the face."

His grievance, as he told crowds of his faithful supporters, was that televised news, newspapers, and news magazines in varying degree were not properly covering the news of the presidential campaign against the background of a stagnant economy and aggravated unemployment. What the president seemed to want was greater recognition, for the benefit of a soured public, of government announcements indicating that the long slump had taken a turn for the better.

He often put his own spin on the news in this manner during the closing days of his reelection campaign to emphasize the best possible treatment of his performance as president: "Have you heard this on television at night? That unemployment claims have gone down to the lowest in two years? Have you heard that inflation is down, that interest rates are down, that total employment is 93 percent, home mortgages are 8 percent?"

To be sure, the country's news organization had put out these, as well as far less favorable figures, as issued by both the government and private sources but not exactly with the kind of spin on them that the president suggested. Unemployment figures, for example, were not issued even by relevant government agencies as the total number of employed people, 93 percent to use the president's figure, but as a high of 7.8 percent of the total American work force, which, month by month, had been reduced to 7.5 percent, or nearly 10 million people.

The president also appeared to object to the large displays of unfavorable public opinion polls that showed him consistently trailing Governor Clinton. Even though some of the polls were narrowing in his favor, the president still was dissatisfied. He called the polls "crazy," dubbed the heads of the opposition Democratic ticket "bozos," and questioned the good faith of the nation's news organizations in not touting his campaign with proper force.

At one rally in what once had been a dependable Republican bastion in the South, he promised to reintroduce prosperity during his second term by making vast changes in the economy. As he explained his position at the time: "People say, 'Well, why do you want to do this? It's ugly out there. You're getting clobbered by the national media over and over again. Can't be any fun.'" He answered his own observation, saying, "The response is that something transcends your own personal well being. And what transcends it for me is, we have literally changed the world. What I want to do is to create more opportunities in employment and education for every young person."

However obnoxious and wrong-headed the nation's free press may have seemed to a proud president trailing in the polls, his complaints did not change the coverage of the news in his favor. Some newspapers, and a handful of television commentators as well, did do some public soul-searching about the degree of fairness shown in the nation's political reportage. In substance, though, nothing changed. The president could not put a spin on the news in his favor except for a few instances of little importance. The opposition Democrats kept their campaign going by stressing the downbeat economy and blaming the president for it.

.   .   .

This is not to suggest that a president, or anybody else for that matter, is bound to accept a bad press, justified or not, without making a forceful attempt to change its opinion and the public's as well. President Bush was well within his rights to argue that news people should report "the water jug as half full" rather than "the water jug is half empty," only that really isn't the way the news business works in America.

Still, even the most admired of presidents during this century seldom hesitated to do a little reportorial arm-twisting for the sake of disciplining the White House press corps. The only four-time president in the nation's history, Franklin Roosevelt, once shamed a *New York Times* reporter who asked him an inconvenient question by telling him to put on a dunce cap and stand in a corner.

There also have been instances in which a President with clever journalistic advisors used the White House press corps to create a somewhat shaky "good press." In the early Carter administration, for example, President Jimmy Carter boldly used the reporters assigned to him to spread a favorable impression of one of his proposed programs for tax reform. What he did was to talk to the reporters informally, on condition that he would not be identified as the source of any information they used—a process known in the trade as "deep background," a term invented by Secretary of State Dean Rusk.

The device worked well for a little while. The White House reporters, while privately acknowledging to their editors that the president was their source, put out a series of important pieces on taxes and other coming governmental actions or problems as seen by President Carter, but ascribed to no source whatever. The president was made to look good, the reporters had a lot of expert-sounding "think pieces" in print and on the air, and the editors went along with the charade until somebody squawked.

The squawker was Seymour Topping of The *New York Times,* then its managing editor, who argued against these "background" briefings as a masquerade. Howard Simons, then the managing editor of the *Washington Post,* agreed, although he conceded, somewhat nostalgically, that the two young reporters who broke the Watergate scandal, Bob Woodward and Carl Bernstein, couldn't have done so if they had attributed their stuff to their sources. The chief source, "Deep Throat," as they called him, may have been named publicly since along with others on a number of occasions, but the *Post* never has admitted his identity—another side of the news business the public seldom understands.

In the Nixon administration, Dr. Henry Kissinger cleverly used diplomatic reporters as a captive audience while he was secretary of state by getting them to agree, in certain sensitive stories, to identify him only as a "senior official." In a number of crises, the "senior official" fairly sparkled with wisdom and the State Department and its people basked in the warmth of a good press that was exceedingly rare then—and ever since.

The "senior official" dodge was so over-used in reporting on Dr. Kissinger's accomplishments that it would have taken a particularly dumb eighth grade pupil not to detect, from news accounts, that a leading government official was being lionized in the diplomatic correspondence of the day. All that ended when William Beecher, the new reporter for the *Boston Globe,* wrote with tongue in cheek of Dr. Kissinger's arrival after an important diplomatic mission by air: "On the ground at 9:30 P.M., the senior U. S. official was last seen entering a long black limousine with Nancy Kissinger."*

The most frustrating experience in my own years as a political writer came in the latter days of William Randolph Hearst, Sr., when he decreed that the term "New Deal" should never again appear in any of his newspapers under any circumstances. Instead, so the order went, his editors would have to change the offensive term to "Raw Deal" in capital letters. All that ended, however, with FDR's re-election in 1936 by forty-six states to two, Maine and Vermont. The "Raw Deal" instruction thereafter was quietly forgotten. On the Hearst paper in New York City, where I worked as a very young reporter, we salved our professional pride by using "Roosevelt administration" to avoid having "Raw Deal" inserted in our news accounts. A small point, perhaps, but important to many of us at a time when jobs were scarce and defiance of a publisher's will was not recommended conduct for beginners.

．　　．　　．

A more acceptable method of influencing public opinion, the televised ad campaign, became a feature of the closing weeks of the 1992 presidential contest. Such material had been used in previous presidential election years, but nothing approaching the volume and expense of the newest electronic commercials had ever been tried before. Mainly, responsibility for the innovation and its staggering cost lay with the independent Perot candidacy. He seemed to enjoy being the star in some of his longer "infomercials," as he called them.

The millions of dollars that Perot spent on his longer presentations became the talk of the presidential campaign. Equally important, his ratings for such work were usually high despite the unsensational nature of his material, the professorial drone he

*Boston Globe, August 15, 1976.

adopted as a featured performer, and his refusal to use attention-grabbing devices. Even if he did not have a chance of beating either of the two major party candidates he opposed, the general conclusion was that he would take votes away from both of them.

In the end, therefore, no matter how he was ridiculed for the undramatic nature of his televised advertising, he became a force in this presidential campaign. The professional politicians treated him with respect, especially on the Democratic side when he centered his attacks on President Bush, regardless of the jibes the political writers and analysts made at his expense.

As for the public response, it was conditioned at first by a general suspicion of all political advertising—and especially the artfully crafted material that appeared on television. Soon, an important poll stressed the credibility of some of Perot's advertising commercials as compared with those of his major party rivals toward the climax of the fall campaign. Although 18 percent of respondents believed Clinton's ads on television were nearly all truthful and Bush's were given one point more in the same category, the poll reported that 37 percent believed Perot's presentations were "almost all truthful."*

Although about half the registered voters interviewed on the effect of televised advertising contended that these displays would not influence their attitudes toward the candidates, the voting totals indicated the ads may have had more of an effect than the viewers conceded. At any rate, for the future, there was no doubt that political televised advertising, for all its drawbacks, was likely to become more of a staple in presidential politics.

For those already convinced that too many millions were being poured into presidential campaigns, it was not good news. For the candidates, in years yet to come, it meant presidential campaigns would mount in expense unless reasonably practical methods were devised by Congress to limit expenditures. For the electorate, the growth of televised political advertising was one more obstacle between candidates and voters that would have to be surmounted somehow to achieve a stronger degree of trust in the governmental process. That, after all, was the principal casualty in the way the campaign of 1992 was conducted, as President Bush must have known because he made it his principal issue in the windup.

All the money that Perot spent on his revived campaign could

---

*New York Times–CBS poll of 1,467 registered voters published in the *New York Times* Oct. 29, 1992, p. A-12.

not buy enough of the public's trust in his judgment. At one of his few public appearances for a down-home rally for his supporters, the band he had hired for the occasion played "The Yellow Rose of Texas." The independent candidate seemed to enjoy himself, although a harsh critic had suggested, after his pullout on July 16, that a more appropriate title for the song might have been "The Yellow Ross of Texas." That, too, was a part of the injustices of presidential campaigning toward century's end.

.   .   .

Probably the least noticed method of communication, radio, was the one that was most used close to election day for floating scurrilous ads, misrepresentations, and downright falsehoods. Those responsible for the worst of these were the most difficult to trace. Even if the political con artists were found and confronted, they invariably denied having any part in anything that might seem to be incriminating.

The legitimate radio ads, too, were difficult to respond to because they ran, for the most part, only in specified areas where one of the three presidential campaigns wanted to pick up a few more votes if at all possible. The Clinton campaign organization, in particular, found these scattered radio attacks difficult to respond to because they ran sporadically and usually could be detected only by accident.

One radio ad sponsored by the Bush organization, for example, accused Governor Clinton and Senator Gore of planning to boost utility bills through "radical environmental taxes." The Clinton people said it was untrue. The Bush sponsors argued that Gore, in his bestselling book about protecting the environment, had advocated taxes to help do the job.

The Clinton campaign put out a radio ad using a reference to President Bush's familiar statement that he would do whatever was necessary "to get elected," then asked, "Isn't it time for a president who will fight for American jobs?"

The Bush people radioed a question about Governor Clinton's position on crime and child welfare: "If he can't care for children and keep the public safety, how can he expect a promotion?"

That opened the door for more back-and-forth, the Clinton headquarters retorting by radio: "George Bush is at it again. Because he can't run on his own record, Bush is resorting to negative attacks against Clinton."

Did this kind of stuff influence anybody? The respective campaign staffs stoutly insisted that radio was just another political weapon and that it could be used effectively, but the documentation was weak at best and never very convincing. All that could be said for radio ads was that they were cheap and sneaky in the sense that the ostensible attack targets seldom knew in advance where such material would be used—and when.

It simply wasn't a very impressive way to participate in an election for the next president of the United States. However, I must admit to a prejudice against the misuse of radio, having been an amateur radio operator at an early age with a homemade station in my mother's kitchen in Seattle, call letters 7 U L. I suppose some of the more extreme television ads, regardless of party sponsorship, were as tasteless and disreputable as the sneak attacks on radio in which candidates were charged with all manner of secret crimes up to and including plots of insurrection The radio advertising seemed much more reprehensible to me, however, because of the comparative youth and political inexperience of a large part of the radio audience.

The mock presidential campaigns and elections in which many underage school children participated in their classrooms seemed to me to be a much more responsible way of indoctrinating the rising generation in the rightful concerns of citizenship. This was one situation in which there never would be any justification for putting a spin on the news.

22

The Scene in October

Governor Clinton still clung to a narrow lead in the opinion polls in October as the presidential campaign headed toward its climax. However, he didn't act like a front-runner. He seemed more comfortable in the role of perennial challenger.

That appeared to suit President Bush. Despite the fumbling nature of his reelection drive, he remained within striking distance of his Democratic rival and tried to look unworried even when a jokester sent a moving van to the White House.

As for Ross Perot, despite the amateurish bumbling of his renewed independent candidacy, his folksy approach to the nation's problems continued to attract dissidents in both major parties and an undetermined number of people who had never voted before. Whether the electorate liked him or not, there was no denying that the spectacle of a billionaire running for president added zest to the campaign.

Given the uneasiness of much of the public in the trough of a long recession, it was evident that this election could be won or lost in the last few days before the polls opened for an estimated 100 million or more voters. No matter what President Bush did or tried to do to deflect public attention from his responsibility for the sagging economy, this was the issue on which the electorate had centered from the outset and this, too, was the basis for Clinton's hope for victory.

When he was fifteen years old, he had been thrilled to shake hands with President John F. Kennedy. Possibly his vision of following in Kennedy's footsteps as the nation's chief executive had begun then. Now that he was within reaching distance of the presidency, he did not mean to let it escape him.

Clinton's rise to a bid for presidential eminence from a home wracked by problems in the village of Hope, Arkansas, had been an inspirational story in itself, a realization of the American dream. Yet, during this squalid presidential campaign, he had been derided and scorned, roughed up and put down.

Under different circumstances, perhaps, the candidate might have been able to project a much more favorable image. However, that isn't the way American politics and journalism are conducted, especially during a hard-fought, no-holds-barred presidential campaign. The images of a successful student, a compassionate husband and father, and a superior public official are dull stuff, after all, when matched against campaign charges of draft dodging in the Vietnam War, illicit love making and pot smoking.

As late as June 2, after nailing down the Democratic presidential nomination after the California primary, Clinton still was a demeaning third behind President Bush and Ross Perot in the opinion polls. Few would have given him a chance then of becoming the forty-second president of the United States.

Still, Clinton and his campaign staff struggled ahead with what seemed at the time like a losing effort against a confident President Bush. Neither the Democratic nominee nor his staff worried then about Perot as the major obstacle he turned out to be. Nor did the Bush people, for that matter, attach importance to Perot's vendetta against the president. It was the president's overconfidence against all opposition to his reelection campaign that gave Clinton his chance for a breakthrough when he finally took the lead in the opinion polls and never relinquished it thereafter.

What helped the Clinton team greatly was the strategy of developing a quick response to any move from either the White House or Perot campaign headquarters in Dallas. The governor, too, boosted his cause frequently through the care with which he supervised every important development during his long and difficult campaign. It was his premise never to take unnecessary chances, to be moderate in his public positions, and to promote the impression that he was leading a "new" Democratic party, not the "tax and spend" Democrats the Republicans had been denouncing for a generation.

In this campaign, the Republicans hurt themselves when they permitted the conservative leaders of the Christian Front to dominate the last two days of their National Convention. By veering from the safe and sane middle position where most presidential elections are won, Bush and his people opened themselves up to criticism within their party on such issues as abortion rights and sexual harassment, both of key importance to women.

The addition of Senator Al Gore of Tennessee and his wife, Tipper, also turned out to be a big plus for the Clinton campaign. Senator Gore, in his unsuccessful 1988 campaign for the presidential nomination, had learned the value of blunting an opposition attack before it could be fully developed. In addition, having acquired enough expertise on protecting the environment as an issue, Clinton's choice for vice president proved well able to carry that fight to the opposition.

Tipper Gore, like Hillary Clinton, also demonstrated early on that she was special. Unlike Hillary, who contented herself with a modest role after her first angry encounter with the opposition, Tipper seemed to enjoy an occasional stump speech, usually delivered with charm and vigor. On the long campaign bus trips with their husbands and the campaign entourage, both wives made a friendly impression on the crowds along the way.

Although some of the Gore children also participated in the barnstorming campaign by bus now and then, it was not until the Clintons realized most people thought them childless that they began bringing twelve-year-old Chelsea with them on weekends and other breaks from her school routine. It all made for pleasant and even attractive family television during the Democratic campaign.

Throughout it all, Clinton remained the dominant figure whether he was making a set speech on an important issue in the campaign or touring by air or bus. The Arkansan's credibility was often challenged by the opposition because of his seemingly habitual attempt to try not to offend a prospective voter, even when he was challenged by a voice from a crowd on his labored explanations for not serving in the armed forces during the Vietnam War. This was one part of the so-called character issue President Bush raised against him from the outset and he never could completely dispose of it.

Clinton put his faith as a politician in what seemed like a plan of sorts for almost everything, which he explained in this manner when challenged: "One of the things I've learned in this business is to make your own strategy, try to stick to it, hope for the best, assume the worst, and go on."

Senator Gore was just as concentrated a campaigner as the head of his ticket, but the often solemn manner in which they both addressed the issues and fielded questions apparently did them no harm. Together, they remained steady and determined through the most trying period of their campaign when their lead over the Bush-Quayle ticket seemed to be slipping away from them. In the end, plain talk worked for them.

. . .

What Ross Perot had going for him besides his $60 million windup advertising campaign, once he resumed his independent candidacy with only a little more than a month to go before election day, was a quirky sense of humor and a string of one-liners that even the rowdiest of political audiences seemed to enjoy. Once he referred to himself as a "hound dog out of a kennel." On what he called "mud wrestling in politics," he added, "The one thing we have now is a system that will completely weed out anybody you'd want as president." Then there was the most famous line of all, in which he pointed to the side of his head in a television appearance and exclaimed, with a delighted grin, "I'm all ears."

Perot's strength in his in-and-out campaign for the presidency was his unconventional pose as an antipolitician in a year in which a large section of the public, with good reason, had had its fill of political promises that couldn't be kept. Up to July 16, when he had dropped out of the race for a whole series of reasons, none of which made much sense to the public, his standing in the polls had been consistently high mainly because he could put into words the uneasy feelings of many Americans about their future.

When he quit so abruptly, there was a feeling among many of his early supporters that they had been betrayed, that the nonpolitician had turned out to be just another politician after all. This was the main handicap he faced upon his return to the hustings, but he confronted it boldly and profited thereby. Although he never again reached the eminence of dominating the opinion polls in the presidential race, as he had in his first appearance, he managed to gain acceptance among a portion of the electorate once again with his breezy style, his countryman's way of expressing himself, and his "aw shucks" approach to the gravest problems of the nation.

No one could imagine either President Bush or Governor Clinton saying, as Perot did, "I can solve the problem of the national debt without even working up a sweat. It's that simple." Although the issue wasn't at all simple and would require a lot more personal discomfort among the electorate than Perot anticipated, many people seemed to like his style despite that. The polls once again documented his slow rise in most samples of public estimates of the appeal of the presidential contenders.

Perot was not the only nonmajor party candidate who had won a place on presidential ballots in all fifty states, but he made a great point upon his return of keeping faith with the volunteers who had put him there. Still, the same thing had been done without fanfare by a little-known candidate of the Libertarian party, one of several also-rans in the 1992 campaign, but it never achieved the recognition that came to Perot for his independent campaign.

During the latter days of the presidential race, it did seem likely that the support for Perot might cut into the vote for President Bush and perhaps for Governor Clinton as well. That meant Perot might well determine the outcome of the election by favoring one or the other of the major parties. As a result, his public utterances were scrutinized more closely than ever before by the rival political camps, the political commentators on television and in the newspapers, and many millions of prospective voters across the land.

For much of the year, Perot hadn't bothered to disguise his impatience, even his anger, with both President Bush and the Republican cause generally. The independent nominee seemed to take a savage delight in attacking the president's current policies and public movements, which brought satisfaction to the Clinton headquarters. To be sure, Clinton himself took a stand-offish attitude toward the whole independent performance for as long as he was not directly concerned, for he stood to gain whenever Bush and the Republicans took a bad hit from Perot.

Once the immunity of the Democratic contender ended, however, and Perot blasted both major party candidates with equal abandon, there still was no counterattack from the Democratic side. The feeling among Clinton and his people apparently was that they could afford to hold back on an all-out assault on the candidacy of Perot on the theory that he could attract more dissident Republican votes than those of Democrats.

Not even the polls that leaned toward the Democratic side offered any substance for the belief at the time. As for the Republicans, the response was still more stress on the main theme of the president's windup oratory: Clinton's failings of character emphasized how little he could be trusted with the responsibilities of government. Evidently, the reasoning of the Republican high command was that a counterattack against Perot would do nothing to help defeat Clinton, who still led the field in the polls. This was the dilemma that President Bush never could resolve.

Bush refused even to think about campaigning for reelection until after the party's National Convention in August. Even then, he was reserved about presenting his case before the electorate and seemed to doubt the extent of the challenge Clinton offered him. He seemed singularly detached very often from the speeches he was making on television that attacked Clinton as someone who could not be trusted at the head of the American government. Only in October did the president show any flash of passion as a manifest of belief in the argument he was presenting to the electorate.

Bush never did argue, however, that Clinton was proposing to do away with free enterprise, much less raise questions about his patriotism. This president seemed much more resigned to defeat, however much he may have deplored the "crazy polls" that continued to forecast a Democratic victory. The attacks on Clinton's character, however, simply didn't work as a campaign issue in a year in which the economy, above all else, was in so parlous a state that millions of Americans were worried about the future, without the help of an organized Republican fear campaign to persuade them that all was lost.

PART THREE
THE ELECTION

23

Down the Home Stretch

There was an overwhelming degree of pretense among all the contenders in the final weeks of the presidential campaign.

Governor Clinton repeatedly challenged President Bush to a series of debates on the issues, fully expecting to be rebuffed. The Democratic nominee even threatened to show up at a predetermined site to shame his adversary into participating.

The president, however, wasn't persuaded. Nor was he shamed into doing anything. The White House's attitude was one of studied indifference. As a tactical matter, the president seemed to want to spread the impression that he still would win, coming down the home stretch, without recognizing the Democrat as an equal.

Standing apart from the two major party candidates, Ross Perot went his own way with his multimillion-dollar advertising campaign and his continual walk-ons at television talk shows. He seemed to be signaling to the public that he could win no matter what the president and the governor did or did not do.

For all three the position was preposterous. Regardless of the president's lofty pretense to indifference about the debates, his situation was precarious. There was no doubt that he still had a chance to win because the opinion polls now showed he was holding his own with Clinton. The Democrat, too, was taking chances with his bluster about Bush's fear of debating him, for a single mistake in such a risky meeting was likely to be fatal for the challenger, and he knew it.

The situation of Perot was the most peculiar of all. Few voters, regardless of Perot's folksy charm, were likely to give him a chance of winning the presidency. He never had been able to push himself out of last place in the polls after resuming his once-aborted presidential quest. Therefore, a far as the debates were concerned, the independent had everything to gain and nothing to lose by participating in a series if it could be arranged.

.　　.　　.

Regardless of all the posturing, there never had been much agreement over the years about the value of presidential debates at the conclusion of a long and difficult campaign.

On television and in the printed press, such sessions over the thirty-two years since the Nixon-Kennedy meetings of 1960 had usually been described in colorful sports language. The opponents sometimes would be pictured as boxers belaboring each other with a flurry of punches, all with the intent of scoring a knockout. Or, as an alternative, the encounters might be described in terms of a horse race.

Actually, most Presidential debates were dull stuff, but the public listened patiently on the supposition, spread by the journalists, that every debate had to have a winner and a loser. There was, however, no way of determining such standings except through opinion polls. And no one could say to what extent such findings would influence voters once they entered the polling booth.

That, perhaps, was the most deceptive posture of all—and the press people themselves were well aware of it. Nevertheless, they did their share toward promoting public anticipation of the debates toward the conclusion of the campaign. There was nothing, either in law, custom, or precedent, to force the contenders to face each other before the nation, much less pin-point their positions on so difficult and unpredictable an issue as the restoration of national prosperity. And there were other issues nearly as tricky for the unwary candidate who took chances on the wisdom of the electorate.

No one could be sure, either, of the good faith of the participants in the debates themselves. So practiced a politician as John Fitzgerald Kennedy, as a senator, thoroughly schooled even then in the traps set by the Boston Irish at election time, was placed at a disadvantage in his presidential debates in the 1960 campaign against Richard Nixon.

The first debate had gone well for Kennedy. He had been jubilant because he felt he had beaten down Nixon's criticism of his youth and inexperience as the Democratic presidential candidate. The second debate, in an NBC studio in New York City, had left something to be desired. Even so, with gentlemanly courtesy, Kennedy had walked over to Nixon after the end of the debate in the television studio to shake hands and exchange a few polite words.

The youthful Democratic nominee should have been on his guard. Just before the debate began, he had tested the position of his chair in the studio and discovered, to his dismay, that four bright lights were shining directly in his face, whereas Nixon had only one. Kennedy saw to it that the disadvantage posed by the lighting, apparently ordered by Nixon, was fixed before the debate began.

During the courtesy call at the end, however, affairs took an unexpectedly nasty turn. A news photographer was taking pictures of the Republican nominee as Kennedy approached. Without altering his manner or raising his voice, Nixon suddenly waved one arm at the unsuspecting Democrat, forefinger extended and face twisted in a menacing scowl, at exactly the moment when the photographer snapped a picture of the two combatants. This was the source of the celebrated mug shot of the debaters with Nixon in what looked like a threatening posture and Kennedy taken aback (which he was at the time). Long afterward, a sympathetic biographer wrote of the victimized candidate's reaction: "Kennedy described this episode with mixed incredulity and contempt."*

The president-to-be was much more circumspect in any approach toward Nixon in the rest of the scheduled debates. The photographic trick had worked once for Nixon. He never again was able to take advantage of his Democratic rival, either in the debates or thereafter.

. . .

Other presidential candidates have had their problems, too, during debates, but not all ended as awkwardly. Ronald Reagan, for one, gracefully ducked answering a question about his age in his 1984 campaign by responding lightly, "I will not make age an issue in this campaign." He won by the greatest landslide in history, forty-nine states to one, and bequeathed to George Bush, his successor, a prosperous nation and a colossal national debt.

Bush profited by the failure of his Democratic rival, Michael Dukakis, to show outrage when asked if, in a hypothetical situation, he would favor the death penalty for somone who had raped his wife. Dukakis later agreed that his routine response had been a mistake.

In the 1980 debates, during President Jimmy Carter's unsuccessful run for reelection against Reagan, the Democratic nominee hardly helped himself as an atomic expert by detailing a talk he had on the

---

*Arthur M. Schlesinger, Jr., *A Thousand Days*, (Boston, 1963) 71.

subject with his daughter, Amy. And President Ford, in 1976, scarcely qualified as an expert on foreign affairs when he announced during that year's debates that Poland was no longer under the influence of the Soviet Union.

In fairness to the candidates, it should be emphasized that they are badgered by philosophical questions, both during debates and elsewhere in their presidential campaigns, that defy a brief and reasonable sound-bite answer. Not often are presidential hopefuls asked, as Ross Perot was in a CBS interview during the 1992 campaign: "Mr. Perot, what do you stand for?" The billionaire hit that one out of the park: "I stand for the principles on which this country was founded."

. . .

A part of President Bush's objection to debating Governor Clinton, as he later conceded, was that the Democratic nominee had a reputation as a first-rate debater, acquired at Oxford as a Rhodes scholar. The president wasn't at all sure that he could hold up his end in a meeting with his Democratic rival. It was this, perhaps, that led him to propose that Perot, as an independent, should also be invited to participate in the 1992 debates when arrangements for them were completed. Evidently, the president and his Republican entourage calculated that Perot, as a debater, would be more likely to injure Clinton's chances than Bush's.

In any event, with three people to be covered in each of four debates, so the Republicans assumed, President Bush would not be under such great pressure to reply to Clinton's challenges. At least a part of the heat, so the theory went, would be directed at Perot as a spoiler.

The troubled Republican state of mind about Bush's chances may perhaps be better understood if the president's known failings as a public speaker are taken into account. Without a prepared script in front of him, Bush invariably spoke in snippets—a few words at a time, usually in partial sentences and incomplete thoughts. It was not that either Clinton or Perot were giants at political exchanges on the spur of the moment. Clinton's tendency to ramble on at length while groping for a suitable answer to a puzzling question was well documented in this campaign. As for Perot, some of his responses to challenges from political audiences ranged from somewhat less than informed to far out speculation.

While the debates were being arranged, a *New York Times*–CBS poll rated the public's expectations of the candidates' performances as follows: Clinton, 41 percent; Bush, 24 percent; and Perot, 8 percent. However, it didn't turn out quite that way.

.　　.　　.

Once the three candidates agreed that they would participate in the debates, all supervised by the Commission on Presidential Debates, the number, time, location, and mechanics of the operation were quickly concluded.

There were to be four meetings, three for the presidential candidates and one for the vice presidential nominees. Each would be for ninety minutes scheduled close together in mid-October beginning with Sunday, October 11, at Washington University in Clayton, Missouri, and followed by the vice presidential contest on Tuesday, October 13, at the Georgia Tech campus in Atlanta. The two concluding presidential sessions were to be on Thursday, October 15, at the University of Richmond in Virginia and Monday, October 19, at Michigan State University in East Lansing, Michigan.

So far, so good. Once the mechanics of all four debates were set down on paper, however, it developed that these were not to be debates at all in the usual sense, something that had also been true of such meetings in previous presidential campaigns.

The first session at Washington University, for example, provided that the candidates for president should not address each other directly but respond to questions posed through a panel of three reporters under the guidance of a moderator, Jim Lehrer, of the Public Broadcasting System. Moreover, the responses to questions by the candidates were limited to two minutes each and only a one minute follow-up was allowed for additional responses. Each candidate then was allowed a brief closing statement.

In that kind of stiff, formal setup, it appeared that it would be difficult to pick winners and losers, stars and also-rans. However, once the contestants confronted each other, it was shown that the planners hadn't taken into account Perot's facility with his one-liners.

The other three meetings were by no means as formal and restricted. The moderator, Lehrer, was the only questioner for the vice presidential debates in Atlanta. The third meeting in Richmond, again for the presidential candidates, offered a chance for questions from undecided voters—the formula so popular with talk shows. The final meeting at Michigan State, one-half moderator-supervised and the other parceled out among three reporters, offered the loosest structure of all with cross-talk among the candidates.

175

The whole business, from start to finish, could scarcely be considered the kind of debate format made famous by Abraham Lincoln and his opponent, Stephen Douglas, in 1858. As Dan Rather of CBS argued from the outset, the meetings between the presidential and vice presidential candidates were not debates in the accepted sense. Rather, in fact, called them "happenings" with some degree of justification.

The only similarity between the 1992 sessions and Lincoln-Douglas was the reluctance, at the outset, of one participant to agree to a meeting until he was virtually forced to do so. In Lincoln-Douglas, Abraham Lincoln was so frustrated by Douglas's continual delay in agreeing to a debate that he called his rival "the little dodger" rather than "the little Giant."

Once Bush decided that Perot should be asked to participate, the arrangements went forward smoothly—so much so that Clinton seemed to have no reservations about the plans as they were developed.

What the challenger hoped to do, it was clear from the outset, was to dominate the debates by repeatedly criticizing the president on the economy whenever he saw a chance to do it. One immediate result was the preparation of thick briefing books crammed with documents and statistics for the use of both major party candidates. In addition, each was put through a series of mock debates by their respective staffs.

The president and the governor, in consequence, were overprepared as the first debate approached. As for Perot, as it was learned later, he was casual about the whole business, didn't bother with briefing books or rehearsals, and came into the talkathons prepared only to put up a confident front. His main purpose was to demonstrate his faith in his own plan to cut the $4 trillion national debt as the highest priority before tackling the grave problems of the recession itself.

.   .   .

So much public interest had been generated in the debates that poll takers reported at least two-thirds of the nation's registered voters planned to watch the first meeting on television. Such a potential audience, if it materialized, would be larger than the baseball World Series games were drawing during the same period. That in itself increased the pressure on the participants.

The Bush and Clinton staffs conceded publicly, during the interminable predebate interviews, that their principal objective was to make sure that each major party nominee performed creditably and avoided damaging errors. Perot appeared completely unworried and relaxed, by contrast. Unlike Clinton, who had to defend his lead in the polls, and Bush, who had to try by all possible means to close the gap with his challenger, Perot's ultimate objective was to sustain his own credibility and make a respectable showing against his more experienced competition.

It was taken for granted, American presidential politics being what it is, that all three organizations had made arrangements before the debates to claim victory for their candidate immediately after the conclusion of each debate and, eventually, the series itself. There was nothing especially tricky about this. It was part of the routine of presidential politics to lay claim to every possible advantage and to deny all fault, a commonplace of much of governmental public relations in the United States toward century's end.

Because the debates were being conducted before live audiences instead of the quiet efficiency of a television studio, the makeup of the witnesses and their behavior became a more serious problem to the Presidential Debates Commission as the bipartisan sponsor. So far as possible, what the commission wanted to do was to admit only undecided voters except for the people in each campaign staff whose presence was necessary. That became the ultimate test of the commission's preparatory work because the televised spectacle of an audience committed to one of the three participants would have ruined the show and made the debates a meaningless exercise toward the close of the presidential campaign.

24

"De Walls Come Tumblin' Down"

It may have been difficult to pick a winner after the first presidential debate but there was no doubt about the ultimate loser. He was President Bush.

Ross Perot's brash one-liners turned out to be the biggest crowd-pleaser at the nationally televised event in Missouri on October 11. However, it was Governor Clinton's soft-voiced criticism of President Bush's inaction in the long recession that produced results next day.

It was then that the president cleared the way for the selection of a new economic team if he won a new term.

The response to the Democrat's mild challenge, in a sense, was like the effect of Joshua's feat with a ram's horn at the biblical battle of Jericho. As the old spiritual sang of the action:

> Den de lamb ram sheep horns begin to blow,
> Trumpets begin to sound;
> Josh' commanded de chillun to shout,
> An' de walls come tumblin' down.*

There was no mistaking the president's intent to drop the three most criticized members of his administration for inaction in the recession: Treasury Secretary Nicholas F. Brady, Budget Director Richard G. Darman, and the top White House economist, Michael J. Boskin. Before the release of a letter from White House Chief of Staff James A. Baker asking for resignations from all cabinet members and other agency heads immediately after the election, the presi-

*As quoted in Louis Untermeyer, *A Treasury of Great American Poems* (New York, 1942), pp. 1018–19.

178

dent announced that the three heads of his economic team in particular would not be reappointed.

Baker's description of the call for staff resignations as routine could not disguise the emergency nature of the president's move to clean house because it came directly after his disappointing showing in the first debate at Washington University. What evidently happened was that both the president and his chief adviser, Baker, believed something had to be done quickly to reassure the public that there would be vigorous action to end the recession if the president was reelected.

As the polls indicated, the Bush campaign still was not going well; the president was seven points behind Clinton after the first debate and Perot was making a surprising jump from only 7 percent before the debate to 18 percent immediately afterward. There was little time to waste now, for the second debate, featuring the candidates for vice president, was directly ahead on October 13 and election day was only three weeks off.

Clinton's jubilant response was predictable. While campaigning in Philadelphia, he paused long enough to tell reporters, "The coach wants to fire the team. But in America, when you have a losing season, the coach gets fired, not the team."

.　　.　　.

The first debate's biggest surprise, to me at least, was the size of the audience. The standard Nielsen rating (one point equals 931,000 homes) showed that the network measurement (minus CBS) was 38.4; the rival World Series baseball game drew only an 8.3 share.

What this meant was that a substantial part of the electorate was far more interested in the presidential contest than in a championship baseball game, in which CBS (for one) had heavily invested to the exclusion of the debate. The Nielsen overnight data directly opposed conventional wisdom that most people found presidential politics to be dull stuff and that World Series baseball was much more absorbing as a matter of interest.

That scarcely meant the evening was exciting or that Ross Perot became an overnight celebrity as a politically minded entertainer, Will Rogers style. His one reliable laugh line, the one done with a toss of the head, "I'm all ears," did bring down a house that was at least half full of Democrats and Republicans. (The rest were Perot fans or independents and undecided voters.)

What he did otherwise was to take sly cracks at the president's

179

weaknesses, which went over well with Clinton people, and the reverse, which pleased the president's adherents. Except for a few of Perot's other lines, which drew applause, the audience was relatively undemonstrative, even seemingly thoughtful at times. Some of the president's remarks didn't even draw a single hand-clap.

If nobody made any glaring errors, it is also true that no novel approaches to campaign logic or illogic were recorded during the ninety-minute television performance.

President Bush continued to center his attack on Governor Clinton's character in an effort to convince voters that he was not to be trusted as a president. It couldn't be done at length under the rules for the debate, limiting comments to two minutes with one-minute rebuttals. So the draft-dodging allegation sounded very much like a presidential attack on Clinton's patriotism.

At any rate, this is how the Democratic nominee responded in his only emotion-charged passage of the evening that he addressed directly to Bush: "When Joe McCarthy went around the country attacking people's patriotism, he was wrong. And a senator from Connecticut, Prescott Bush, stood up to him. Your father was right to stand up to Joe McCarthy. You were wrong to attack my patriotism."

Later in the evening, the president came back with a crack at Clinton's campaign against the White House's handling of the economy, saying, "He thinks, I think he said, that the country is coming apart at the seams. Now, I know the only way he can win is to make everybody believe the economy is worse than it is. But this country's not coming apart at the seams, for heaven's sake. We're the United States of America."

That was about the best the president could do for the evening. Clinton, seeming content to plod along with sound bites out of his set stump speech, which he used in one- and two-minute bites whenever possible, also showed no disposition to make waves.

So it was that Perot, from whom so little was expected, carried off the evening's honors with light jabs at anybody who seemed at the moment to displease him. That didn't bother the Clinton people unduly although they tried to make more out of their candidate's performance than was warranted. As for the Bush campaign staffers, they appeared relieved to settle for applause for Perot on the theory that he was taking votes from Clinton.

It was only the next day, when the president and Baker decided they had to shake things up somehow after failing to do so in the

debate, that the country learned how effectively Clinton had campaigned for the highest office in the land.

.   .   .

There was a postscript to the first debate, a paid ad filmed the
next morning at the International House of Pancakes in St. Louis, in
which eight actors made approving remarks about the president's performance and dirty cracks about Clinton. This was supposed to persuade voters that ordinary people believed the president to be a
winner and the governor a loser.

The quickie began:

First booth: I saw the debate last night and I just got one conclusions. It's all George Bush.

Second booth: I still have a lot of confidence in my president.

Third booth: I feel we need Bush to keep us from a big-spending
Congress.

Fourth booth: I don't trust Clinton.

Fifth booth: The man says one thing and does another.

The rest was no strain on the imagination. Nor did it seem to
convince anybody, least of all the responsible advertising agency,
that Bush was the winner in the first debate. It may have been a
terrific idea in the advertising agency that was given the contract to
produce it but it didn't seem to change the adverse polls among the
electorate. However, it was an example of how far politicians were
willing to go to try to persuade the public of their candidate's genius
when he wasn't doing very much to help himself.

The truth about the campaign was easier to come by. It didn't
take great discernment on the part of any reporter who followed Clinton as he campaigned in South Philadelphia on the morning after the
debate to realize how solid an impression he had made on most people in a poor neighborhood there. Whether the conclusion was fair or
not, the president bore the blame for hard times, as was shown by
one jobless man who wrung Clinton's hand and said: "Get that Bush
out of there. I need a job."

Curiously, among the people in the neighborhood who had seen
the president on television the night before, there seemed to be an
appreciation of the way the challenger had handled himself in his
meeting with Bush and Perot. For all his vague talk about improving
the lot of the average family, the Democratic nominee seemed to
have come across to the hard-pressed folk of South Philadelphia as

someone who cared very much about what was happening to them. As a small businessman described his situation, "Too many taxes, too much crime, too few jobs."

Plainly enough, in that neighborhood, the president had forfeited the confidence of the few hundred people who caught a glimpse of Governor Clinton. There and elsewhere, in similar working-class areas in the nation's large cities, it wasn't so much a case of great enthusiasm for the Democrat; rather, the feeling generated by the sparse, even apathetic crowds was that President Bush simply wouldn't do for four more years.

(By contrast, both that day and on many others when Clinton campaigned in more affluent neighborhoods, the position was the reverse: a troubling suspicion among voters who still had something to lose that it might be better to stick with a president whose foibles were known than to take a chance on someone like Clinton who might try to raise taxes and do much worse.)

There didn't seem to be much sentiment for Perot in the battered working-class section in which Clinton campaigned that morning. Indeed, Perot appeared to the few who talked about him to have made a freakish impression—something that turned out to be fairly general in poor, working-class neighborhoods such as the one in South Philadelphia. Nor was Perot's appeal any greater with the lower middle classes generally.

There is little doubt that Perot's wisecracks at the expense of President Bush and Governor Clinton the night before had found an appreciative, even an amused, audience of millions of people throughout the land. The instant polls that night and the next day credited him with having found himself an appreciative audience, but it was evident that his standing in the election depended entirely on how many votes he could take from the president and his Democratic challenger. As to which one he would hurt the most, and whether his showing would be strong enough to influence the election in any decisive way, that still remained to be determined in the other so-called debates.

For political sophisticates who had brushed off the first night's performance as meaningless, therefore, it was a grievous error to conclude that the meetings of the candidates would have no influence whatever on the election day outcome. Because much of the electorate was demonstrably uneasy about the prolonged economic slump and skittish about the three presidential candidates, there was every possibility of a sudden and dramatic shift in mood. Like the first confrontation, whether or not it was called a debate, the other three could not be taken for granted.

People on all three campaign staffs knew quite well that these meetings would go far toward determining the outcome of the election. The nation already had learned, once the White House determined that the president had failed to make out a good case for himself in the Missouri meeting, that he would bring in a whole new economic team if reelected. So, if the economic walls already had come tumblin' down, other consequences were likely to follow before election day dawned.

This was by no means an electorate that could be taken for granted.

.   .   .

Another consideration still had to be taken into account in the climactic struggle to influence the electorate just before election day. That was the furious activity among the movers and shakers who are so much a part of the Washington Establishment and the White House itself.

As so frequently happens within a presidential administration under heavy strain, President Bush's brigade of loyalists began fighting among each other, some arguing for bold new tactics to avert defeat on election day and others seeking to avoid blame for a presidential failure at the polls. Inevitably, the mechanism used by the contestants was the White House leak—the technique that destroyed the Nixon administration. Only this time there was no picturesque "Deep Throat" to guide the opposition *Washington Post* in its latest foray against a Republican administration.

Instead, Bob Woodward, the Pulitzer Prize–winning senior partner of the team of Woodward and Bernstein, published a series of articles in the *Washington Post* that clearly reflected the views of one or more White House insiders. One striking point in the series, which ran just before the debates, had an insider criticizing President Bush for "sheer idiocy" in apologizing for abandoning his pledge: "Read My Lips, No New Taxes." The insider argued that Bush's decision to sign a tax increase proposal, sent to the White House from Congress, had been "the right thing to do."

The loyalist *Wall Street Journal* editorially identified Woodward's principal source as the much-criticized budget director, Richard G. Darman, and accused him of an "attempt to set the tone of all future histories of economic policy during the Bush years." Although the president defended Darman at the time, he did concede that the timing of the Woodward articles was "peculiar."

The outcome was reflected in the president's announcement after his unimpressive showing in the first debate that Darman, Treasury Secretary Brady, and Financial Adviser Boskin wouldn't be around for a second-term Bush presidency, assuming there was one.

That, however, did not stanch the damage from the continued back stabbing that seemed to have become a part of the White House's routine for the balance of the presidential campaign. The intrigue, as it developed for the remainder of Bush's term, sometimes became Byzantine in its intensity. In describing the situation within the White House as he saw it at the time, a former Bush administration official, William J. Bennett, was quoted using his knowledge of Shakespearean drama to describe what was going on behind the scenes: "Woe is England for here are cynicism, betrayal and treachery, to talk about their President, their friend, their sponsor, as the doddering old fool in the attic."*

. . .

The most powerful figure behind the scenes in the closing days of the president's reelection campaign, Secretary Baker, maintained a disarmingly low profile despite these disquieting events. To his critics, he seemed to be trying to distance himself from responsibility for the president's faltering campaign, which was absurd on the face of it after he had been brought in to run both the campaign and the White House. To his admirers, now fewer in time of travail, his discretion was appropriate under the circumstances.

Much was made of Baker's secretiveness, his refusal to take public positions in his new post unless the president virtually demanded it, and how he limited his public appearances. It became a bad joke among the White House press corps when they exchanged tactical information on what they called "Baker sightings," which generally translated into a brief appearance by the chief of staff at a White House function. Generally he gave no news conferences, and issued only the most necessary statements in his name.

However, in fairness to the secretary, as the president's closest friend and adviser, he had been put in an impossible position in the last days of the Bush campaign. From the State Department, where he had served creditably as secretary, and sometimes with distinction,

*New York Times, Oct. 11, 1992, p. 15.

he had been plunged into the very heart of a thoroughly disorganized presidential reelection drive when it was too late to do much to reverse its fateful direction.

It had been often said in Baker's behalf that this was a job he had never sought, didn't want but couldn't refuse. The critical decisions on the conduct of the campaign already had been made. He could not undo them.

About the most he *could* do was to protect the president from further fallout and hope, perhaps, for some thundering error on the Democratic side that would tend to reverse Governor Clinton's progress toward a goal on November 3 that few, even among his own supporters, had been confident that he could achieve after his weak beginning in the New Hampshire primary vote.

As for the business at hand, the second of the presidential campaign debates—this one for the three vice presidential candidates—loomed dead ahead only two nights after the disappointing first venture by President Bush. This time, the advance verdict of the commentators on television and in the press was that little could be expected from Vice President Quayle that would improve the president's position. Some even said that the vice president was being shoved into an untenable situation to make the best showing he could against the highly regarded senator from Tennessee, Al Gore.

Nothing seemed to be working well for the Bush team so close to election day.

25

The Hidden Issue

The second presidential debate, which featured the three major vice presidential candidates, aroused scant advance public interest.

In the American political tradition, vice presidents were to be seen and seldom heard. Accordingly, vice presidential candidates usually received comparatively little attention in most general elections, which was both shortsighted and unwise.

For an office whose occupant remained just a heartbeat away from the presidency, the vice presidency deserved much greater attention from the presidential nominees and the electorate. Of the sixteen presidents to date in twentieth-century America, five had acceded to the highest office from the vice presidency in emergencies—more than 30 percent of the total. Among them were some of the strongest—and weakest—chief executives. Theodore Roosevelt, at forty-two, had succeeded the assassinated President William McKinley in 1901. In 1923, upon the death of Warren Gamaliel Harding in San Francisco, Calvin Coolidge had become President. Harry S Truman had taken over the Oval Office in 1945 upon the death of Franklin Delano Roosevelt. When John Fitzgerald Kennedy was assassinated in 1963, Lyndon Baines Johnson succeeded him. And in 1974, upon Richard Nixon's forced resignation in the Watergate scandal, Gerald Ford—the only unelected Vice President—had become President.

In the light of such a record, the nation's leaders and challengers in this election should have been prepared for any eventuality at the outset of the vice presidential debate on October 13 at Georgia Tech in Atlanta. Nothing much happened, however, until a grizzled, white-haired veteran of the U.S. Navy muttered into a microphone over national television: "Who am I? Why am I here?"

.　　　.　　　.

Nominally, the speaker was Vice Adm. James B. Stockdale, Ross Perot's candidate for vice president, the only nonpolitician on the platform. For some time he had been listening to his opponents belaboring each other—Vice President Quayle for the Republicans and Senator Gore for the Democrats. The issues were familiar, ranging in importance from unemployment and the sagging economy to the failures in public education, public health, and the environment.

In responding to a nod from the moderator, Hal Bruno of ABC, the admiral, by implication at least, had raised a far more important subject: "What is truth?"

Throughout this campaign, as much of the electorate already suspected, truth had taken a beating although each major candidate had posed as a citadel of virtue and blamed all the others seeking public office—a familiar charade in American politics. That morning, the issue had been raised once again in direct, even virulent, fashion.

President Bush had led off on NBC's "Today" by once again accusing Governor Clinton of dodging the draft in Vietnam and this time had urged him "to come clean." News people, in a follow-up, had aroused Clinton by asking him for comment, upon which he had challenged the president instead to give an honest account of his part in the Iran-contra scandal, saying: "It's time for President Bush to make public the transcript of his questioning [in the Iran-contra case]. Since his current story is now different from his original alibi, Bush either told the American people one thing in public and told investigators another in private or misled both."

The Democratic presidential nominee apparently took to this revived issue with relish because it enabled him to charge President Bush with changing *his* story as well.

There was some truth to the accusation. Since 1986, when he had been President Reagan's vice president, President Bush had argued repeatedly that he had taken no part in the Iran-contra scandal— the sale of American weapons to Iran to obtain the release of American hostages with part of the proceeds going to support the contras, the revolutionaries in Nicaragua. In return, Democrats in Congress already had contended that Bush, as an important player in the proceedings, had misled both Congress and the American public.

Predictably, the president had brushed off his opponent's demand for a transcript of the questions of a special prosecutor that he had answered—questions that may or may not have had a bearing on those that had led more recently to the indictment of his colleague in the Reagan cabinet, Defense Secretary Caspar Weinberger. The charge in the Weinberger case was misinforming Congress.

This was strong stuff, for it at least implied that a criminal arms conspiracy had been under way at the time in defiance of the will of Congress and that perjury may have been committed. Without presuming to pass on the guilt or innocence of any of the participants, news people already had published and broadcast reports that President Bush, while still in office, whether reelected or not, would be asked for pardons in advance, Nixon style, for any in high rank in the Reagan administration who had been involved.

Because so sensitive an issue was still developing outside the opening discussion in the vice presidential debates at Georgia Tech that night, it is not to be wondered at that Admiral Stockdale's seemingly innocuous queries, "Who am I? Why am I here?" constituted a reminder of a query that Pontius Pilate had posed two thousand years ago: "What is truth?"

No proper responses were forthcoming then. Nor were there any that were more satisfactory at the second of the presidential debates in 1992. However, as every major participant fully realized, the issue of truth telling could not remain hidden much longer with election day so close at hand.

Then, if ever, it would be the American people who would have to demand a proper accounting. The final reckoning in the Iran-contra scandal could not be put off forever. Eventually, the nation would have to be told the answer to the most persistent of the remaining questions: "What did George Bush know and when did he know it?" and "What did he really do about it?"

. . .

Unlike the first debate between the presidential candidates, there had not been any concern over prospective winners and losers in the vice presidential discussion. Like their principals who had preceded them, the candidates had tried to maintain reasonably safe positions in which there would be little possibility of damaging error—the horror factor in all these encounters.

Vice President Quayle had been shrill to the point of seeming desperation in arguing that Governor Clinton could not be trusted to be president on the basis of the so-called character issue, as exemplified by the Vietnam draft allegations. In reply, Senator Gore had hammered away at the Bush-Quayle ticket's responsibility for the nation's slumping economic condition and its failure to reduce unemployment substantially.

Not until Admiral Stockdale by inference accused his major party rivals of not paying enough attention to other important lapses did there seem to be a chance of approaching more sensitive issues. But Vice President Quayle was not to be swayed from the same kind of personal attack against Governor Clinton that President Bush had been conducting. Senator Gore, instead of swerving from his apparent assignment, the continued assault on the Bush administration's economic faults, redoubled his efforts to develop that issue along the lines Clinton had followed.

Thus, neither of the principals wanted to take chances in their ninety-minute nationally televised appearance. As for Admiral Stockdale, who had tried to move the discussion into the far more sensitive field of national security, there was a curious indecision by both the major party candidates to go into the reopened Iran-contra scandal at any depth.

For Vice President Quayle, that was understandable. He had nothing to gain and a great deal to lose by delving into an issue in which so many suspicions still were being raised against the White House and as quickly—and furiously—denied. There would have been much more justification for going on the offensive in the renewed scandal investigation had Senator Gore wanted to take a chance on it. However, the Democratic ticket still enjoying a smaller, though still definite, lead over the Bush-Quayle ticket in the opinion polls, he apparently decided, as did his advisers, to leave well enough alone.

That late in a presidential campaign, neither Republicans nor Democrats were likely to be venturesome except if they truly believed they now had a knockout punch ready for the opposition. Because Admiral Stockdale swerved off course without result and seemed somewhat bewildered thereafter, there was a lot of sympathetic murmuring that the old sea dog had been out of his depth in a hard-fought national campaign.

Had he been able to arouse his opposition, he would have been right on target. At least, he had tried, but his colleagues had chosen to remain on familiar ground that already had been cleared by the presidential nominees. The moderate couldn't do much about that.

.   .   .

As if to make up for his overly cautious approach to the president's shortcomings during the debate, Senator Gore returned to the attack against Bush two days later. I must say it was done with style. It was not that anything Gore said about the president was new, but the reporters seemed to think his audience, the National Conference of Editorial Writers, had been impressed, mainly because he broadened his criticism of the Bush administration's role in the Middle East to include the devious manner in which the United States had gone about rearming Iraq before the Gulf War.

It was one thing, as Gore emphasized to the journalists at Lexington, Kentucky, for the United States to deal with Iran to free American hostages but quite another to rearm Saddam Hussein as the dictator of Iraq after the end of the eight-year Iran-Iraq War. That, the senator charged, was President Bush's mistake, for it led directly to Saddam's attack on oil-rich Kuwait, a prime source with Saudi Arabia for America's supply of foreign oil. "I think the president has a great many questions to answer about Iraqgate," Gore said.

The foremost question, and the one that bothered the opposition Democrats in Congress, was why the Bush administration would have rearmed a dangerous Middle East dictator who had prevented a sweeping victory by his much larger Iranian foes in the Middle East. It was an easy answer to point out, as some Republicans did, that Iran—after the war with Iraq—had become the dominant military power in the Middle East and was reportedly developing an atomic capability.

However, with America in the grip of a long recession, the loan guarantees for Iraq might well have been used instead to reduce the economic damage on the home front. Eventually, when Iraq defaulted on its loans and thereby cost the United States more than $1 billion in losses, criticisms that had been lodged by Gore and other Democrats in Congress seemed justified.

This is how Senator Gore stated the case against President Bush in switching from appeasement of Iran to the rearming of Iraq: "I believe what we're seeing right now is George Bush presiding over a cover-up that is significantly larger than the Watergate cover-up. Watergate was described as a two-bit burglary. Iraqgate by contrast includes the largest bank fraud in the history of America."

That, in effect, introduced a whole new element in the Bush administration's conduct of the Persian Gulf War against Saddam's Iraq, in which Saddam had used his American-supplied arms against his benefactors. At its victorious climax, that conflict had been regarded as the shining star in the president's accomplishments with an 88 percent approval rating from the public. That, in turn, had seemed at the time to be a virtual guarantee of the president's renomination and reelection.

Only that isn't what happened. This was when the role of the Italian government became known through its very large interest in the Banca Nazionale del Lavoro, which had supplied the American-guaranteed money to Saddam's Iraq through its small American branch in Atlanta.

That, too, was when the matter became so serious in the United States that three of the most secretive American investigative agencies—the CIA, FBI, and the Justice Department—blamed each other for concealing the affair from congressional investigators. This was what Senator Gore emphasized when he openly discussed the crime in all its ramifications. If he could not shed more light on the source of the conspiracy, he at least stressed the correctness of public suspicions about such plotting in government and he also shredded President Bush's reply that he had acted only to bring Saddam Hussein into the family of nations.

The Democratic vice presidential nominee compared the Bush administration's position in the Iraqgate scandal to that of the Nixon administration after that president's reelection in 1972 when the Watergate scandal seemed to be heading toward presidential impeachment proceedings in the U.S. Senate.

As Gore stated the comparison: "After the inauguration in 1973, the Nixon administration became consumed with defending itself in the midst of that scandal. You are seeing the same thing happen right now with the Bush administration except it is happening at a much faster pace."

Gore predicted, however, that no impeachment test would be brought against President Bush because he was likely to be defeated for reelection in 1992 whereas Nixon thought he was safe when he won reelection in 1972. Still, even if the notion of impeaching another president could be set aside, the senator couldn't suggest what could be done about the internal feuding between the CIA, the FBI, and the Department of Justice.

Nor was there any real appreciation, publicly, of the reasons for the reluctance of these three agencies to face a postelection trial of the issues. To insiders, it still appeared important to conceal from the public the secret maneuvers of American and British intelligence that had failed to uncover Saddam Hussein's widespread preparations for his attempt to take over Kuwait's oil fields.

This much already had been leaked to the press to try to account for the interagency feuding during the presidential campaign.

The CIA had prepared still another story to explain its nonaction

191

in a bank fraud case through which Saddam got his money by pleading that it would have involved the publication of classified material damaging to American security interests. It was at this point that it became known that British intelligence, in its close relationship with the CIA, had also been involved in the bartering with Saddam. But unlike the procedure in the United States, the British insisted on a refusal to specify exactly what their hush-hush intelligence operation had done for or against the rearming of Saddam—and why they had so acted. That would be determined after election when and if the matter appeared for adjudication before a British court.

For the remainder of the presidential campaign, therefore, the American part of the inquiry blacked out to conceal who helped Saddam get American money and why the CIA and the Department of Justice were privately blaming each other. As for the FBI, it politely disassociated itself from further inquiries by pointing out that its director, Sessions, himself was under investigation for alleged personal indiscretions.

The absurd part of the whole silly business was that insiders around Saddam knew the whole story and some of it leaked from Baghdad. Still, Attorney General Barr stonewalled the Democratic demand to appoint a new special prosecutor once his choice of former Judge Lacey had satisfied nobody. The CIA director, Robert Gates, had tried a similar dodge by asking the inspector general to investigate, but that also had gone nowhere.

What it all came down to was that the government's chief investigative agencies all looked foolish before the public at election time. If any special prosecutor ever was to determine responsibility, it would have to be done after the election.

While all this was going on, the White House was maintaining a grim, almost a painful, silence. It was apparent that the president, in his familiar position when presented with a confusing situation, decided to do nothing on the theory that it might just go away. This was what the White House had done with the development of the recession beginning in 1990 and it hadn't resolved anything. Nor did the head-in-the-sand attitude turn out to yield any better results in the bank fraud case that had provided Saddam Hussein with the sinews of war.

So late in a presidential campaign for reelection, nothing much could be done either to clear reputable officials with a good record of service to the nation or to produce public evidence at a trial that would resolve the bitter interagency dispute over the responsibility for creating Saddam Hussein's war machine.

That would be left for the next administration to handle. No one should have pitied Admiral Stockdale under the circumstances for asking, at the second presidential debate, "Who am I? Why am I here?" After all, who was there now on earth to give adequate response to Pontius Pilate's even more difficult question of two thousand years ago: "What is truth?"

26

Bush in Retreat

$\mathbf{I}$t was bound to happen.

Sooner rather than later, President Bush's floundering reelection campaign spread doubt and disillusion through even the most important of the federal government's operations.

Although the Republican old guard remained faithful to their president, the far right of the Christian front and the fragmented liberals, the disconsolate remainder of the Rockefeller wing, began criticizing the conduct of the campaign. Yet, except for absentee ballots, not a vote had been cast and even the most discouraging among the polls showed but a few percentage points separating President Bush from both his rivals.

Under much worse circumstances, gritty Harry Truman, sometimes Bush's role model even though the Missourian had been a lifelong Democrat, had won a surprise victory over the New Yorker, Tom Dewey, in 1948. Truman's grinning picture, holding aloft the *Chicago Tribune*'s banner headline proclaiming his defeat, remained a comforting assurance to a gloomy White House that the polls could be wrong.

For 1992, President Bush still clung to that precious bit of hope. It remained his life jacket in a mounting sea of confusion as some in the White House already began making fitful preparations for imminent departure and the fainthearted among the party's professionals began updating their résumés for the anticipated job hunt beginning with the coming of the new administration in the new year. As for President Bush, it was almost fatefully accepted in the White House that he already was in decline.

.   .   .

Once even the most successful politicians begin to slide downhill in the nation's capital, almost everything affecting their future seems to go wrong as well. Such was the uncomfortable position in which President Bush found himself in mid-October with election day only about three weeks off.

Between the second and third presidential debates, even the austere State Department showed symptoms of panic. In a misguided attempt to help the president out of a jam, several officials at State became involved in a secret search of departmental files in Washington and London to determine if Governor Clinton, at the time of the Vietnam War, had ever sought to give up his American citizenship to duck the draft.

No one really knew where the rumor had begun, but latterly it was attributed to several conservative congressmen who seized on almost anything that might be derogatory to Governor Clinton in the hope that it might undermine his chances for election to the presidency. His trip to Moscow while he was a Rhodes scholar at Oxford, for example, had led conservative gossips to speculate that he might have done something suspicious while he was in the Soviet Union. But alas for their hopes, it was just the kind of a brief expedition that any American might have taken at the time out of sheer curiosity.

The rumor about a supposed effort to change citizenship, however, led to far more serious consequences, not for Clinton, but for his detractors. When the story was picked up for checking by several news organizations, notably the Hearst Newspapers and the Associated Press, application was made to the State Department under the Freedom of Information Act for any indication in its files that Clinton had ever made a request for a change of citizenship.

Now the department's rules came into play, for these regulations specified that requests of this nature had to be taken in the order in which they were received unless there was some demonstrable need for emergency action. In the Clinton case, as it developed, some officials at State decided on a rush act to determine if there was any truth to the rumor affecting his citizenship.

Somehow, the *Washington Post* learned of the search of Clinton's records, which, as matters turned out, had been coupled with similar examinations of his mother's files and Ross Perot's. The *Post* also determined that the examination had turned up nothing that was derogatory in any way either to the two presidential candidates or Clinton's mother.

When Clinton heard about the incident at State while he was campaigning in Seattle, he let fly. "It turns out," he commented, "that the State Department was not only rifling through my files, but actually investigating my mother, a well-known subversive. It would be funny if it weren't so pathetic. This is a crowd so desperate to hold onto power that they have forgotten the purpose of power in government is to help people and lift them up."

To conclude his remarks, in a lighter mood, he suggested that his mother, Mrs. Virginia Kelley, a devoted horse-racing fan, might have been telephoned nightly from Moscow by Leonid Brezhnev, who was in power at the time, for tips on the third race at Oaklawn.

Senator Gore, as Clinton's running mate, added for good measure, "I think the American people have a right to be outraged."

Outraged or not, the public was treated to a full-dress exposé of this political farce created by Republican fantasies and executed for political purposes just before election day. A State Department official thereupon named Elizabeth Tamposi, assistant secretary of state for consular affairs, as the official who had taken charge of the search of the passport files for Clinton, his mother, and Ross Perot on an emergency basis.

The department's inspector general, Sherman M. Funk, was authorized to conduct a thorough investigation into Ms Tamposi's actions along with others who may have been involved, the objective probably being to push the disagreeable business under the rug until after the election.

Meanwhile, Lawrence Eagleburger, the acting secretary of state, offered his resignation as a formality but President Bush rejected it. As for Secretary Baker, still on leave to the White House, he remained discreetly silent about the whole curious business although it was evident that the White House must have known about the search.

For President Bush, it was an embarrassment he could have been spared when his reelection campaign still was lagging with election day just ahead. The passport files were supposed to yield devastating information that would blow the Democratic presidential campaign out of the water, but nothing happened.

As usual in such situations, no matter which party is in the White House, those supposedly involved in the affair at State swore to high heaven that their motives were pure and that no wrong had been committed.

However, the damage to the Bush campaign could not be undone. Nor was it possible to brush aside the public amusement over the inept display of political skullduggery within the State Department. In vain did Acting Secretary Eagleburger, a respected career diplomat, insist that the department under all conceivable circumstances had to be rigidly nonpartisan. No politician in the nation's capital, however, believed so detached a viewpoint was possible in a department so closely linked with the president's political fortunes.

The upshot of the departmental embarrassment over the search in the files of two presidential candidates and the mother of one of them was to disclose to the public the extent of the federal government's disorganization in the closing period of the presidential election.

Unless the polls were "nutty," as President Bush occasionally proclaimed them to be, it was apparent that his administration now was functioning under mounting difficulties in the closing days of what appeared to be a losing reelection campaign. Clinton was taking the long view by appealing to his own constituency against overconfidence. Setting himself up as a role model for his campaign organization, he seemed to be working harder than ever as election day approached.

. . .

Next to the president, Secretary Baker now became the responsible top-ranking official for maintaining some semblance of order in the federal government. However, the trouble with dependence on Secretary Baker was that he seldom could be easily located because of his manifold duties both as White House chief of staff and political campaign director. Nor were the people he had taken with him from State to the White House any more in evidence at top level than their chief. His well-advertised reluctance to exercise his authority persisted despite the less than admiring publicity it was bringing him.

Much of the White House press corps already had concluded that the secretary was making every conceivable effort to separate himself from the stigma of a probable Republican defeat on election day. It was a position, incidentally, that some of those closest to him were trying to emulate.

Like Vice President Quayle, Secretary Baker was widely believed to hope for the Republican presidential nomination in 1996 now that the 1992 race was apparently already lost. These two weren't the only ones who seemed to be trying to salvage something out of what appeared likely to become the wreckage of the Bush administration on election day. Among others who modestly were calling attention to themselves as influential figures for 1996 were Jack Kemp, the moderate secretary for housing and urban development, and the Reverend Pat Robertson, who had been somewhat influential during the latter days of the party's National Convention.

As the enveloping shadow of gloom spread from the White House, it also affected the operations of the president's economic team, all of whom had been notified publicly by the president that they would be replaced even if he succeeded in being reelected. Still, Treasury Secretary Nicholas Brady, Budget Director Richard Darman, and the chief economic adviser, Michael Boskin, realized all too well that nothing they could do in the short time before election day would make their departure any easier to bear.

Even in the Pentagon, the once untouchable Defense Department and the uniformed services were bracing themselves for major cuts in spending and manpower. Regardless of America's vital interests in the Middle East, Europe, and the rim of the far Pacific, the time for withdrawal of the nation's armed outposts on foreign soil had at last arrived with consequences that now were too difficult to forecast.

No one could logically accuse the Pentagon's civilian directorate or the Joint Chiefs of Staff of preparing for a more insular nation, centered mainly on defending the home front. Yet, regardless of the outcome of the election, the requirement for a massive reduction in the $4 trillion national debt seemed to outweigh all other considerations except the urgent need to create work to relieve unemployment. One approach, favored by Governor Clinton during the campaign, was to repair the nation's infrastructure: its roads, bridges, tunnels, and regulatory systems.

.   .   .

The surest sign of top-heavy Democratic support in the presidential race came in a year that began with most contributions, large and small, going to the Republican ticket headed by President Bush and wound up with even more money going to the Democratic ticket topped by Governor Clinton. There was nothing unusual about this. Historically in this century, winners in presidential campaigns may not receive all the contributions but they generally come away with more money than the losers. That, at any rate, was the way the election shaped up midway between the presidential debates, Clinton still leading in the polls.

In line with standing operation procedure at the corporate level, the large donors who weren't sure which side to back often wound up giving to both. That, as has already been emphasized, was reported by the Federal Election Commission in a listing of contributors who gave more than $100,000 to each party.

Had the record of all gifts—large and small—been confined to roughly the first part of the presidential drive, there is little doubt that the Republicans would have had more than the Democrats by at least 3 to 1. Just before the end, though, it was shown that the Democrats had raised more than $70 million for their presidential ticket, about $20 million for October alone. As for the Republicans, their early lead in financing shrank so quickly that toward the end they had to settle for about $62 million including $13 million for October.

These gifts were besides the previously reported receipt of $55.2 million in federal financial aid for the presidential campaign of each major party. Atop that, Ross Perot reported spending at least $60 million of his own money on his independent candidacy. Those figures would seem to indicate that more than $300 million in publicly listed gifts was devoted to the election of a president, certainly a record for the era.

How much else was contributed through political action committees, unacknowledged gifts to individuals or offices representing one of the presidential candidates, and other devices for concealed contributions is always a matter for intense speculation toward the end of every campaign for the highest office in the land. It may be to the interest of the candidates and their fund-raising staffs to play down the role of large contributors, but that doesn't necessarily coincide with the public interest.

Those who give the biggest bucks invariably turn up as White House influentials in one way or another. In any event, based on a lifelong interest in presidential elections as a sometime reporter, observer, writer, and teacher, I would suggest that as a nation toward century's end we were approaching the half-billion-dollar mark in electing a president, a danger signal for those who have had experience with the way pressures on presidents are created.

That seemed to me to be ample reason for Governor Clinton to proclaim, if elected, that he would make presidential election reforms one of his first priorities. No one had any right to expect miracles in new ways to finance presidential campaigns from a newly elected chief executive. Yet, assuming Clinton did win and did take presidential election reform seriously, whatever he would be able to do was likely to create just a little more confidence in the system than the public exhibited in the 1992 election as a whole.

.   .   .

The falling off in Republican campaign financing, coinciding as it did with large gains in the field made by the Democrats, raised a serious question about how far public opinion polls foreshadowed the outcome of the election. Even a slight decline in the polling figures for President Bush in mid-October of that election year had to be taken with the utmost seriousness. It had been a long time since the polls had been open to such doubt that both campaign financing and voter confidence in a candidate had suffered just before election day, as was the case in 1992 when President Bush was being so badly put down.

CBS News put Clinton sixteen points ahead of Bush, 47–31 percent and only 11 percent for Perot. ABC News made the margin even broader, giving Clinton an eighteen-point lead over Bush, 49–31 percent, and 12 percent for Perot. The most conservative poll, *Newsweek*'s, gave Clinton a fifteen-point lead over Bush, 46–31 percent, and 14 percent for Perot.*

Even though there was some evidence at the time that the Clinton-Bush race might be tightening and Perot might be getting more of the vote than these polls indicated, such changes obviously were not reflected in the polls cited here with the findings for the two most important debates in the presidential series yet to come.

Had the voting shift begun earlier, would it have made any perceptible difference in President Bush's chances? No one can say after the fact. The outcome long since has been recorded in the history of the American presidency.

*CBS News dated its poll Oct. 15–17; ABC News, Oct. 15–17; and *Newsweek*, Oct. 15–16. The dates of the four debates were Oct. 11, 13, 15, 19.

27

Putting Down a President

$\mathbf{M}$idway through the third presidential debate at the University of Richmond in Virginia on the night of October 15, a woman asked the three candidates: "How has the national debt personally affected your lives? And if it hasn't, how can you honestly find a cure for the economic problems of the common people if you have no experience in what's ailing them?"

It was the crux of the encounter between 209 uncommitted voters and the candidates—an informal town meeting in which the nation's problems were discussed. The audience already had rejected the mudslinging that had been President Bush's strong suit in his attacks on the character of Governor Clinton. Now Ross Perot was called upon by Carole Simpson of ABC, the moderator, to respond to the deeply personal aspect of the question.

First of all, he confessed his private life had been disrupted because the issue had made him an independent presidential candidate. Then, he added that he wanted to reestablish a strong basic economy for future generations, and his children and grandchildren in particular.

The president was quite deliberate in making his initial response. He said he wanted to think just a bit about the problem because the national debt affected everybody, himself included. And as a parent, he explained, he wanted to believe that his grandchildren would be able to afford an education.

When the moderator pressed him for a further response, he asked if she was suggesting that "if somebody has means, the national debt doesn't affect them?"

The questioner who had started the discussion then intervened, causing the president to say that she might help him respond if he understood something of her circumstances.

The woman said, "Well, I've had friends that have been laid off jobs. I know people who cannot afford to pay the mortgages on their homes, their car payments. I have personal problems with the national debt. But," and she repeated, "how has it affected you? And if you have no experience in it, how can you help us? How can you help us if you don't know what we're feeling?"

Ms Simpson tried to be helpful to the president. She explained to him during a brief pause, "I think that she means more the recession, the economic problems today rather than the deficit."

President Bush seemed in firmer control now. "Well, you ought to . . . you ought to be in the White House for a day and hear what I hear and see what I see . . . But I don't think it's fair to say, 'You have not had cancer, therefore you don't know what it's like'. . . . So I think it's sad, but I think in terms of the recession. Of course you feel it when you're president of the United States. And that's why I'm trying to do something about it by stimulating the exports, investing more, better education system. Thank you. I'm glad to clarify it."

Governor Clinton took over then, saying, "Well, I've been governor of a small state for twelve years. I'll tell you how it's affected me. I've seen what's happened these last four years in my state. Middle-class people, when they lose their jobs, there's a good chance I know them by their names. When a factory closes, I know the people who ran it. When businesses go bankrupt, I know them. And I've been out here for thirteen months in meetings just like this one ever since October with people like you all over America, people that have lost their jobs, lost their livelihood, lost their health insurance.

"What I want you to understand is the national debt is not the only cause of this. It is because America has not invested in its people. It is because we haven't grown. It is because we've had twelve years of trickle-down economics. . . . It is because we are in the grip of a failed economic theory. And this decision you're about to make better be about what kind of economic theory you want. . . . What I think we have to do is to invest in American jobs, American education, control American health care costs, and bring the American people together again."

In a sense, the discussion touched on the heart of the presidential campaign of 1992. Because it did, attracting the attention of a national audience larger than that for a recent World Series baseball game, it became a significant part of the presidential election. To be sure, Governor Clinton was better prepared for the questions from the uncommitted audience than President Bush, but that was because the Democratic nominee had suggested this format. He was used to it much more so than the president and Perot.

By contrast, the president, in his somewhat mechanical responses to questions posed at random from the audience when the moderator saw a raised hand, gave the impression that his plans for the debate had been aborted. In a sense, that was true, for it was clear enough that what he had really wanted to do here was to keep on attacking Clinton on the character issue—the alleged draft dodging, the adulterous affair, the admitted one-time bout with pot, and so on.

In the vice presidential debate, the second in the series, Vice President Quayle had seemed to be making progress by battering away at Clinton for these alleged shortcomings. What the president evidently had been set to do was to argue that someone who behaved as erratically as he believed Clinton had done could not be trusted to run the country as president.

However, from the very outset of this nationally telecast debate, the handpicked audience of uncommitted voters had made it clear to all three candidates that they were to discuss the relevant issues of the campaign, not the invidious personalities and the mudslinging that to date had turned off most other audiences. Now, therefore, the president was both puzzled and uncomfortable.

It really wasn't entirely his fault that his showing at the University of Richmond was so indifferent. He seemed, through no fault of his own, to have been outmaneuvered by being forced to play Clinton's game—the discussion of domestic issues—whereas the Arkansas governor was being let off the most important part of Bush's presidency, his expertise in foreign affairs.

Perot, too, wasn't measuring up to the lively promise of his appearance in the first debate, something that had concerned President Bush when Perot had, by common agreement, been the star of the proceedings with his wisecracks and his homespun wisdom. There had been little chance for the third man in the presidential debates to shine this time and he, too, seemed to realize it.

Clinton, so far at least, appeared to be doing better than he had in the past. Unless he stumbled, the Arkansan was likely to carry off the honors in this latest encounter. Because only one more debate was left, and Clinton was still leading in the polls, it would take an upset to revive the president's chances of reelection.

.　　.　　.

The president, at the outset, had attacked Clinton, for leading anti-Vietnam War demonstrations against America while he was a Rhodes scholar in Britain. Bush had followed up by again criticizing his Democratic rival for shifting positions on several issues in what appeared to be an effort to please everybody. "You can't turn the White House into a waffle house," the president said, demonstrating that Perot wasn't alone in getting off a sharp-tongued one-liner.

Clinton broke in then, seeming willing to throw verbal punches at the president. He recalled that a *Washington Post* editorial had called Bush a "political chameleon" for frequently changing his position, then added: "I'm not interested in his character. I'm interested in changing the character of the presidency."

One of the questioners in the audience stressed the point the moderator had been making about the electorate's displeasure over the conduct of the campaign, saying: "Can we focus on the issues and not the personalities and the mud? . . . I think there is a real need here to focus at this point on needs."

In this manner the president at last had to give up his emphasis on attacking Clinton's fitness to be president. As for Perot, he took one last crack at his major party rivals: "Now, just for the record, I don't have any spin doctors. I don't have any speech writers. Probably shows. I made those charts you see on television. But you don't have to wonder if it's me talking. What you see is what you get. . . ."

Clinton shot back: "The ideas I express are mine. I've worked on these things for twelve years and I'm the only person up here who hasn't been a part of Washington in any way for the last twenty years. So I don't want the implication to be that somehow everything we say is cooked up and put into our head by somebody else."

Nevertheless, the ill feeling between the two major candidates persisted. From the outset, they had differed over the proposed North American trade agreement when Clinton charged the federal government already was giving low interest loans and job training money to companies that eventually moved abroad "but we won't do the same thing for plants that stay here." He called for "more trade, but on fairer terms and favor investments in America."

It wasn't long before the president got back at the Democrat domestic program in which higher taxes were proposed for wealthy Americans and foreign corporations doing business in this country. Bush said: "I don't see how you can grow the deficit down by raising people's taxes. You see, I don't think the American people are taxed too little. I think they are taxed too much. I went for one tax increase. And when I make a mistake I admit it. Say that wasn't the right thing to do."

Perot meanwhile was belaboring both candidates at every turn.

His style was to announce what he'd do if president without going into the dull business of how he proposed to fix all the country's woes. "Put it to you bluntly, America," he said at one point. "If you want me to be your president, we're going to face our problems. We'll solve our problems. We'll pay down our debt. We'll pass on the American dream to our children and I will not leave our children a situation that they have today."

Perot also wasn't above calling attention to his expensive thirty-minute commercials being put on national television in the closing phase of the campaign. "I'm spending my money, not PAC money, not foreign money, my money, to take this message to the American people," he said.

Bush, too, complained, "When you're president, you expect this—everybody's running against the incumbent. They can do better, everyone knows that." He then boosted his proposal to improve the lot of impoverished inner city dwellers by creating urban enterprise zones to bring more business—and more jobs—to the crumbling ghetto areas.

Here, Clinton once again centered his attack on the president, charging he had vetoed such a measure earlier in the year when it was passed by Congress because it would have levied higher taxes on wealthy Americans to help pay for urban improvement. "This is not mud slinging," he added. "It is fact slinging." He plugged his proposal to set aside $20 billion a year for the next four years for investment in needy areas together with investment tax credits.

So it went through relatively brief discussions of what could be done about reducing crime and insuring better gun control, and an almost meaningless few minutes on foreign affairs, in which President Bush's substantial accomplishments were largely glossed over. Nor did he seem unduly disturbed because he did not have a chance to expand on his views about the creation of a new world order.

The surprise of the evening was how far the candidates differed on the fourteen proposals in affected states, to be voted on election day, in which term limits would be fixed for some elective offices not now covered.

President Bush was all for applying strict limits to congressional terms in line with the two-term limitations for presidents. He pointed to the Democratic control of the House of Representatives for thirty-eight years to justify his proposed limitation of service in the House to twelve years.

Among the results of the long period of Democratic control of the House, he went on, were "a sorry little post office that can't . . . do anything right and a bank that has more overdrafts than the Chase bank and Citibank put together." He concluded, "We've got to do something about it and I think you get a certain arrogance, bureaucratic arrogance, when people stay there too long. And so I favor, strongly favor, term limits."

Clinton was diametrically opposed, saying term limits would pose a problem for a lot of the smaller states that now have trouble getting a fair hearing in Congress. It would also increase the power of the unelected congressional staff people, he went on, then argued that there already was enough prospect for change with the expected election of 120 to 150 new members of Congress on election day. What he favored instead was "strict controls on how much you can spend running for Congress" plus firmer limitations on spending by political action committees.

As for Perot, he volunteered to serve only one term as president if elected and reject all compensation. He insisted, however, setting term limits for Congress wouldn't work unless widespread government reforms also were adopted.

In this manner the candidates for president responded to the public mood that continued to be so critical of incumbents during that election year and so greatly in favor of change, although no one to date had been able to put into words a proposal for change that was likely to win universal approval. It had been that strange kind of campaign from the outset and it was that kind of campaign to the very end.

. . .

There seemed to be agreement in principle among the candidates that the nation and its people deserved better national health care, particularly because many Americans had no health insurance of any kind. But all were far apart on how it was to be done with Clinton proposing greater government regulation and Bush favoring as little government participation as possible. Perot wanted something done and called for widespread government reforms but offered no specifics.

Clinton, having presented a detailed plan during the campaign, stressed the responsibility of employers to cover their employees for health insurance on the assumption that government would similarly cover the unemployed. He also argued for regulating insurance companies in rating clients, checking the rising cost of pharmaceuticals, and cracking down on medical fraud. His plan also included national practice guidelines for physicians, public preventive clinics, and a system of managed competition in the entire health care industry to keep down costs.

President Bush wasn't as specific, except for his stress on reducing malpractice lawsuits and, through a system of government vouchers and tax credits, making health care available to those unable to afford it.

Similarly, all the candidates wanted a better educational system but the mounting costs and the range of ideas for improvement scarcely supported even a modest hope for nationwide acceptance of a system that functions mainly at the public level through the control of local school boards.

What the evening's town meeting came down to at the end was familiar enough.

President Bush reverted to his issue of trust, asking the nation: "Who has the perseverance, the character, the integrity, the maturity to get the job done? I hope I'm that person."

Perot challenged the electorate to accept him at face value as the candidate who could do the job without laboring over specifics. "If they just want to keep slow dancing and talk about it, but not do it, I'm not your man," he said. "I'm results oriented. I'm action oriented."

Governor Clinton, in his final appeal of the evening, rested his case on change: "You have to decide whether you want to change or not. We do not need four more years of economic theory that doesn't work. We've had twelve years of trickle-down economics. It's time to put the American people first, to invest and grow this economy."

What the nation had witnessed for ninety minutes in this televised town meeting was the response of mostly undecided but distinctly worried voters who put the questions that bothered them to the presidential candidates. For the most part, these were not the queries posed by skilled professional journalists experienced in national affairs (the moderator's questions, those of the only professional on the televised scene, mainly consisted of clarifications and elaborations).

The outcome was nothing more nor less than the put-down of a president.

28

Middle-Class Blues

Throughout much of the final presidential debate, there was an aggrieved sense that taxes on the middle class would be raised within the next four years.

Although none of the three candidates would admit to so heinous a fault, each accused one or both of the others directly or by inference of considering the possibility. It was, clearly, an issue of importance in the campaign.

President Bush, having been burned because he had violated his 1988 campaign pledge, "Read My Lips, No New Taxes," was the most fervent in his protests that he never again would do such a thing, especially to the middle class. He had his doubts, though, about Governor Clinton, warning, "Watch your wallets, Mr. and Mrs. America."

The Arkansas governor, in return, took the pledge against increasing taxes on the middle class except in the event of an emergency, the nature of which was undefined. He criticized the president on his broken no-tax promise and accused Ross Perot of proposing more taxes on the middle class and working poor.

As for Perot, who called for a general policy of sacrifice by all Americans, he admitted to a proposal for a fifty-cent-a-gallon gasoline tax but chided both his rivals for their respective plans to salvage a damaged economy because, in his view, their programs didn't add up.

In response to Governor Clinton's proposed tax program of imposing new levies on only the wealthiest Americans and foreign corporations doing business inside the country, the independent candidate immodestly reminded his nationwide audience that he, at least had paid billions of dollars in taxes. He also used the occasion to plug his separate television programs that dealt with his proposals for restoring the nation's economic health.

However, all that did nothing to resolve the most puzzling part of the possibility for greater taxation for the middle class. Simply put, what that amounted to was a complete lack of information, except possibly in the code of the Internal Revenue Service, on how the American middle class could be defined.

That, in all likelihood, would become the basis for what might be called the Middle-Class Blues in the event that more taxation did come its way during the next presidential term.

However, even under the IRS code, no one could be sure of the upper and lower limits of an American middle-class tax system. The best that could be guessed at was that it might begin with the $200,000-a-year lower limit of Clinton's proposed new taxation for the wealthiest Americans and extend downward to the official poverty level for the working poor.

(Unlike the British, who divide their middle class into social layers of lower, middle-middle and upper middle, most employed Americans still like to call themselves middle class although they don't seem to object to being listed by collars—blue, white, or none at all.)

In effect, the discussion left the possibility for greater middle-class taxation in limbo, dependent almost entirely on circumstances. In all probability it damaged President Bush more than the other two candidates. As the nation's chief executive, he could scarcely have avoided a share of the blame that was heaped on him before, during, and after the final debate on October 19 at Michigan State University in East Lansing.

．　　．　　．

The third presidential debate began with a question about Governor Clinton's credibility as the Democratic challenger to a second term for President Bush. The moderator, Jim Lehrer of PBS, stated the position this way: "You are promising to create jobs, reduce the deficit, reform the health care system, rebuild the infrastructure, guarantee college education for everyone who is qualified among many other things, all with financial pain only for the very rich. Some people are having trouble, apparently, believing that this is possible. Should they have that concern?"

Right off, Clinton denied there was cause for concern that he had promised more than he could deliver but at once tackled the disturbing question of added middle-class taxation saying, "There are many people who believe that the only way we can get this country turned around is to tax the middle class more and punish them more."

However, he tried to assure the nation that that was not his intention. By contrast with the wealthiest Americans, whose incomes have increased even though their taxation level went down, the Democratic candidate pointed out that the middle class had been paying more taxes on lowered incomes for at least a dozen years.

That was what he called a part of "trickle-down economics" and added, "It's also a departure from tax-and-spend economics because you can't tax and divide an economy that isn't growing."

What he proposed, besides heavier taxes on the wealthy and on foreign corporations, was $100 billion in tax credits to revive business, $140 billion in spending cuts mainly in defense, investment in new transportation and communications, and an environmental cleanup system among other innovations that would produce more revenue.

Right away, President Bush argued that reducing the $4 trillion deficit might be a more necessary priority and again opposed all tax increases. Referring to Clinton's tax-the-rich plan, the president warned, "Mr. and Mrs. America, when you hear him say, 'We're only going to tax the rich,' watch your wallet. Because his figures don't add up and he's going to sock it right to the middle-class taxpayer and lower if he's going to pay for all the tax programs he proposes."

To that analysis, Perot added his warning, "This is going to take fair, shared sacrifice," by which he referred to his six-year proposal to cut the deficit and balance the budget.

This was when Clinton turned on Bush for raising middle-class taxes in violation of his "Read My Lips" pledge and vetoing a bill to raise taxes on the rich. The Democratic nominee's reply to Perot was just as harsh, accusing him of seeking higher taxes on the middle class and working poor besides his proposed fifty-cent-a-gallon gasoline tax. "The answer," Clinton insisted, "is to invest and grow this economy. That's what works in other countries and that's what'll work here."

.   .   .

There was a lot more of this back-and-forth throughout the ninety-million session, but the climax came when one member of a panel of three reporters asked Clinton: "Will you make a pledge tonight which income level you will not go below [to tax]?"

Clinton fired back his qualified pledge: "I am not going to raise taxes on the middle class to pay for these [income-producing] programs. Now furthermore, I am not going to tell you to read my lips. On anything. Because I cannot foresee what emergencies might develop in this country."

Again, the president argued that Clinton would have to tax people with incomes of $36,600 and under instead of confining added taxation to the rich, that there would be 21 percent interest rates, and that inflation "would go through the roof." He also attacked the governor's twelve-year record in Arkansas, which led to a lively argument and enormous differences in figures for the state's economy.

Perot concluded that part of the discussion by saying, "Our real problem here is that they both have plans that will not work."

As can be seen, this was not a debate any more than the previous sessions had been. It was called that mainly because it was the name adopted by the bipartisan presidential commission appointed to oversee the discussion among the candidates.

Still, regardless of what the sessions were called, there was a decided difference between this final meeting and the previous discussion involving the presidential candidates because questions then came from some of the 209 undecided voters whereas news people once again were posing the issues now.

Regardless of the professionals' criticism that questions from the public were easier for the candidates to answer, it did seem that the news people tended to try to revive controversies without much regard for their relevance. For example, one of the professionals veered aside from the concern of voters for the possibility of added middle-class taxes to review Governor Clinton's state of mind about the Vietnam War. Another suggested that President Bush might now have a different judgment on permitting American assistance to flow to Saddam Hussein in Iraq before the Gulf War.

The diversions, as Ross Perot suggested, came under the heading of history that blocked him, at least temporarily, from pressing his interest in trying to reform some of the federal government's practices. Clinton, too, appeared to favor the voters' questions over those of the journalists but that, probably, was because the Democratic candidate had been the first to suggest the dominance of ordinary citizens in the town-meeting format.

As for President Bush, it seemed that he might well have preferred avoiding questions entirely, given his shaky standing in the opinion polls, although at one point he did flare up in favor of his campaign to annoy the press. For the professionals it was significant that one of the most prominent among them, Dan Rather of

CBS, called the citizens' questions more interesting. Regardless of who asked the questions, the final session was estimated to have drawn 88 million television viewers, the largest of the debates.

. . .

Jim Lehrer of PBS, who had handled the questions for the first half of the final session, deferred to three other professionals for the questioning of the candidates in the latter part of the debate: Susan Rook of CNN, Gene Gibbons of Reuters, and Helen Thomas of United Press International, who is also the senior member of the White House Press Corps.

Ms Thomas asked Governor Clinton: "Your credibility has come into question because of your different responses on the Vietnam draft. If you had it to do over again, would you put on the nation's uniform and, if elected, could you in good conscience send someone to war?"

Clinton recalled that Presidents Lincoln, Franklin Roosevelt, and Woodrow Wilson were among the nation's commanders in chief who had never served in the armed forces before they had to order soldiers into battle. "So the answer is," he said, "that I could do that although I wouldn't relish doing it but I wouldn't shrink from it. I think the president has to be prepared to use the power of the nation when our vital interests are threatened."

On the Vietnam War, he repeated an explanation he already had made when the matter of the draft first came up: "If I had it to do over again, I might answer the questions a little better. You know, I've been in public life a long time and no one had ever questioned my role and so I was asked a lot of questions about things that happened a long time ago. I don't think I answered them as well as I could have. . . . I was opposed to the war. I couldn't help that. I felt very strongly about it and I didn't want to go at the time. It's easy to say in retrospect I would have done something differently."

President Bush got in the final word on that issue saying, "A lot of decent, honorable people felt as he did on the draft. But it is this pattern. . . . You might be able to make amendments all the time, Governor, but you've got to, as president, you can't be on all these different sides. And you can't have this pattern of saying, well, I did this or I didn't. Then the facts come out and you change it. That's my big difference with him on the draft. It wasn't failing to serve."

On Saddam Hussein and Iraq, however, the president found himself under criticism, this time by Ross Perot. The argument arose over a discussion of leadership and accountability for a leader's actions when Perot turned to the president, saying: "If you create Saddam Hussein over a ten-year period, using billions of dollars of U.S. taxpayer money, step up to the plate and say, 'It was a mistake.' . . . Now, leaders will always make mistakes—and I'm not aiming at any one person here. I'm aiming at our government—nobody takes responsibility for anything. We got to change that."

The subject changed then, as it often did in these four debating sessions, with a discussion of how and why leadership often requires the building of a consensus. President Bush picked up the challenge on Saddam Hussein: "Look, you have to build a consensus but in some things—Ross mentioned Saddam Hussein. Yes, we tried. And yes, we failed to bring him into the family of nations . . . but then, when he moved against Kuwait, I said this will not stand. . . . A president has to do that. Sometimes he has to act, and in this case I'm glad I did because if we had let the UN sanctions work, and had tried to build a consensus on that, Saddam Hussein today would be in Saudi Arabia controlling the world's oil supplies and he would be there maybe with nuclear weapons. Anyway, we busted the world's fourth largest army and we did it through leadership."

Perot, however, wasn't satisfied. Later, he came back to the Iraqi attack on Kuwait, demanding the release of instructions sent to the American ambassador to Iraq, April Glaspie, just before Saddam moved to try to seize Kuwait's northern province. The independent candidate charged the instructions would show that the warning to Saddam was so weak that it virtually encouraged him to attack, something the State Department has repeatedly denied.

"Who will get hurt if we lay these things on the table?" Perot demanded in seeking release of the Glaspie instructions. "The worst thing is, again it's a mistake. Nobody did any of this with evil intent. I just object to the fact that we cover up and hide things, whether it's Iran-contra or Iraqgate or you name it, it's a serious thing."

Governor Clinton broke in then to argue that the real mistake was to "coddle" Saddam Hussein "when people in high levels in our government knew he was trying to do things that were outrageous." To that, the president retorted, "What you're seeing, on all this Iraqgate is a bunch of people who were wrong on the war trying to cover their necks here and trying to do a little revisionism. And I can't let that stand because it isn't true."

Clinton didn't bother to point out that he had supported the Gulf War. Perot contented himself with a denunciation of what he called Republican "dirty tricks" in which he alleged his wife and children were spied upon. There the discussion of the origins of the Gulf War ended in a whirl of confusion—so often the inconclusive result of these open-ended though fragmentary examinations of the issues. Probably, it was one of the reasons President Bush did not make a better impression in the debates. It didn't do much, either, to advance the cause of his opponents.

These touch-and-go considerations of pending issues of consequence to the electorate were confusing in the extreme when they applied to pocketbook issues as was illustrated by a question from Gene Gibbons, the Reuters reporter, to Governor Clinton: "Now there are rumblings that a commercial bank crisis is on the horizon. Is there such a problem, sir? If so, how bad is it and what will it cost to clean it up?"

Clinton's response was vague. Under new regulations, he said, the government was given the responsibility to close some banks that "are not technically insolvent but that are plainly in trouble." Still, he gave assurance that this situation was not another crisis like the savings-and-loan crash saying, "The banking system in this country is fundamentally sound despite the weakness of some banks." To that, President Bush agreed in substance but added that financial reforms were needed to modernize the banking system.

Perot, however, took a shot at the president anyway on the S & L crisis, alleging that as vice president he had been in charge of deregulating these institutions but hadn't acted until after the 1988 election. He also quoted a published estimate that there now were 100 problem commercial banks and added, "It'll be a $100 billion problem," if it turned out to be true. The discussion then turned to reforming the government itself—another issue covered briefly and without much substance in a few minutes.

Other problems of magnitude for the nation were given even less attention, among them the U.S.–Canada–Mexico trade treaty and free trade generally, the difficulties of the nation's automobile industry and the airlines, and even such hardy perennials as the regulation of lobbyists and the virtues of the oft-proposed federal budget line-item veto and a balanced budget law.

One of the most important issues of the campaign, pro-choice vs. right to life, wasn't even mentioned.

.   .   .

Finally, the prospect of middle-class taxation, with which the final debate had begun, seemed to have been forgotten by the participants in their summations, limited to two minutes or less at the end of the ninety-minute discussion. Necessarily, the vision of a new America with the approaching twenty-first century also was uncomfortably squeezed by the candidates' desire for votes, as witness the following excerpts:

Governor Clinton: "I offer a new approach. It's not trickle-down economics. It's been tried for twelve years and it's failed. More people are working harder for less, a hundred thousand a month losing their health insurance, unemployment going up, our economy slowing down. We can do better. And it's not tax-and-spend economics. It's invest and grow, put our people first, control health care costs, and provide basic health care to all Americans. Have an education system second to none and revitalize the private economy. That's my commitment to you."

President Bush: "I don't believe in trickle-down government. I don't believe in larger taxes and larger government spending. On foreign affairs, some think it's irrelevant. I believe it's not. We're living in an interconnected world. The whole world is having economic difficulties. The U.S. is doing better than a lot but we've got to do even better and if a crisis comes up I ask who—who has the judgment and the experience and, yes, the character to make the right decision. . . . I need your support. I ask for your vote."

Ross Perot: "The question is, 'Can we govern?' The 'we' is you and me. You bet your hat we can govern because we will be in there together and we will figure out what to do and you won't tolerate gridlock, you won't tolerate endless meandering and wandering around, and you won't tolerate nonperformance. And believe me, anybody that knows me understands that I have a very low tolerance of nonperformance also. Together we can get anything done. The president mentioned that you need the right person in a crisis. Well, folks, we got one. And that crisis is a financial crisis."

. . .

Altogether, the vision of a nation in crisis wasn't very encouraging almost on the eve of the next-to-last presidential election of the twentieth century. Middle-class blues weren't the greatest consideration. The state of the union itself required urgent repair.

29

The Race Tightens

When the final two weeks of the presidential campaign began with the end of the presidential debates, Governor Clinton was still ahead but by a diminished margin.

President Bush hadn't gained on the Arkansan to a perceptible degree, as far as most public opinion polls were concerned, but Ross Perot's multimillion-dollar advertising campaign on television was beginning to show results. He averaged 18.7 in seven national polls taken immediately after the debates, almost double his standing before they began.*

In the same seven polls, Clinton still was coasting along in first place with a 42.4 average, not spectacular but still comfortable; Bush was still ten points behind with 32.4 as his average. Even if Perot had no chance of winning, it was clear now that he was taking votes away from both the major party candidates.

Perot, without doubt, was demonstrating once again how important it was not to underestimate his dynamics in this strange presidential contest. Even if he probably couldn't attract enough votes to win in any of the fifty states in the union, his detractors now had to admit that he could very well represent the difference between victory or defeat for one or the other major party candidates in states with a big electoral college vote, such as Texas or Florida. That, in turn, represented a threat in a presumably close election.

Under such circumstances, the determination of Perot's motives became all-important in the opposition Republican and Democratic camps directly affected by his huge expenditure in a presidential campaign he couldn't win. True, in the three presidential debates in which he had

*The polls were *New York Times*—CBS, Oct. 20–23; *Newsweek*, Oct. 22–23; Harris, Oct. 20–22; *Los Angeles Times-Mirror*, Oct. 20–22; *Time*-CNN, Oct. 20–22; *Washington Post*, Oct. 19–22; and *U.S. News and World Report*, Oct. 20–21.

participated, he had frequently taken the position that he would not indulge in personal attacks either on President Bush or Governor Clinton.

Yet, no one who had heard his televised protests against "Republican dirty tricks" could doubt his animus toward President Bush's run for reelection. To date, there had been no specifics. However, on more than one occasion, Perot had muttered impatiently about Republican "spying" on his wife and daughters.

What he was doing in effect was to let his money talk for him—and he was throwing more millions into his televised programs in the final two weeks of the run for the presidency than either the Democrats or the Republicans. He also announced for the first time that he intended to campaign in person during the windup in two eastern states crucial to Bush's reelection, New Jersey and Pennsylvania.

"It's going to be like seeing the Virgin Mary or an apparition or something," said the manager of the Perot drive in New Jersey, Jay Goodwin. At the same time, federal disclosure reports showed that Perot was spending almost $25 million on his televised national campaigning for the first two weeks of October.

As President Bush once had said, it was "bizarre" conduct for an independent presidential candidate who had no possibility of victory. But outside the continually vague rumors of a feud with President Bush in the dim dark past, Perot kept his anger in check and allowed himself only parenthetical references far from complimentary to the Republican cause. Now and then, he even threw in critical references to Governor Clinton's Democratic campaign to indicate a proper sense of balance against both major parties in his independent run.

The Democrats and Republicans, baffled by Perot's behavior, both stepped up their attacks on each other during the campaign windup mainly because they didn't really know what to do about the Perot candidacy. For the time being, he got off without suffering a major attack from either of his major party rivals. Nothing like this had developed in presidential campaigning in this century.

Perot had made it abundantly clear that he wouldn't be anybody's vice president; nor would either of the major party nominees in 1992 have accepted him. This contest would be taken right to the end of the presidential election and settled at the ballot box. Perot wasn't about to give up again, as he had on July 16.

.　　.　　.

Among the journalists whose duty it was to try to assess the effect of the presidential debates, there was general agreement that

Perot hadn't hurt President Bush to date as much as he had hurt himself. That didn't mean, however, that Governor Clinton had come off a clear winner by any means; what he had been able to do, by the most disinterested appraisals, was to avoid making the kind of devastating error that might have caused him to injure his campaign irreparably.

Except for a few distressing lapses in the choice of language, President Bush, too, had avoided plunging into fatal error. In the three debates in which he had figured, the president had shown little spirit; in fact, his seeming impatience in glancing at his watch during his second debating session had been widely commented upon. By contrast, Clinton appeared to have maintained a calm front and a steady flow of comments, which, if not particularly remarkable, at least made a good impression on the televised audience.

Perot appeared to have been the only one of the three candidates whose plain talk and homespun humor made the discussions interesting. After the first debate, in which he seemed to have been a clear winner, even he sounded dull and repetitious at times. None of the three participants, for that matter, sparkled in the presidential discussions; in backing away from explosive subjects, such as pro-choice vs. right to life, for example, their play-it-safe attitude was clearly evident.

All of which was bound to raise the general question, "Why have debates if they aren't debates and all the participants are too cautious, in discussing most controversial subjects, to speak their minds forcefully and effectively?" It was something for the electorate to mull over, for by the time the debates were held, the end of the presidential campaign was in sight and the candidates began to show more verve and spirit.

It may be argued, as many did, that the electorate in 1992 wanted information, not theatrical fireworks. Perhaps so, but it is hard to believe that many minds were changed other than those who were so uncertain about both major party candidates that they swung to support of Perot.

Was so negative a response worth all the effort? I doubt it. If it had been possible for both major party candidates to risk something more than a dispassionate discussion of the major issue, the sinking economy, perhaps the debates might have taken a more significant turn. President Bush, in particular, backed away from almost anything having to do with the downturn in general and joblessness in particular because that was the weakest point in his argument for reelection. That was why he finally centered on the question of whom to trust in the election with consequent criticism of Clinton on the "character" issue.

This reluctance on the part of the president to face up to the real issues in the campaign was what made the discussion so heavy-handed during the debates. It also accounted for the tendency of all three candidates, in preparation for their meetings, to argue more about technicalities than substance. This was why President Bush's people were more interested in having three reporters ask the questions than in Governor Clinton's proposal for more of a town-meeting atmosphere with voters posing the issues.

The presidential debate in which the 209 uncommitted voters ran the show through a moderator turned out to be the most interesting in the series. I doubt, however, that whatever form the questioning took would have made much difference in the outcome of the debates. The fact that Perot probably gained more through the discussions than his major party rivals would seem to be one valid indication that this was so.

In the postdebate review of the four sessions, several academics insistently made the point that the best way to insure a real debate among presidential candidates was to put them together in a television studio without moderators or questions, and let them go at each other directly. However, to anybody who has survived year upon year of unproductive wrangling at faculty meetings, this seemed to be the least promising suggestion.

What it all came down to, once the debates ended and election day loomed directly ahead, was that there always would be a desire by any presidential candidate to center on advantageous subjects and avoid embarrassment on lesser matters. Naturally, if professional journalists did the questioning, the press in general would take the kind of licking from some candidates that led President Bush, for one, to agitate for a campaign to annoy the media. This is something professional journalists have to cope with daily in trying to produce information from sources not always willing to provide it.

No one seemed to have any objection to Governor Clinton's version of a town meeting as a model for future debates. As long as all sides were content with questions that were more likely than not to produce routine answers, I suppose that might well become the most popular method for future discussions among presidential candidates, if they could agree on time and place. Otherwise, the notion of having ersatz debates might well disappear.

There were more serious objections to the format of the debates. One was the likelihood that spur-of-the-moment questions and answers could result in charges of suspicious or objectionable government actions being made in public without a shred of proof. Another possibility, even more difficult for the body politic, was a confused or even a mistaken concept of a desirable governmental proposal that would create unnecessary difficulties for all concerned.

As to the undocumented accusation, one instance during the debates was Perot's intimation that President Bush was concealing secret orders that had been sent to Ambassador Glaspi in Iraq just before the Gulf War that in effect convinced Saddam Hussein he could grab the northern province of Kuwait without objection from the United States. This was when Perot demanded that the president make public the relevant correspondence with the ambassador and others; the president heatedly denied anybody in the federal government had ever given Saddam the idea that he could get away with his Kuwaiti invasion.

Governor Clinton felt it necessary then to defend the president by pointing out there was no support for Perot's suspicions. Instead, he went on to criticize the president's pre-Gulf War conduct on more relevant grounds. The incident, therefore, passed off without undue harm, but future presidents might not be as lucky.

As for confusion that could be created by an ad lib discussion of an important and desirable new government program, one of the leading examples during the debate was the premature exploitation of so complicated a proposal as government-supported health care protection.

There was no doubt that all three candidates fully supported the necessity for available and affordable health care for all Americans. They also agreed that the system should be administered so efficiently that medical costs would be kept within reasonable bounds and insurance also would be made available for all Americans.

However, even the most sympathetic insurance executives estimated that insurance premiums alone would cost at least $20 billion a year—some estimates were even higher—if reliable health insurance were to be made available to all citizens. What bothered me about the discussion was that all the candidates seemed to assume that the money would be provided in some magical manner. At any rate, I heard no specifics from them or anybody else during the debates on exactly how these insurance costs would be provided and defrayed.

President Bush took refuge almost at once in his pet peeve, the towering cost of malpractice lawsuits increasing in cost and complexity year by year with lawyers as the main beneficiaries, in his view. Governor Clinton, too, chose not to try to meet the issue squarely by contending that both insurance firms and government bureaucrats could be made to resolve the problem for the common good. Again, no specifics.

Perot said on the health care insurance issue, "We've got plans lying all over the place in Washington. Nobody ever implements them. Now I'm back to square one. If you want to stop talking about it and do it, then I'll be glad to go up there and we'll get it done."

The only possibility for paying for health care insurance that I heard, even by indirection was Governor Clinton's suggestion that affluent people who also draw Social Security should have their retirement benefits made subject to taxation. However, this was not a specific proposal; it was given as a matter of social philosophy that Perot seemed to share for the time being. As for President Bush, he was firmly opposed to all increases in taxation for everybody.

.   .   .

Of the three candidates, President Bush's position was by far the most difficult because he was under almost continuous attack by both Clinton and Perot on every major issue. The president also had been the least enthusiastic at the outset about participating in the debates under any format. As the incumbent, he provided the largest target for his rivals and he also had the most to lose in the debates.

However, the president did try continually to take the offensive against the Democrat by calling him a "taxer and spender," a "waffler" on key issues, and a candidate plagued by indecision who wanted to be on "all sides" in every major issue. The Republican strategy didn't work, however.

Clinton kept his cool and remembered to try to look presidential. President Bush, finally, seemed to be frustrated and even upset at times. As for Perot, he didn't appear to let anything bother him unduly. When he seemed to be pinned in a corner, he always had his escape clause: "See, it's that simple."

Only it wasn't.

30

Perot's Troubles

It was difficult to separate truth from fantasy in the final week of the presidential campaign.

While Governor Clinton still was protesting a State Department inquiry affecting him and his mother, Ross Perot's independent campaign exploded with embittered charges of "Republican dirty tricks."

In the White House, a distressed President Bush called Perot's accusations "crazy." At the same time, it developed that Secretary of State Baker, the president's campaign director, may well have known that the Clintons and Perot were the objects of an unauthorized search of State Department passport files but did nothing to stop it.

When all this spilled over into appearances by the three presidential candidates on a scrambled processional of television talk shows and special features, the American electorate had just cause for wonderment. Even the fabled Man from Mars, dropping in on an American presidential election, could scarcely have been blamed for muttering, "What on Earth is going on here?"

It was a good question, for which easy answers were not immediately forthcoming.

In the case of the passport files, the question of White House culpability would not dissolve despite the voluble, even pained, denials by deputized officials around the president and secretary of state. Yet, the strangest part of this queer business, which even Acting Secretary Eagleburger denounced as unlawful, was that nothing discreditable was found that would have reflected on either Governor Clinton, his mother, or Perot.

The operations, to put it mildly, turned out to be both a political aberration and an embarrassment to the president at a time dangerously close to election day when he still seemed to have at least a chance of overtaking Governor Clinton's diminished lead in the public-opinion polls.

As for Perot and his continual accusation of "Republican dirty tricks" against him and his family, the rationale behind that performance was even more difficult to understand. If the combined printed press and televised comment had to be summed up in one word, it would have been "incredible."

President Bush already was in deep enough difficulty over the lapses in his State Department without loading him down with responsibility, as Perot was trying to do, for a supposed plot against the Perots' daughter on her wedding day.

.   .   .

Granted, as so many have long since pointed out, that Perot had a history of suspecting plots against him, his various business operations, and his family. Granted, as well, that the designated federal, state, and local authorities had not been able to find any substance to his past complaints, ranging from an alleged Texas Republican spy plot to a foiled attack on Perot's North Dallas estate by five Black Panthers carrying rifles in the 1970s. Still, should not Perot have disclosed his reason for quitting his independent presidential campaign on July 16, when he walked out, instead of waiting to make his charges until the final week of his resumed presidential effort? This was the question dispassionate critics were asking as election day approached and, once again, there were no credible answers.

On the contrary, when reporters continually questioned Perot's story about a Republican attempt to disrupt the August wedding of his daughter, Caroline, he angrily accused them of trying to reflect on his integrity. Shortly afterward, Orson G. Swindle III, the head of Perot's political organization, pleaded with reporters: "We're trying to stop talking about it. If you'll cooperate, we'll quit talking about it."

In retrospect, that raised still more questions.

.   .   .

The millions of Americans who watched the presidential debates already knew that Perot was obsessed with the notion that the Republicans had been playing "dirty tricks" on him and he also had complained that unnamed Republicans had been investigating him, his wife, and his daughter. However, the first time he mentioned the supposed plot to ruin the wedding of his daughter, Caroline, on August 23, came in an interview with the *Boston Herald* in October.

Perot himself brought it up, according to the *Herald*'s account, saying that the whole story would be in his appearance on CBS's "60

Minutes" on Sunday, October 25. The *Herald* used the story the preceding Friday. After Perot's account of the supposed plot to disrupt Caroline's wedding created a sensation on "60 Minutes," it developed that this was the basis for his accusation of "Republican dirty tricks" that had caused him to quit the presidential race on July 16.

However, he offered no explanation for varying his reasons for dropping out. Nor did he make public any evidence beyond unnamed Republicans who had warned him that an effort would be made to embarrass his daughter on her wedding day by circulating a spurious and highly defamatory picture of her in advance.

In admitting a lack of evidence on the "60 Minutes" broadcast, he added, "It was a risk I did not have to take and a risk I would not take where my daughter is concerned."

Next day, October 26, he repeated his charges against his supposed Republican enemies in two campaign appearances. To account for his return to his presidential campaign on October 1, he explained that he had feared both President Bush and Governor Clinton were not properly addressing the importance of attacking and eliminating the $4 trillion national debt, which he had made the major issue of his revived drive.

Later, he went beyond the accusation that unnamed Republicans planned to disrupt his daughter's wedding by adding charges that the same unnamed opponents had also planned to tap his office equipment in Dallas and bug his telephones there. In the latter instance, the Federal Bureau of Investigation confirmed that he had made such a complaint, that the FBI had created a "sting" operation to trap the perpetrators, but that nothing had come of it.

President Bush's campaign chairman in Texas, Jim Oberwetter, expanded on the story by complaining that the FBI had tried to trap him into paying $2,500 for an audio tape and other materials from Perot's Dallas office, but that he had refused to participate in the deal. He even complained to President Bush about it, Oberwetter said.

The first White House response, from the president's press spokesman, Marlin Fitzwater, was an indignant comment of "Nonsense!" He went on, "I don't want to attack Perot but I don't know where he's getting it from—fantastic stories about his daughter and disrupting her wedding and the CIA. It's all loony."

President Bush was just as emphatic in endorsing another of Fitzwater's statements: Perot was "a paranoid person who had delusions." Said the president, "I agree that this recent incident is crazy."

Perot wouldn't back down. He let it be known that he had asked well before the "60 Minutes" telecast for an interview in which he had intended to confront President Bush with his charges, but the president refused to see him. After the telecast, Perot did meet with Secretary Baker twice but neither seemed satisfied with the outcome. Someone representing Baker at the White House called Perot's charges "farfetched."

. . .

The public response to Perot's part on the "60 Minutes" program so close to election day was disastrous.

Up to that time, Perot had been viewed as a respectable alternative to the two major party presidential candidates among many largely conservative people who had had their doubts about reelecting President Bush or swinging over to Governor Clinton, still an untried national leader, as an alternative Democratic nominee. Perot seemed to have drawn from both major party candidates.

In response to arguments that a vote cast for Perot was "wasted," many of these perfectly reputable dissidents had pointed out that their purpose was to send a signal to Washington of public dissatisfaction with the kind of government both major parties offered.

In a sense, the independent movement Perot had stimulated might well have been taken as the forerunner of a new party, supported by dissatisfied fragments of Democrats, Republicans, and substantial independents who had seldom bothered to vote in previous elections. (The 50.1 percentage of eligibles who had cast ballots in the 1988 presidential election demonstrated how little public enthusiasm there was for a government in which the two major parties offered only fragmentary prospects for change.)

Perot's eccentricities hadn't alienated the basic support that came to him to any profound degree until he publicized his charges that unspecified Republicans had threatened to disrupt his daughter's wedding with "dirty tricks." That was too much for the shakiest part of the protest vote he was attracting to so surprising a degree.

Within a few days after the "60 Minutes" telecast, there was no doubt that his independent campaign had stalled despite the millions of dollars he was pouring into his effort toward the end. Tracking polls (cumulative daily polls spread over three or four days at a time) also indicated a sudden drop in the independent's support.

A week before election day, ABC News reported a five-point drop in its Perot polls from 21 to 16 percent of respondents, with a three- to four-point margin of error. A CNN–*USA Today* poll with a similar margin of error at about the same time also showed a steep falling off, this one from 20 to 16 percent. As for the audience level for Perot's multimillion-dollar advertising campaign for votes on television, that too showed a sharp decline. For one thirty-minute Perot "infomercial" for the final week of the campaign, there was a reported 25 percent slump in viewer interest from about 16 million to 12 million.

After that, to nobody's surprise, Perot's campaign staff simply refused to answer any question about Perot's suspicions of Republican "dirty tricks" directed against him and his family. Whatever effect he may have had on the outcome of the election now seemed to be largely nullified. Except for the bitter-enders who would have dropped dead rather than be caught voting for either Bush or Clinton, Perot's independent campaign seemed to be all over except for the shouting.

Now the choice for most of the electorate clearly was Bush vs. Clinton and take your pick.

.   .   .

Why did Perot's actions vary so greatly from his declared purpose of making the presidency an instrument of change for a better and greater United States?

To his detractors, without doubt, he was all too often viewed as an irresponsible figure who believed the power of his vast fortune could buy him anything he wished. To those who had faith in him, despite his errors in judgment, he was more of an idealist who sincerely tried to improve the lot of the American people suffering through a long recession.

Perhaps there was a bit of both in the makeup of this altogether strange independent candidate for the modern presidency. It is tempting, at any rate, to dismiss his bungled candidacy as a political accident of little consequence for the future of the nation. Yet, that isn't a justifiable conclusion, either, for Perot really *did* have an impact on the presidential campaign of 1992 as witness his brief lead in the polls during the early part of his independent run and the millions of votes he won from his major party rivals toward the end.

Had his behavior appeared to the electorate to be more rational as an independent candidate, who is to say that he might not have changed the ultimate outcome? I do not mean to suggest that he could have won without a dependable political organization and a more convincing approach to the problems of the nation's economic ills. With all his faults and his incredible performance at the end, he did manage to introduce massive changes in American presidential campaigning and, much more than his major party rivals, he induced millions more people among the electorate to go to the polls on election day.

To me at least, this was no mean achievement, based on a lifetime in observing, reporting, writing, and teaching about presidential elections.

· · ·

Perot is by no means the only American presidential candidate or sitting chief executive whose judgment was flawed in one way or another and who exhibited signs of paranoia under pressure. I would present Richard Milhous Nixon and the Watergate caper as exhibit A and Lyndon Baines Johnson's debilitating effort to win the Vietnam War as exhibit B.

This is not intended as a defense of Perot's strangely-oriented independent run for the presidency. Nor is it an effort to excuse Perot's puzzling behavior when he was presenting his ideas to the nation, without credible proof, of what he called Republican "dirty tricks." It is not that there never have been "dirty tricks" in American politics. With a printed mountain of proof, the *New York Times* presented the once-suppressed Pentagon Papers to the nation to expose a government-sponsored effort to hide the truth about our entry into the Vietnam War. With day-by-day performances in his *Atlanta Constitution*, Ralph McGill, its editor, documented the suppression of civil rights among helpless minorities in the South.

What Perot lacked in his allegations was such stunning proof of "dirty tricks" directed against his family and himself—the kind of unprofessional "shooting from the hip" that more often than not does more harm than good. Were his charges true? I doubt if we shall ever know. Surely, however, he is not the first enormously wealthy American who has imagined—or experienced—threats against his person and his family that led him to take immense precautions for the safety of those he loves.

· · ·

Whatever animus there may have been between Perot and President Bush, it was completely overshadowed toward the end of the presidential campaign by Bush's assaults on the character of Bill

Clinton, and the equally reprehensible Republican efforts to attack Hillary Clinton mainly because she preferred a legal career to being a housewife.

It is true that Clinton is not the only modern president who has been obliged to withstand that kind of abuse in a presidential campaign. Nor is Mrs. Clinton the only possibility for first lady who has had to accept ferocious attacks because she chose to lead an active and useful life outside the home as wife and mother.

It is worth noting that Governor Clinton paid back President Bush for Republican criticism of Hillary by expressing sympathy for Perot's complaints of Republican "dirty tricks." Toward the end of his campaign, Clinton said: "Mr. Perot may not be able to prove these charges, but the Bush campaign has been the most reckless campaign that I've seen in modern American history."

All this scarcely served to assauge Perot's hurt feelings over his rough treatment by the president and the Republican campaign people. In consequence, he intensified both his spending and his anti-Bush campaign oratory as election day approached. The increased feuding between the Bush and Perot forces couldn't help benefiting Clinton's campaign in the crucial last days before the voters went to the polls.

It was also difficult for the president to contain the damage done by some of his political appointees in the unauthorized rifling of State Department passport files for material that might be damaging to Clinton. The scandal hurt most when the White House couldn't set at rest persistent rumors that stimulus for the invasion of the files had come from the highest level of government. Mere denials in no way deflected continued criticism by State's professional career diplomats that this department of government, above all others, should have maintained a nonpolitical status.

To that extent, the issue became still another festering sore in the floundering Bush campaign during the last days before the presidential election. As matters turned out, therefore, Perot was not the only candidate for high office who was in deep trouble. The president himself, as the polls continued to indicate, would not have an easy time of it on election day.

31

Iraqgate

The president's formula for disposing of difficult problems didn't work in the case of Iraqgate. The issue simply wouldn't go away.

Shortly before election day, the Democrats in Congress renewed their charges against the Bush administration in the case by demanding punishment for those responsible for passing $5 billion to Saddam Hussein in American loan guarantees to help him rearm for the Gulf War and also try to develop atomic, chemical, and biological weapons.

The Democrats insisted that American taxpayers, in effect, had unknowingly been used as pawns to make possible Saddam's arms buildup for the war, which, as Senator Gore had said, should never have been fought. The allegations involved the branch bank in Atlanta that was in effect owned by the Italian government—the conduit through which money intended for Iraq's use to buy American grain was used instead for armaments.

So close to election day, the Democratic charges took strident form, but on the Republican side the posture was one of injured innocence. At the White House, the demand for a special prosecutor was turned aside as unworthy of attention, but then, no one expected a special prosecutor, even if appointed virtually on election eve, could have taken any effective action.

Meanwhile, the president's punishment for Saddam and his people, a stiff set of United Nations sanctions, effectively reduced food and other necessities of life for the defeated nation to the barest minimum. In all probability, the sanctions had obliged him to permit UN inspectors to search for the rest of his hidden experimental materials he supposedly had been using to try to create atomic weapons.

That, the president's foes in Congress contended, did not excuse him of responsibility for having permitted Saddam to use American money to buy arms. This was more than preelection-day posturing.

What the Democrats were trying to do was fix responsibility on Bush for the Persian Gulf War.

Ross Perot was in on the anti-Bush movement, too. During the presidential debates, he had demanded disclosure of instructions given to the American ambassador to Kuwait, April C. Glaspie, plus documents passed between the White House, the State department, the Pentagon, and Baghdad immediately before the war began on August 1, 1990. The independent presidential candidate had stressed that the messages to Saddam Hussein were so weak that they amounted to a go-ahead to invade his virtually helpless but oil-rich neighbor and take its northern province.

Some in the Pentagon had adopted a similar line, it now developed, when efforts were made to persuade the White House to take a tougher position against the threatened invasion. These were not, so far as could be learned, disappointed Democrats; mainly they were career officials in the Defense Department, some of whom remained in service, but finally had decided to air their grievances.

Certainly, these present and former members of the military establishment had more than enough evidence at the time to stimulate their concern that Saddam was ready to move for control of the entire oil-rich Gulf area. With the leaks of documentary evidence, nothing was secret about Saddam's intentions. Under his direction, his foreign minister, Tariq Aziz, had published them in a letter to the Arab League toward the middle of July 1990 when the Iraq arms buildup on the Kuwaiti border already was under way.

The letter virtually demanded settlement of all outstanding differences between the two countries under the threat of war. These were the issues, as Iraq's foreign minister spelled them out:

1. Immediate settlement of the dispute involving Kuwait's northern province, the subject of the long argument over the delineation of their common border

2. Agreement on what should be done about Iraq's debt to Kuwait, estimated at many millions of dollars, and which Saddam quite naturally was reluctant to pay

3. Conclusion of a long argument between the two nations on both oil production schedules and prices

As if that hadn't been enough warning, taken together with the Iraqi arms buildup, Saddam delivered a speech in conjunction with the letter in which he threatened to use his army to make Kuwait come to terms. At the same time, King Hussein of Jordan and President Hosni Mubarak of Egypt, in a friendly admonition to the American government, played down Saddam's threat and tried to persuade Washington against showing alarm.

This was the usual line that moderate Arab rulers had been taking for years in an obvious effort to keep the United States from assuming a stronger role in the settlement of Middle East disputes. It was understandable Arab policy to try, by all possible means, to weaken the American position in an effort to isolate Israel. However, when it came to accepting Saddam's domination of Kuwait, which with Saudi Arabia remained a major source of American oil supplies in the Middle East, that was an entirely different issue, at least as far as the Pentagon was concerned. No one in the E Ring, the seat of civilian authority over the military, felt strongly enough then about defending Kuwait to protest the White House's leisurely approach to the problem. On the contrary, President Bush still was at the height of his popularity. The nation still was basking in the reflected glow of the Reagan boom, which was just tapering off. Only months afterward did leading economists fix mid-July 1990 as the start of the long recession.

Under such circumstances, it would have taken an exceedingly rash Pentagon official to tell a sitting president what to do about a Middle East issue that then seemed of little concern to the American people. This was why Saddam felt emboldened by the lack of any strong response from either the United States or Britain to his threatened offensive against Iraq. The fact was that, unknown to the American and British publics, both Western governments were then playing along with Saddam, evidently unconvinced that he meant to make war on Kuwait as threatened.

It was only through twenty-twenty hindsight that the protesters surfaced at the Pentagon and the State Department and the British, too, began worrying that they had been taken in. By then, however, it was too late. Saddam already had struck against Kuwait on August 1, which obliged President Bush to form his American-led opposition force.

.   .   .

So far as could be learned by penetrating the fog of intelligence that blanketed the final negotiations to avert war in the Middle East, a stream of apparently routine cables from Washington in the last days of peace produced only a soothing response and mealy-mouthed assurances from Saddam and his wrecking crew.

The American ambassador seemed to have been working in a

diplomatic haze. Neither the White House nor the State Department seemed particularly alert, either, as the crisis approached. By the time a few troubled midlevel officials had raised hesitant questions about the dangerous game being played with Saddam, it was too late to stop the Iraqis.

The sequence of events now became known. Various versions of the texts Perot had demanded in the presidential debates appeared unofficially, without in any way quieting the political storm created about American "coddling" of Saddam just before the Gulf War.

The Democrats were still demanding a full-scale inquiry even though it could not have been held in the final days of the presidential campaign. Nevertheless, they were still intent on pressing the issue against President Bush, whether or not he was reelected.

The administration's defense of the weakness of the various American responses to Saddam's threat was a case in point. The following appeared to be the sequence of events once it was determined that the president should caution Saddam in what amounted to a personal communication to Baghdad.

After a routine expression of American hopes for a peaceful settlement, made orally in mid-July 1990 to the Iraqi ambassador to the United States, Secretary of State Baker cabled Ambassador Glaspie to ask Hussein for a statement of his intentions. Nothing much happened.

Another Baker cable on July 24 restated the American position, which, though friendly in tone, cautioned against the use of force but took no position on the Iraqi disputes with Kuwait. The Glaspie response was a classified cable after a meeting with Saddam the next day in which he expressed worry about American concern. The ambassador helped him by indicating that further American criticism might not be helpful.

That cleared the way for the controversial Bush message, which was based on the expectation that Saddam would be willing to resume negotiations with Kuwait despite the massing of at least one hundred thousand Iraqi troops on the Kuwaiti border. It has been said since that some State Department people wanted a temperate presidential message that would urge further negotiation by the aggrieved parties but a few in the Defense Department hoped for a much tougher line.

In substance, the paper that Bush signed stressed American friendship for Iraq while emphasizing this country's interest in further negotiations. However, so far as is known, even that message, characterized by a former Defense Department civilian official as a "piece of pap," was delivered orally by Ambassador Glaspie before leaving Baghdad for consultation on July 30.

Still, a few senior officials in both State and Defense were enough concerned, even though Kuwait and Iraq representatives had resumed talks in Jedda, second largest city in Saudi Arabia, to decide on an August 1 meeting to draft a tougher line. That day, however, the Iraqis broke off the Jidda talks and Saddam sent his troops storming across the disputed border to try to take by force what he couldn't achieve through diplomacy.

The United States then froze Iraq's assets, led a UN Security Council move the day after the invasion to condemn it, then started building up a coalition force in the Persian Gulf after Iraq completed its conquest. On January 17, 1991, the American-led forces wrecked Iraq's army in a lightning air war and freed Kuwait, but still left Saddam in power in Iraq after a four-day ground attack that ended on February 28.

All told, the war lasted forty-three days. In his enlarged status as a victorious commander in chief, President Bush then proclaimed the creation of a new world order under American leadership with the collapse of the Soviet Union. However, the new world order never assumed the dominant status that the president had intended. Instead, toward the end of his wavering reelection campaign, he was thrown on the defensive while trying to justify his help for Saddam before the war over Kuwait began.

.   .   .

The reason the Democrats continued to press the attack on President Bush's arms buildup for Saddam Hussein primarily had to do with the issue of trust that the president originally had raised against Governor Clinton. Clinton had argued in return, toward the end of the campaign, that it was the president who could not be trusted.

It made the president's conduct suspect during the buildup for the Gulf War. In a speech in Louisville, Kentucky, Clinton said on Oct. 28: "Every time Bush talks about trust, it makes chills run up and down my spine. The very idea that the word 'trust' could come out of Mr. Bush's mouth after what he has done to this country and the way he's trampled on the truth is a travesty of the American political system."

There had been more of this that same day in the president's adopted home city of Houston, where Clinton said: "There's just no such thing as truth when it comes to him. He just says whatever sounds good and worries about it after the election."

Next day at Grand Rapids, Michigan, President Bush retorted in kind to his Democratic challenger by questioning both his credibility and his character, saying: "What's catching up with him now—what's catching up with him just as we go down to the wire—is this pattern of deception.

"He said on April 17, 'I'm going to reveal my draft records,' and we haven't seen them yet. You can't say that you're going to have one position, then another. You've got to stand up and take a position and lead. And that's what being president is all about."

It was such bitterness between the two major party candidates that made this presidential campaign so shameful in tone. Perot's multimillion-dollar advertising campaign on television, too, tended to drag down the electoral process. Among some of the most distinguished of the nation's commentators on the developing news of the campaign in general and the president's performance in the Iraqgate matter in particular, all restraint also seemed to have been disregarded during the campaign windup. In the august column of the *New York Times,* William Safire, a Pulitzer Prize–winner, now was calling Attorney General Barr the "Coverup General" for dawdling on the appointment of a special prosecutor in Iraqgate.

The measurement of trust, honesty, character, and personal honor was being put to uses in this deplorable presidential campaign of 1992 that were passing strange. It could not help making comprehension all the more difficult for much of an electorate already discouraged by the limpness of the national economy.

.   .   .

The puzzlement of the American public over the continuing Iraqgate scandal did not end at the water's edge. In a London courtroom, another act of this strange drama revealed still more circumstantial evidence of collusion in high places to maintain a steady flow of arms to Saddam Hussein before the Gulf War.

The following is the barest outline of the case, as seen through the sharp eyes of the prosecution, before a single witness took the stand.

The defendants were the responsible officials of a company called Matrix Churchill, important mainly because it was owned in Iraq but had its main office in Britain and an American subsidiary in Ohio. The firm was accused of violating both American and British export control laws by falsely declaring that its products destined for Iraq were for civilian use when they were intended to build up Saddam's military machine for the Gulf War.

Among the company's products, the prosecution contended, were tools, such as computer parts and others of importance, that could be used to manufacture armaments. The Banca Nazionale del Lavoro, largely owned by the Italian government, also figured in the prosecution's case by reason of its loans, negotiated through its Atlanta branch, that supplied money for some of Matrix Churchill's operations.

It was, the prosecution contended, an elaborate cover for what seemed to be an intelligence operation to keep tabs on Saddam's attempts to produce nuclear, biological, and chemical weapons of mass destruction.

There is no doubt that, once the London trial began, it would be carefully followed in both the United States and Britain for fear that secrets bearing on national security of both Western powers might be disclosed. Before the unusual legal action, there already had been rumors that it could be interrupted for reasons of state security. Yet, because it bore on the relationships between President Bush and Saddam Hussein before the Gulf War, this case commanded international interest.

That it was put off as long as possible so that it would not interfere with the presidential election spoke volumes about the converging interests of Britain and the United States in the Middle East. The tensions over Iraqgate, certainly, would not end with the tally of the votes in the United States. Nor would the fate of the conspirators diminish the deadly rivalry for the control of the fabulous oil resources in the Persian Gulf area.

For both the United States and Britain in the closing days of the presidential campaign, the emphasis seemed to be on dragging out the trial procedures in London in an effort to prevent any release of information affecting the security of both Western powers through the testimony of witnesses for the defense. When and if that was threatened, observers openly speculated, the British might be willing to end the trial abruptly at the risk of freeing the defendants. That eventually is what happened—but the decision came after the election in America ended.

32

Surprise!

Going into the last weekend before election day, the opinion polls showed President Bush was closing in on Governor Clinton. Ross Perot's independent candidacy, too, seemed to be picking up a little more support although he still wasn't much of a threat to anybody.

Out on the campaign trail, the president suddenly seemed invigorated. He shouted, made faces, flailed his arms, and denounced the opposition, Clinton and Al Gore, as a couple of bozos. Gore, a respected environmentalist, became Mr. Ozone in the president's vocabulary. Together, he said, his Democratic opponents didn't know as much about foreign policy as his dog, Millie.

"Who do you trust to be president of the United States?" he continually demanded. As he dipped into the South where support of the Atlanta Braves baseball team was an article of faith, he slapped hard at Clinton in particular, saying his Democratic opponent's aspirations for national leadership were akin to putting "a Little League guy in to coach the Braves."

It was, all in all, a remarkable turnaround for a president who, only a few weeks before, to some had seemed resigned to defeat. Nothing his despairing Republican campaign people could do to reinvigorate his campaign seemed to please him. Even the ever-confident first lady, Barbara Bush, had become thoughtful, even a little depressed, sometimes.

The final surge for the president began to be noted in the polls. As that last weekend approached, the figures looked very, very good to the Bush team. The *Wall Street Journal*/NBC News poll cut Clinton's lead to five points, 43–38 percent, and put Perot at 11 percent. ABC News gave Clinton four points over the president, 41–37 percent, and 17 percent for Perot. *Newsweek* reduced the Democrat's margin to two points, 41–39 percent, and CNN–*USA Today* gave

Clinton only a one point lead, 41–40 percent; Perot was stuck at 14 percent in both these polls.*

Assuming a three-point margin of error for these polls, it was possible for the most ardent Republicans to contend that the two major party candidates were locked in a virtual tie for the presidency that last weekend. That is what many of them did. To his supporters on that last swing through the South, the president pumped out his confident message: "Remember, things are decided in the last couple of weeks in this campaign. And now people are going to decide." Invariably, he concluded with his challenge, "Who do you trust to be president of the United States?"

Even the skeptical national reporters who tagged along with him on that last campaign tour began to waver about Clinton's chances. The president, they realized, wasn't making a last despairing campaign pitch for victory. He truly thought he was about to win reelection.

. . .

Then, just when the Democrats around Clinton and Gore were getting a bit shaky themselves, the president was hurled back on the defensive with the disclosure that he probably knew a lot more than he had admitted about the Iran-contra scandal while he was vice president. The story broke on October 30, the Friday before election day with the publication of hitherto secret notes of a high-level meeting called by President Reagan, at which Vice President Bush was said to have agreed on the sale of arms to Iran for the release of American hostages.

The notes, taken by Caspar Weinberger, then secretary of defense, directly contradicted Bush's contention that he had been "out of the loop" when the deal was made. The notes, dated January 7, 1986, read: "Met with President, Shultz, Poindexter, Bill Casey, Ed Meese, in Oval Office. President decided to go with Israeli-Iranian offer to release our five hostages in return for sale of 4,000 TOW's [missiles] to Iran by Israel—George Shultz and I opposed—Bill Casey, Ed Meese and VP favored—as did Poindexter."

Governor Clinton, quick to turn the issue of trust against President Bush, trumpeted the news during a campaign stop in Pittsburgh as a reflection on Bush's character, saying: "Secretary Weinberger's note clearly shows that President Bush has not been telling the truth

*The timing for the polls was as follows: *Wall Street Journal*/NBC News, Oct. 28; ABC News, Oct. 28–29; *Newsweek*, Oct. 28–29; CNN–*USA Today*, Oct. 28–29. The election was Nov. 3.

when he says he was out of the loop. It demonstrates that President Bush knew and approved of President Reagan's secret deal to swamp arms for hostages."

Bush commented, in turn, that the notes did not contradict what he had said under oath. However, the record did show that he claimed he was out of the room when the decision to swap arms for hostages was made, that he didn't recall any serious objection to the Reagan plan, and didn't realize until later that the arms sales to Iran were made to obtain the release of the hostages being held then in Lebanon by a pro-Iranian group.

Still, there was no disputing the text of the Weinberger notes that showed he and Secretary of State George Shultz opposed the deal and that Bush was listed in favor with the CIA director, William Casey; Attorney General Edwin Meese, and National Security Adviser John M. Poindexter. The notes were handwritten.

The Iran-contra special prosecutor, Lawrence E. Walsh, made public the document with the disclosure of a new federal indictment of Weinberger, in which he was charged with making false statements to Congress in its inquiry into the arms-for-hostages swap. The "contra" part of the scandal, the distribution of leftover money from the deal for the benefit of the Nicaraguan rebels against their pro-Communist government, was not involved in the Weinberger case.

The new indictment, returned four days before election day, replaced a previous indictment dismissed in November because a federal judge ruled it was deficient in proof of obstructing Congress. Instead of a mere paraphrase of the Weinberger notes in the original indictment, the new one gave the full text as the former defense secretary had written it.

Weinberger denied the charges and faced trial in 1993. His lawyer, Robert S. Bennett, called him a "pawn in a political game." At the White House, a spokesperson also imputed a political motive to Walsh, the special prosecutor, for acting so close to election day. Walsh denied it.

Although Bush's campaign people were dismayed by the dramatic turn in events, the White House remained steady in trying to spread assurance that "nothing had changed" when, in fact, a troubled issue had suddenly been revived. Gore, campaigning in Maine, said as much when he charged that President Bush hadn't "told the truth" about "one of the worst scandals in the history of American foreign policy." For the four remaining days of campaigning, the Iran-contra scandal and Bush's frequent denials remained in the forefront of the news, much to the dismay of the Republican high command. It was something on which Bush's people had not counted, and they had a difficult time rallying their forces to try to counteract the revived Democratic offensive, now centered on Bush's character rather than his continual criticism of Clinton as untrustworthy.

The one point in the president's favor was the impression that the Democrats somehow had held back this last-minute surprise so that the Republicans would not have enough time to answer the charges. This was something that reflected directly on Special Prosecutor Walsh and he took pains to see that the story of the disclosure of the Weinberger notes was fully understood.

According to the special prosecutor's office, the search for the notes arose from the dismissal of the original indictment in the case. The notes became pertinent, so the prosecutor insisted, because he charged that in 1987 Weinberger falsely declared that he had kept no records of his activities although he had maintained extensive diaries about his daily work.

These diaries, it was said, had been deposited by Weinberger in the Library of Congress along with other personal records of his years as secretary of defense. There the prosecution finally uncovered the text of the notes that were then recorded in the replacement for the original indictment.

The action that once again placed the president's reelection campaign at a disadvantage was one of the last in the five-year term given Walsh as special prosecutor. In his investigation, he had had only limited success and several expensive failures, notably the dismissal of guilty verdicts he had obtained against two of the major figures in the scandal, National Security Advisor Poindexter and an aide, Lt. Col. Oliver L. North. As far as the Bush people were concerned, the feeling was that the sooner the books were closed on the Iran-contra inquiry as conducted by Walsh, a lifelong Republican, the better it would be for the president's reelection campaign.

.   .   .

In barnstorming through the mid-South that black Friday when the Iran-contra surprise seemed to stall his eleventh hour effort to overtake Clinton, President Bush's handicap was more psychological than anything else. The polls had stimulated him. He had come to believe that this presidency was truly his, that as long as he bore down hard on his opposition he still could win his second term.

Four years ago, he had been behind, too. Dukakis at one point had led him in the polls by seventeen points. Yet, in the end, he had triumphed. Those about him seemed discouraged now by the renewed doubts about his position in the Iran-contra scandal, but he still exuded confidence that he would beat Clinton.

In campaigning through Tennessee, the home state of Al Gore, Mr. Ozone, there was a Mason-Dixon poll that indicated a virtual tie between the president and Clinton. That, certainly, was cheering news, the opposite of what was coming out of Washington, D.C., on the meaning of the new Weinberger indictment and the Weinberger notes on the meeting in the Oval Office during the second Reagan term.

So the president persisted in his attack on Governor Clinton's character, his fitness and dependability as the nation's leader. To Bush, that truly was the issue. To his audiences from Nashville to St. Louis and beyond, in a swing through the Midwest, he argued as follows: "The real question is not who is for change, but whose changes will make your life better and your world safer."

In his mind's eye, he believed that the electorate would decide on election day that his way would be the best both for the American people and the world at large. In that manner, he resumed a windup for his campaign that would take him through more than a dozen states with selected appeals in each to get out the vote on election day.

As his associates described it, this was the position he adopted to deflect the adverse responses from the late break in the Iran-contra affair. What he had determined to do was not to let it get him down when he had to be at his best. There still was time for him to get out the votes that would beat Clinton.

. . .

For Clinton, that last weekend had to be adapted to combating any belief that the president's rise in the polls could be the decisive blow against a Democratic return to power in the White House. It made him think of three hastily scribbled phrases on a sign at his campaign headquarters:

> Change vs. more of the same.
> The economy, stupid.
> Don't forget health care.

That summed up what Clinton's message had to be that final weekend of combat against a president who simply and naturally wouldn't believe he was licked. True, the issue of trust and character now could be used, as well, but it could not be decisive because the

Iran-contra scandal lay half-buried in the public consciousness and, by itself, it could not produce victory at the polls the following Tuesday.

What Clinton had to do, in that final get-out-the-vote swing through the states he needed to win, was to knock the president off stride with the doubts about his position in the Iran-contra scandal, then hammer home the Democratic plea for change in the interests of a strengthened nation.

As the scribbled note at Clinton's headquarters had it, the decisive issue still remained "the economy, stupid."

So, that last weekend, Clinton's jetliner touched down in Pennsylvania and Ohio and on through other contested states in the Midwest and South. When the Democratic nominee learned in Pennsylvania of the president's reversal in the Iran-contra scandal, he began varying his attack on Bush's performance on various economic problems by hitting hard at the issue of trust: "The president repeatedly has said something that is not true. He has seriously called into question [his actions] on those issues and now he has to answer your questions on all."

This was the way the Arkansas governor programmed himself on the issues that counted the most: He argued his prescription for an economic revival that would make life more promising for middle-class America while fighting the battle against poverty and adding taxation only for the wealthiest citizens. He promised basic health care for all people, looked forward to an era of change, and asked for a vote of confidence in himself and Gore by saying: "I am the one person in this race who comes from the great American middle class and understands the American dream."

Between campaign stops, what the Democratic nominee also had to do was to persuade his entourage of reporters and commentators that President Bush's surge in the polls had been halted. The Democrat claimed to have stabilized a lead of seven points over the president. His private poll-taker, Stan Greenberg, was available to challenge claims of the president's ascendancy from skeptical press people.

Was it true that Clinton was in so seemingly impregnable a position? Regardless of polls, private or public, the conclusion was obvious that predictions in a close race were bound to be difficult to document convincingly. As the veteran George Gallup had emphasized on more than one occasion, "The plain fact of the matter is that you have to be lucky."

Still, on this last go-around, Clinton did feel lucky. He seemed

241

relaxed and comfortable despite his heavy schedule of travel and speech making as he zig-zagged across the country. He even tried to make a few jokes, definitely an unacceptable risk for so serious-minded a candidate. It was evident for him, too, that the response from the new disclosure about the president's role in the Iran-contra scandal was mainly psychological. This foreign scandal, like its companion in the Middle East, Iraqgate, simply was too difficult for a mass public to absorb easily.

The Democrat's strong point was his insistence on putting the home front above foreign affairs and making his promised repairs in the economy as his number one issue.

.　　.　　.

What, then, of the independent, Perot, who had changed the way this presidential campaign was being conducted and in all likelihood would also have some surprises for his rivals in the outcome? True to his faith in the power of television advertising and the millions of dollars he had set aside to invest in the final weekend of campaigning, most of his drive was conducted from television studios. He did try two short trips, neither of them of any real importance, but open-air campaigning simply wasn't his style.

What he had to do that last weekend, if he hoped to make any impression whatever on the electorate, was to stall harsh criticism that he was trying to buy the election with his investment of millions of dollars in television programs of up to one hour for his campaign windup. Even more troublesome, he had to recover as best he could from the adverse response created by his unproved charges that the Republicans had planned to disrupt his daughter's wedding.

There is no doubt whatever that Perot's ranting about Republican "dirty tricks" had created doubt among some of his less-devoted followers that he had the judgment and stability to seek the highest office in the land. Yet, mainly because of continuing doubts about both major party presidential nominees, the outspoken Texan still commanded a substantial following and could well attract a far larger vote on election day than his critics could anticipate.

As Perot's general counsel, Clayton Mulford, had said in trying to choke off the critical feeling about him, "We need to get back to our message." For all his faults, and they were many, the Texan also had some surprises left for election day.

33

Winding Down

$\mathbf{A}$t last, it was over. Across a downcast and sometimes bewildered America, the presidential campaign of 1992 dribbled to an untidy end.

The last broadcast had been made, the last trip taken, the last dollar spent, the last promise uttered, the last insult sent winging toward a despised rival.

For President Bush, Governor Clinton, and Ross Perot, reality finally had replaced an orgy of self-delusion in the wee hours before the polls opened on election day—the signal for a dubious electorate to exercise its will.

As ordained by the peculiarities of the American political system, all three contenders for the highest office in the land had suffered all manner of indignity. Yet, in accordance with custom, each in his own way had solemnly pledged to bring about better times for rich and poor and a much-abused middle class that existed somewhere between the extremes.

So elaborate a vision of upward mobility for 250 million people could only strain belief.

This, however, is the way the system of democratic choice had developed over the years in the United States even though a thoroughly skeptical public majority invariably had its doubts about fair words forced from eager candidates in response to cruel political pressures.

The public's remedy, however, had been even more drastic toward century's end.

When prosperity vanished under the rule of one major party, it was generally expected during so massive an era of change that the preferred candidate of the opposition would come to power. This is the way the electorate had operated for much of the century. Barring physical attacks made against sitting presidents, this also is the way the electorate had voted without a shot being fired in anger when a new chief executive was elected.

Such was the outcome foreshadowed for the latest presidential campaign with the last preelection polls showing a renewed and enlarged lead for the Democratic team of Clinton and Gore. These were the principal forecasts directly before election day:*

New York Times–CBS: Clinton by nine points, 44 to 35 percent for Bush and 15 percent for Perot.

Washington Post: Clinton by eight points, 43 percent to 35 percent for Bush and 16 percent for Perot.

Wall Street Journal–NBC: Clinton by eight points, 44 percent to 36 percent for Bush with 15 percent for Perot.

ABC: Clinton by seven points, 44 percent to 37 percent for Bush and 16 percent for Perot.

CNN–*USA Today:* seven points for Clinton, 44 percent to 37 percent for Bush and 16 percent for Perot.

Harris: six points for Clinton, 44 percent to 38 percent for Bush and 17 percent for Perot.

President Bush's response was subdued. At first, he blamed the "nutty pollsters" who were making him look bad. Then, as he renewed the customary American campaign technique of redoubling the insults to the opposition before election day, he added somewhat gratuitously that such criticisms should not be "taken personally." Although the president still tried to put up a stout front in the windup, he was once heard wondering aloud when somebody predicted his reelection, "Are we kidding ourselves?"

At the same time, Clinton remained reserved over the prospects of a Democratic victory. Instead, he pushed himself to continue racing back and forth across the country by air in the final days, sometimes posing, gesturing, and speaking to crowds and on TV for sixteen to eighteen hours a day. The strain Americans impose on their presidential candidates just before election day has to be witnessed up close to be appreciated.

As for Perot, the outsider, he spent a fortune over the last weekend on still more television advertising, mainly glorification of self and a proclamation of confidence that he knew how to run the country to everybody's advantage. He was short on detail except for the

*Timing of the polls: *New York Times*–CBS, Oct. 29–Nov. 1; *Washington Post,* Oct. 28–Nov. 1; *Wall Street Journal*–NBC, Nov. 1; ABC, Oct. 28–Nov. 1; CNN–*USA Today,* Oct. 31–Nov. 1; Harris, Oct. 30–Nov. 1.

campaign book bearing his name. Toward the end at a rally in his home city, Dallas, he commanded a band to play "Crazy," then whirled one of his daughters through a fast routine while the band played on.

.   .   .

Were the polls right about forecasting a major victory for Clinton?

There was a lot of behind-the-scenes comment about the sudden shrinkage of the Democrat's lead just before the last weekend and the equally fast turnaround in which he once again dominated the field by six to eight points.

Nominally, among the industry and its customers, the rapid on-and-off movement affecting Bush's chances was attributed to the disclosure of the president's ambivalent attitude in the Iran-contra scandal—the revelation of the damaging Weinberger notes four days before election day. In taking the notes at face value, it was said, they demonstrated that Bush had been "in the loop" that decided the United States should sell arms to Iran in return for the release of American hostages—something he had steadfastly denied.

Among Bush's campaign staff from Secretary Baker down, there already were loud protests that the Democrats had been able somehow to hold back this eleventh hour blow at the president's credibility until it was too late to counteract it effectively. Ron Brown, the Democrats' national chairman, scoffed at that, as did others who took the Republican outcry as an attempt to duck responsibility for a coming defeat.

There was, however, another side to the back-and-forth switching of the polling figures. Critics of the industry argued it was far more likely that there was a minority among the pollsters that worried over discounting the president's strength at the polls and giving him a chance thereby to duplicate Harry Truman's feat of pulling off an unexpected victory.

This, the critics said, could have accounted for the brief upward blip in the president's status among a few polls just before the weekend, which was corrected in the final reports. To be fair to the critical element, it has not been unknown for a worried pollster to make technical adjustments based on data added (or subtracted) from raw figures to tie in with his guesswork.

Whatever the reason for the wavering attitude among a few strays, however, the stalwarts of the industry stressed that the polls

245

indicating a substantial Clinton victory were uniform at the end. That, they emphasized, is what counted.

Now it remained to be seen what the electorate would do once the last television ads were flashed on the bland faces of sets in millions of American homes and the final words of the candidates had been heard.

.   .   .

Clinton's last cross-country expedition was an epic of politics in itself. Between 9:00 A.M. On November 2 and 11:00 A.M. on election day, he led a convoy of three aircraft in campaigning visits to eight key states in which he either was narrowly leading or contesting for the lead: Pennsylvania, Ohio, Michigan, Kentucky, Missouri, Colorado, New Mexico, Texas, and back home to Arkansas to vote.

The Democratic nominee began his last day at the Mayfair Diner on the outskirts of Philadelphia because it had been one of John Fitzgerald Kennedy's last stops in his 1960 campaign. It was a good luck omen for the Arkansan to follow in the footsteps of his admired predecessor, and he took advantage of it with enthusiasm.

To a small crowd outside the diner, he spoke in glowing terms of "the mystery of democracy" and urged them to go to the polls on the morrow. There was no criticism of President Bush or Perot, just a reminder that the voting booths of the nation were more powerful than any president and to take advantage of them.

It was much the same everywhere else he went that day at brief stops in large cities and small towns, among them Cleveland, Romulus, Michigan, Paducah, Kentucky, and St. Louis, and on to the mountainous west in Colorado and the great plains of Texas. The crowds were usually small, but enthusiastic, and the candidate frequently was cheered as "the next president." One of the largest and loudest rallies was in St. Louis where his ever-present wife, Hillary, introduced him as follows: "After November 3, Missourians will have a president who knows what Missouri needs."

This extensive effort was made, not so much to impress the few thousand loyal supporters who turned out to see Clinton and his entourage from the bustling eastern part of the country to the Rockies and back to the south, but to stimulate a large Democratic turnout at the polls. The method was familiar: a play to the local television stations and local newspapers in each area along the route to enlarge on the candidate's visit, and his plea for votes to carry the decisive states he needed to win.

The twenty-eight-hour air marathon could have worked only in

America. Throughout, Clinton seemed supremely confident and the staff people about him were just as upbeat. As for the press crowd in the three planes, they had the climactic story of the campaign, all the incentive they needed to spread the urgent message of voting for the morrow.

Still, despite all the augury for success on election day, Clinton was careful not to be carried away by the possibility. For the sixteen years since Jimmy Carter's victory in the 1976 election, the Democrats had wandered in the wilderness of defeat. Too often, despite their control of Congress as a whole or in part, they had seen victory snatched away from them when Republican candidates were able to plaster them with the damaging label of taxers and spenders, which was fatal to the best of their presidential nominees.

This time, at least, Clinton was not to be caught in that trap. Throughout his campaign, he had tried to portray his party as an entirely new organization, businesslike in operation. Yet, somehow, he had maintained distinctive Democratic liberalism in showing his sympathy for the dispossessed and the poor, his concern for middle-class values, and his campaign philosophy of "tax the rich and spare the middle class."

Would it work? Only the morrow would tell.

. . .

President Bush's campaign finale was much more relaxed and gaited to the defensive style of a trailing nominee. In the two days before election day, he too, tried to hit some critical spots, far fewer than Clinton as the acknowledged leader. His argument continued to be almost entirely negative—a warning that Clinton as president would be raising taxes generally on an unsuspecting nation and that he was not to be trusted.

To the president, Clinton was a draft dodger in the Vietnam War, a philanderer, and a "bozo." Aside from the charge that Clinton was lying about his proposal to tax only the rich, the president stuck to his practice of name calling even though it simply had not worked earlier in the campaign and wasn't likely to help much at the end.

As for the disclosure that the Weinberger notes had shown that he had not been honest about his part in approving the sale of arms to Iran to release American hostages in return, Bush mostly left the issuing of denials to others. For example, he let a White House spokesman argue with reporters in saying, "It's just another Clinton opportunity to try to smear us."

Now and then, at a fresh campaign stop, Bush would vary the

monotony of name calling by using a somewhat feeble scare tactic tied to the spirit of the season. One version he tried went like this: "If Clinton is president, every day is going to be a Halloween, fright and terror." Only he didn't act as if he believed it.

Like the people who tuned out for Clinton, the president's crowds at campaign stops were small, consisting mainly of the party faithful and campaign workers. In one of the few positive responses to the elaborate programs Clinton had presented to try to stimulate national recovery from the long recession, Bush argued for less government action, not more, saying: "The answer is not to have government investing by taking more of your taxes. The answer is for us to stimulate small business by tax relief, less regulation, and less lawsuits."

The president, however, seemingly paid no attention to such caustic reflections. Nor did he seem at all concerned that he was likely to be beaten by his rival on election day. He seemed content to pose as being above the battle in presidential style.

The principal recognition the president gave to his less than favorable position with election day just beyond the horizon was his frantic activity in some of the nation's leading television network studios. This was the way he had chosen to play "catch-up" in the last hours before the polls opened. Even so, his frequent predictions of victory seemed hollow, no matter how often he repeated them.

There was still another method Clinton had exploited to pull ahead and stay ahead in the polls, his seeming pleasure at plunging into crowds to touch hands, that the president could not emulate. On a few limited occasions, and these under careful guard by the Secret Service, he did go through a handshaking crowd routine on those final days of the campaign, but his heart wasn't in it and it didn't come off very well.

Clinton, on the other hand, gave the Secret Service fits by his wish to mingle physically with the masses whenever an opportunity presented itself, even at the end of the campaign, during which he deliberately laid himself open to personal attack. President Bush was too cautious and too reserved to take such reckless chances.

This was the note, whether his public liked it or not, on which he ended his campaigning, saying: "Barbara and I can hardly believe it."

Then it was back to Houston for the president and Mrs. Bush to cast their vote on election day. He had argued his case for the economy throughout his campaign, asking the electorate to believe him when he maintained that times were improving and there was nothing to fear. Now, within hours, he would find out whether the public was on his side.

. . .

For Perot, who had done so much to set both the pace and the tone of this campaign despite his much-criticized July dropout and October return, the end came with a $3 million splurge of television self-advertising.

"We're all going to win and lose together," he told the nation in his final appeal. "You own this country. Pick the person that will do the job you want done."

That and a dance with his daughter, Katherine, before a small crowd of supporters in a downtown Dallas arena marked the conclusion of one of the strangest and most illusory campaigns in the history of the presidency. There were no uproarious claims of victory that final night before the Texas polls opened in the morning. No one of consequence would have believed them anyway.

To the very end, Perot's purpose in spending so much money and investing so much energy in a cause he could not win remained completely obscure. Possibly in answer to the frequently voiced suspicion that his campaign was principally aimed at defeating President Bush, Perot criticized both the president and Governor Clinton that last night.

If any of his supporters had had to guess at his purpose, it may have been that he had decided he wanted to launch an independent political movement based on what had happened to him during his presidential campaign in 1992. The most he could expect during this, his first campaign, was that he might hold the balance of power in states with large electoral totals, such as Texas and Florida, if the voting turned out to be as close between Bush and Clinton as the polls indicated.

However, unless the national vote cast for him in the fifty states turned out to be much less than the polls predicted, it was a fairly good bet that Perot would be heard from again in elections yet to come.

Gridlock, the issue he had raised to describe the election of a president and a Congress of opposing political views, had brought him to national attention. His championship of the movement for one party to dominate both these branches of government would not soon fade away.

34

The Election

It was all over at 9:45 P.M., Little Rock time.

At that hour, when Ohio's 21 electoral votes went into Bill Clinton's column, he exceeded the majority of 270 necessary to win the presidential election.

A half hour later, President Bush conceded defeat, which made it official. In that quiet and essentially undramatic manner, the governor of Arkansas, one of the poorest and least populous states, became the forty-second president-elect of the United States that November 3.

As late as June 2, when he had assured himself of the Democratic presidential nomination by winning California's primary election vote, he had finished last in a public opinion poll that pitted him against President Bush and Ross Perot.

Now, by campaigning for thirteen months against continued economic relapse and unemployment, it had become Clinton's responsibility to lead the nation toward better times.

In the electoral college, his winning total had been 370 to 168 for Bush, with Perot completely shut out, a respectable victory, although it was scarcely overwhelming as his critics were quick to point out.

In the popular vote, the president-elect won by 5.6 million votes over Bush, which amounted to 4.4 percent of the 104 million votes cast—much less than a majority. The totals were Clinton, 43.7 million; Bush, 38.1 million and Perot, 19.2 million.

Translated into percentages, the totals were Clinton, 43 percent; Bush, 38 percent; and Perot, 19 percent.

Even if he had been unable to score in the electoral college, Perot had reason for satisfaction and encouragement for creating a more cohesive political organization. Almost one in every five voters had cast ballots for him—the strongest showing by an independent candidate since Theodore Roosevelt's in 1912 when he finished second to the victor, Woodrow Wilson, with President William Howard Taft in last place.

President Bush, despite abundant evidence of both his surprise and chagrin over his defeat, came back to the White House after election day to try to assist his successor in the always painful transition for an outgoing chief executive. Although he had averted the ultimate humiliation of ending his political career in a last-place finish, he had been only the fourth elected president of this century to be defeated for a second term.

．　　．　　．

President Bush may have tried to make an effort toward a smooth transition of power to the president-elect the morning after election day, but Senator Bob Dole of Kansas, the Senate minority leader, would have none of it. The new number one Republican said of President-elect Clinton at the first available opportunity: "They [the Democrats] want change. Well, we want to be responsible and deliver change, whatever that means. But we're skeptical, so we'll wait and see."

Clinton was more tractable. Despite all the pressure on him to set up a new cabinet and a panel of advisors to shape the new government, he pursued his first priority, easing the position of the home front with such attitudes as these: "Today I say to our business and financial leaders that although change is on the horizon, we understand the need to pursue stability even as we pursue new growth. The changes I seek will strengthen America's market systems, not weaken them. It will not be easy but we will spare no effort to restore growth, jobs, and incomes to the American people."

With that, he and his vice president-elect, Al Gore, went on about their business. Their transition team, headed by the future secretary of state designate, Warren Christopher, took over the sensitive task of building the core of the incoming Clinton-Gore administration. The transition people were given their orders at their first meeting with Clinton in the Arkansas State House in Little Rock and soon were hard at work.

The strongest part of the team was assembled with little trouble. Besides Christopher at State, Senator Lloyd Bentsen of Texas was the designated secretary of the treasury, Representative Les Aspin of Wisconsin took over the Department of Defense, and Thomas F. McLarty, an old friend of the president-elect, was made the next White House chief of staff.

They became the backbone of the new administration, and none expected trouble over confirmation, although lesser lights that were selected did have some embarrassing times right up to the celebration of the new president's inauguration and thereafter.

Before that great day for the incoming administration, Clinton learned to his dismay that the intricacies of foreign affairs were likely to distract his attention from the home front in ways that he had not anticipated. The principal villain turned out to be President Bush's old nemesis, Saddam Hussein of Iraq, who was trying by all possible means to stall resolutions voted by the United Nations Security Council that sought to find and dispose of his suspected laboratories and factories for the creation of an Iraq atomic bomb.

When Bush threatened military action on behalf of the UN inspection team, which had been continually frustrated, Clinton immediately gave the president his full support despite the hard feelings generated during the campaign. The incoming president warned Saddam not to take advantage of the lull during the transfer in leadership by trying to test American resolve. For the time being, Saddam seemed more agreeable to receiving the UN inspectors.

There was little doubt, though, that more trouble was brewing in the Middle East, and this time it had nothing to do with Arab hatred for Israel. In keeping with his interests, President Bush concentrated on this and other aspects of foreign policy vital to the nation, regardless of dissension in the ranks of the Republican faithful over whom to blame for their defeat at the polls.

.   .   .

The struggle for control of the Republican party began on the day after election. As the campaign director who had shifted from secretary of state to White House chief of staff, James A. Baker had to take more heat than anybody else for President Bush's defeat.

Vice President Quayle was among the first to attack Baker. He told White House reporters that the Republican campaign had been poorly managed and that the Clinton-Gore team, by contrast had run a good show. Among less exalted members of the Bush team, the president's part in his defeat was also discussed without hesitation. He was often faulted for being overly optimistic that the country would lift itself out of recession without government help and that he seemed too little interested in promoting his cause with the electorate until the final weeks before election day.

If the president resented such reflections as these on his political leadership, he gave no indication of displeasure. Instead, he seemed to be more concerned about keeping the jittery coalition between the moderate wing of the party and the conservative right from clashing in what might have been a savage internal battle.

The least fathomable part of the equation bearing on the future of the Republican party was the course that might be taken by the former Republicans who had deserted to vote for Perot as an antiparty independent. Most poll-takers already had estimated that 38 percent of those who had cast ballots for Perot formerly had been Republicans and an equal number consisted of so-called Reagan Democrats, the rest being independents.

Assuming the 38 percent estimate of Republican deserters was reasonably correct, it would have amounted to more than 7 million of the 19.2 million votes Perot received. In forming his long-term America United organization, Perot's first appeal was to this group because most analysts believed fewer Reagan Democrats would rally to his standard. After the Clinton victory, millions of these renegade Democrats were believed more likely to return to their party.

However, there was little disposition among the leaders of either major party to believe that Perot would ever become a significant threat as an independent regardless of his unexpectedly large vote in the 1992 presidential election. The argument against him was mainly that he had too many diverse interests, most of them related to money making, to become a dedicated political leader of consequence. Yet, he remained a potent influence—so much so that both major parties adopted some of his ideas for making this a better and more competitive nation. It seemed to many people that it was far too early to sell him short.

.   .   .

Although more than one hundred new members of Congress were elected with Clinton, the legislative branch was far less affected by the outcome of the election than the executive. The big change was that Democrats, for the first time in twelve years, controlled the presidency as well as both houses of Congress.

Changes in the Senate and House of Representatives were relatively minimal. With one-third of the Senate up for reelection, the Democrats made a net pickup of one seat on election day when their majority stood at 58 to 42 but a short time later, in a special election in Georgia, they lost a seat and returned to 57 to 43. In the House, the Democrats dropped six seats but their majority on election day still was a substantial 261 to 173 with one independent.

As second in line for the presidency after the vice president, House Speaker Thomas S. Foley of Washington called the new 103d Congress more representative of the American people as a whole than its immediate predecessor and more responsive to the prospect of the kind of change President-elect Clinton had advocated during the campaign. However, in view of Congress's balky record against the previous Democratic administration of Jimmy Carter, Foley's views amounted merely to assurance of friendly intent.

Although the extent of Democratic control of both houses was impressive, it had its limitations. In the Senate, there still were not enough votes to halt a Republican filibuster, a talkathon the minority sometimes undertakes to kill a majority proposal. It takes sixty votes to stop a filibuster. Accordingly, despite the end of gridlock—the presidency and Congress under control of different parties—the minority still had enough power to impede and, in a few instances, to defeat pending legislation if it wished to do so.

Aside from numbers and procedure, the change in the appearance of Congress was striking. The 110 new members who appeared at the first meeting of the 103d Congress constituted the largest change in the legislative branch in forty-four years. Women, blacks, and Hispanics all made notable gains. For the first time, an American of Korean descent, Jay Kim, a Republican, was elected to the House from California. A native American, the first in more than fifty years, Ben Nighthorse Campbell, a Democrat from Colorado, took a seat in the Senate.

The first black woman senator, Carol Moseley-Braun of Illinois, boosted the number of women in the upper house to six although she faced challenges. Her five colleagues were the newly elected Barbara Boxer and Diane Feinstein of California, Patty Murray of Washington, and the reelected Barbara Mikulski of Maryland. Nancy Kassebaum of Kansas was a holdover until 1997.

In all, there were forty-seven women in the House, thirty-five of them Democrats and twelve Republicans, a net gain for the Democrats of nineteen.

Blacks, too, scored notable increases in the House, a total of thirty-eight that included the first five to represent constituents in this century in the Carolinas, Virginia, Florida, and Alabama. This was an increase of thirteen over the previous House total. In addition, seven more Hispanics were chosen for the House, giving that group a total of seventeen.

President Bush, when he returned to Washington after election as a lame duck in the White House, observed merely, "The government goes on. . . ."

.   .   .

Even so, for the new president, there was uncertainty over the extent of the cooperation he could expect from the Congress dominated by members of his party. Nobody was willing to predict that his congressional colleagues would give him a blank check for the major legislation he was putting before Congress in his first one hundred days in office and thereafter. This was seldom due to bad temper or personal dislike. Inevitably, in a nation of a quarter of a billion people spread across fifty states, the interests of Congress all too often were likely to be sectional, whereas the president, of necessity, had to take account of broader national and international relationships including trade and national security.

Based on Jimmy Carter's experience as president, the incoming administration also had warning that it could not hope to move ahead with a bold new program of change by overloading Congress. To have tried at once to produce a national health program, a boost for the economy, greater employment, and improvements in the nation's programs for education, the environment, and civil rights would have been courting disaster. By so doing, the Carter administration choked up, accomplished none of its objectives, and suffered a miserable defeat after a single term.

In selling the White House's program to Congress and the nation, therefore, the new president-elect realized well in advance that he could not push his fellow Democrats in Congress beyond their ability to produce the necessary legislative changes he wanted. Everything, therefore, would depend on a wise choice in priorities and the first, surely, would be, in the inelegant language of the notice still visible at the otherwise deserted Clinton campaign headquarters, "The economy, stupid."

.   .   .

Along with improvements in the economy, which already were visible soon after election day, the president-elect counted on fulfillment of his campaign pledge for all-inclusive national health care to stimulate greater public support for his administration.

The promise of affordable health care for all Americans was President-elect Clinton's best bet for starting another American revival toward century's end in the FDR manner. Next to a realistic attack on persistent unemployment, the health issue had aroused the most interest among the electorate during the campaign and, in all probability, it had accounted for a sizable chunk of the 5.6 million majority by which Clinton had been voted into power.

As expected, most of the nation's insurance companies modified their opposition to national health insurance immediately after election day. Clintonian magic wasn't really involved in that decision. What had caused it was the application of one of the oldest of American political maxims: "If you can't lick 'em, join 'em."

In all truth, some of the top people in the health insurance industry at last had come to realize that national health insurance was inevitable. The soaring costs of medical and hospital services and the inability of the once-powerful insurance lobby to twist Congress to their will had combined to create public pressure for Clinton's national health plan. If the British could afford it, so the argument went, Americans could find a way to follow their example. However, despite the retreat of the insurance lobby, the medical profession, the hospitals, and associated laboratories mounted a fearful protest. The outcry was that Clinton would bankrupt the country. The collapse of the Soviet Union meant that the conservatives couldn't very well stir up the public with the old sure-fire warning of a Communist threat. What had to suffice was the battle cry of bigger tax-and-spend Democratic policies to meet an estimated $50-billion-a-year cost for national health protection.

What bothered business and industry about the Clinton health plan was that employers would be obliged to share at least a part of the bill for insuring their employees. The argument also was used that Social Security benefits would have to be taxed to help subsidize health costs, something that produced a spasm among the elderly.

However, all the clamor against national health care succeeded only in arousing greater support for the proposal among the public at large even before the new president took the oath of office. What the more sensible conservatives did then was to try to shape their own program to reduce the risks for themselves.

One proposal urged upon government by a combination of insurers, hospitals, and medical people was called managed competition. The theory was that this kind of thing would keep down costs and thereby do away with the notion of government-imposed price ceilings on medical and hospital care. Naturally, that was beneficial for the health industry and wealthy patients who could afford to pay such outrageous costs as, say, $10,000 to care for a broken leg and $12,000 and up to treat a blood condition. Managed competition, too, could scarcely interfere with imposing an increase in annual fees of 25 percent, such as New York state granted in 1992–93 to Empire Blue Cross–Blue Shield.

At the outset, what had to be decided was whether the prospect of managed competition within the insurance industry could be considered a practical alternative, as far as the public was concerned, to government regulation of costs. That issue was so contentious that it couldn't easily be resolved. Nor could other difficulties be disposed of without long and painful delays that threatened Clinton's new order for the home front before he even entered the White House.

·　　·　　·

Like FDR, who had to shout for help when he found himself alone in the Oval Office with the nation's problems on his first full day as president, Clinton might well have made a postelection fuss about the continued battering he and his program of revival for America were taking long after the votes were counted that made him president.

Instead, the president-elect maintained his cool.

What he did do, as a practical politician was to embark on what amounted to a perpetual campaign for public support. Several weeks after election day, he still was plunging into crowds and seeming to enjoy it, shaking hands with perfect strangers, engaging unsuspecting citizens in conversations. Once, on a short holiday in California, he burst into a beach volley ball game with a bunch of astonished youngsters. Almost every day he was visible on TV, taking his daily jog of up to three miles in sweatshirt and shorts with a snug-fitting cap. Whether he was home in Little Rock or on the road, he seldom missed regular exercise and seemed in good physical shape.

After a while, in the interim between election day and the inaugural in Washington, D.C., the president-elect seemed just as likely to pop up in a classroom with teenagers as to hold a news briefing. He also was known to drop into a McDonald's for a hamburger.

What he obviously wanted to do was to make himself known as more of a public president than his more recent predecessors. Apparently, where he drew the line was against any invasion of the privacy of twelve-year-old Chelsea Clinton, once the family moved into the White House on January 20, 1993.

It was off limits, too, for the new president to be interrupted at dinner with Hillary in a public restaurant when the working press and photographers swarmed in for pictures and interviews. He still liked being in a public place, however, where strangers might approach him to shake hands and ask for his signature. All this, plus the jogging and other public excursions, gave the Secret Service fits. It also did not make for smooth relations with the press.

This, however, seemed to be the way the president-elect wanted to conduct his public relations, and the working press—and his own public-relations people—had to make the best of it.

35

The New President

Some funny things happened to Bill Clinton on his way to the White House. George Bush, on the way out, experienced others that were not at all funny.

As John Nance Garner remarked to a reporter at the height of the wheeling and dealing in the 1932 Democratic National Convention in which he became Franklin Roosevelt's vice presidential running mate, "Politics is funny."

There was, however, nothing particularly humorous about the Clinton-Bush transition. It was from time to time, strange, embarrassing, and occasionally downright peculiar. In the end, the inaugural was magnificent. At long last, according to some, a sense of hope seemed to have animated the enormous crowds in the nation's capital that witnessed the induction of the new president.

That, too, may have come shining through to some of the vast public beyond who viewed the proceedings on television, as the nation's poll-takers reported. It may have been a balky and delayed start for the new administration but it was a good one for both the new president and his vice president, Al Gore.

• • •

With the fortitude of a Democrat who had unexpectedly broken the chain of presidential successes by the opposition, Clinton had learned to be skeptical of Republicans bearing gifts. So it developed that he was wary, and with justification, of a report by the Bush Commerce Department three weeks after the election that the nation's damaged economy had "turned the corner."

Instead of a 2.7 percent national growth rate for the 1992 third quarter that had been criticized as excessively gloomy when it was issued just before election day, the department had put out an adjusted postelection figure for the same period of 3.9 percent.

Commerce Secretary Barbara J. Franklin laid it on thick, saying, "I think we've turned a corner. This is a big present to President-elect Clinton as we're going out the door." To that President Bush added, "The economy is living up to our predictions."

President-elect Clinton cautiously speculated that he might not have to spend as much on short-term repairs for the economy if the rate proved accurate but stood by his long-term plan of cutting in half the $4.3 trillion national debt within his four-year term.

Otherwise, Democratic skepticism continued. The incoming labor secretary, Robert B. Reich, commented, "We probably can't count on that figure to signal the beginning of a recovery." The incoming communications director, George Stephanopoulos, dismissed the supposed good news brusquely, calling it "good but not good enough."

Still, the Bush administration persisted in trying to put the best possible face on the still-wobbly economy with an announcement that there had been a drop of 800,000 by December 1 in the nation's unemployment since the previous June. The latest figure was put at 7.2 percent of the work force, or about 9.2 million people who couldn't find work, down from 7.8 percent in June.

That, however, added to the 30 million recipients of federal food stamps, showed hardship still stalked the land with Christmas approaching. As a result, the president-elect, in his first postelection news conference, warned that the nation's economic problems were of long duration and "there won't be any overnight miracles." Unlike the outgoing president, who had hoped against hope that the dawdling economy would right itself, preferably before election day, the president-elect tried, at least, to be more realistic. What he expected to do, in a broad sense, was to stimulate job growth through widespread repairs of the nation's roads, bridges, and other parts of the infrastructure, grant tax credits to businesses that stepped up employment, and decrease the national debt through new although indefinite investments in expanding the economy.

All that, however, had to be reviewed in a hurry when President Bush's final budget report to Congress, issued the previous July, suddenly was revised barely three weeks before he bowed out of office to show a thumping increase in estimated deficits for future years. In the July report, the president had predicted that the budgetary deficit would drop to $274.2 billion in 1994 and shrink still more to $236.7

billion in 1997. In the revised report put out on January 6, 1993, the White House estimated a deficit of $292.4 billion for 1994 and $305 billion in 1997.

President-elect Clinton, after learning of these increases in deficit estimates of $18.2 billion for 1994 and $68.3 billion for 1997, called the totals unsettling, and predicted the loss, if unchecked, could reach $400 billion by century's end. As a result, some of the incoming president's campaign pledges appeared to have been put on hold.

The first to be shadowed with doubt was the Clinton plan to cut the national debt in half within four years. Next to seem even more shaky was another campaign promise of a tax reduction for the middle class. What the inflated deficit figures would do to a proposed national health plan also was hard to determine. All this happened before the new president had even entered the Oval Office for business.

As for the Bush Commerce Department's assurance that the nation had "turned the corner" toward recovery and reduced unemployment by 800,000 since June with a jobless rate of 7.2 percent as of December 1, the final projection for the Bush administration wasn't quite that good. The rate of unemployment, in fact, rose a point to 7.3 percent before Bush left office, a reputed loss of about 127,000 additional jobs in a month and an estimated total unemployment figure of 9,327,000.

In sum, if there was any recovery at all, it was lamentably weak, as the incoming president discovered before his inauguration. It meant that his overly ambitious program for promoting recovery would probably have to be scaled down. As for the Clinton prospects for reducing health care costs as an opening thrust toward broad national health care for all, the Bush Commerce Department estimated 1992 health costs at $838.5 billion with a projection of an increase of more than $100 billion for 1993.

· · ·

There was still another Bush surprise on his last Christmas Eve. He issued pardons to former Defense Secretary Caspar Weinberger and five other former officials in the Reagan administration for their part in the Iran-contra scandal. There already had been three guilty pleas among the six who were pardoned; one other conviction and two cases including Weinberger's were pending.

Special Prosecutor Lawrence E. Walsh, who had worked on the scandal for six years, attacked the president for his action, saying that the Iran-contra cover-up "has now been completed." The pardon wiped out a trial for Weinberger that had been scheduled to start January 5 for his alleged lying to Congress about secret American arms sales to Iran, the proceeds of which were used to help the Nicaraguan rebels—the contras—in their effort to overthrow their pro-Communist government.

Walsh indicated that he might try to involve President Bush in the scandal to a greater extent, if at all possible, to try to show that a conspiracy had been undertaken in the Reagan administration, in which Bush had served as vice president, "to lie to Congress and the American people." In that connection, the prosecutor also accused Bush specifically of misconduct. All of this the retiring president denied. He defended his pardon of Weinberger, calling the former defense secretary a "true patriot," and argued that the five others also deserved executive clemency.

The others who were cleared included the three who had pleaded guilty to withholding information from Congress and received probationary sentences: Robert C. McFarlane, former national security adviser, who also was fined $20,000; Alan G. Fiers, Jr., former chief of the CIA's Central American Task Force, and Elliott Abrams, former assistant secretary of state.

The remaining two were Clair E. George, former chief of CIA secret operations, convicted of lying to Congress and awaiting sentencing, and Duane R. Clarridge, a CIA official facing trial on charges of perjury in connection with secret missile shipments to Iran.

The only defendant in the scandal, which began as a well-intentioned effort to ransom American hostages held by a pro-Iranian group in the Middle East through arms sales to Iran, was an ex-CIA agent, Thomas Clines, who was convicted of perjury, jailed for sixteen months, and fined $40,000.

A retired Air Force major general, Richard V. Secord, and three others pleaded guilty to various charges stemming from the operation and received probationary sentences. John M. Poindexter, former National Security advisor to President Reagan, and two others were cleared through court actions.

Thus, the Christmas Eve pardons by President Bush closed the book on an expensive inquiry that lasted for more than six years. Except for the possibility of a further examination of Bush's diaries and notes as the special prosecutor had threatened, further legal actions thereafter seemed unlikely.

.   .   .

That, too, appeared to be the end of the postcampaign uproar over who had ordered and carried out furtive late-night searches of the passport files of the president-elect as well as those of his mother and Ross Perot. The incident came to light late in the presidential campaign.

In the cleanup between the change of administrations, President Bush summarily dismissed Elizabeth M. Tamposi, the assistant secretary of state for consular affairs, accusing her of having ordered the illegal passport searches. She denied wrongdoing, saying she had acted on the basis of press requests under the Freedom of Information Act.

However, the State Department's inspector general, Sherman M. Funk, primarily blamed Ms Tamposi in his written report saying, "Never, in our opinion in the annals of the Freedom of Information Act, has there been a search conducted with such urgency, scope, thoroughness, and grade levels of participants."

Besides Ms. Tamposi, the report said, several junior officials had been disciplined for participating in the search and others had been demoted or made subject to eventual dismissal. The report agreed that the rifling of the files had been "politically motivated to influence the outcome of the election" but contended there had been no evidence involving the White House.

The assumption throughout was that the Bush campaign people, in a desperation move, had tried to find evidence that Clinton had been so opposed to the Vietnam War that he had sought to change his citizenship, something of which the British Foreign Office had no evidence. Nothing was found in the passport files, either, to make credible the reason for the late-night activities against the president-elect, his mother, or Perot.

So ended the last of what many believed to be the Republican-originated "dirty tricks" during the 1992 campaign. Afterward, Clinton objected to the delay of seven weeks in the postelection release of the Funk report, saying that if anything like that happened while he was president he would fire the culprits at once without waiting for election day. To that, Perot agreed, calling the incident a "gross abuse of federal power."

.   .   .

As president-elect, Clinton also objected strenuously to a recommendation by federal regulators to wind up the savings-and-loan scandal with a $50 billion increase to bilked depositors and payments to the depleted Federal Deposit Insurance Fund. The collapse of the thrift industry appeared to be very much on his mind, as was the condition of the nation's banking industry as a whole during the continually weak recovery from the long recession.

Soon afterward, by curious coincidence, two of the largest organizations in Wall Street, one a major accounting firm for S & Ls and the other a prominent brokerage, agreed to costly settlements of federal government claims. The new president's decision, well before assuming office, had struck home.

The accounting firm, Ernst and Young, agreed to pay $400 million in settlement of federal charges that its audits of some federally insured failed S & Ls and banks had been improper. The settlement was said to be about one-tenth of what four of the worst S & L busts had cost the government already in making good the losses of depositors.

The Office of Thrift Supervision also conducted a continued check on the auditing firm's additional agreement to change some of the practices criticized by federal regulators in connection with the settlement. That, however, did not avert broader federal scrutiny of perhaps as many as a dozen other auditing firms that generally served the banking industry.

Another settlement, this one a civil suit against the Salomon Brothers brokerage, committed three of its top officials to pay $225,000 in fines to dispose of charges that they had failed to give their employees proper supervision in bidding at U.S. Treasury auctions.

By far the worst punishment in any prosecution of financial fraud was given to Charles H. Keating, Jr., head of the collapsed Lincoln S & L, and his son, Charles H. Keating III. Their conviction of fraud and racketeering in a Los Angeles federal court, with the prospect of lengthy prison terms for both, seemed in large degree to justify the president-elect's hesitation to authorize huge new grants from the hard-presssed U.S. Treasury to close the S & L inquiry.

The elder Keating already was serving a ten-year sentence on conviction of similar State charges and, at sixty-nine, was likely to spend the rest of his life behind bars with the imposition of an even stiffer federal sentence. Federal prosecutors frequently pointed to his case as the most extreme among all the frauds perpetrated in the S & L scandal because it is expected to cost the taxpayers more than $2 billion before all the Lincoln's victims are paid off.

Said Attorney General Barr in the closing days of the Bush administration: "Mr. Keating [senior] as much as any man has come to symbolize the excesses that led to the collapse of the thrift industry."

It was still another coincidence that the comptroller general, Charles A. Bowsher, announced the day after the latest Keating verdict that the federal government's bookkeeping was seriously deficient and, in the closing days of the Bush administration, could have hidden liabilities of many billions of dollars.

Although Bowsher's report was in no way connected with the attorney general's denunciation of the Keating fraud in the S & L scandal, the comptroller general's key finding indicated that the government's leading departments also had some internal inquiries to conduct. He said: "Widespread financial management weaknesses are crippling the ability of our leaders to effectively run the federal government."

Specifically, the comptroller general's report attacked the federal government's annual expenditure of $1.5 trillion. "It doesn't keep track very well," he wrote. It was a case, he said, of "abysmal" and "rudimentary" bookkeeping. To the incoming Clinton administration, he also issued a stiff warning against easing up on federal banking regulations. He cautioned, too, that current bank regulation and inspection were so ineffective that no early warning could be expected of trouble ahead. What he urgently recommended to Clinton's financial team was an entirely new set of banking regulations that would do more to insure the nation of the safety of its banks. Coming after the S & L mess, the incoming administration had been put on notice of the possible consequences of relaxing banking standards to promote more lending, lower interest rates, and a speedier recovery from recession.

That was how the problem of control for financial excesses in the nation was handed over to the Clinton administration even before it took office on the basis of the president-elect's deepening concern for the home front after a dozen years during which the outgoing Reagan-Bush administrations had necessarily concentrated mostly on foreign affairs.

The incoming budget director, Leon Panetta, was the first among the Clinton appointees to heed the warning. In testifying before the Senate during his confirmation hearing, he backed out of the president-elect's campaign pledge for a tax reduction for the middle class. The proposal, Panetta said, should be abandoned for greater emphasis on public investment and deficit cuts to stimulate long-term economic growth.

The new president at long last was being exposed to the realities of governing the nation. He couldn't expect to please everybody. In obtaining confirmation of his cabinet appointees from his Democratic-controlled Senate, he lost his nominee for attorney general, Zoe Baird, over public protests that the prospective chief law enforcement agent of the government should not have hired two illegal aliens as domestic servants for herself and her husband. Ms Baird withdrew as an appointee the night after President Clinton took the oath of office to uphold the laws of the nation, and he accepted full responsibility.

．　　．　　．

The new president also had to take much more account than he anticipated of the nation's dominance in foreign affairs as the world's surviving military superpower after the collapse of the Soviet Union.

Much as he wanted to concentrate on much-neglected domestic affairs in keeping with his campaign pledges, he became involved long before assuming office in American interventions in Somalia, Iraq, and Bosnia-Herzegovina. It also became his responsibility to approve for ratification such major treaties as the Start agreement with Russia for limiting atomic armaments, the ban on chemical weapons of mass destruction signed by 120 nations including the United States, the Canada–United States–Mexico trade agreement, and various commitments to the UN for aid in threats to peace from Cambodia to the stalled peace talks between Israel and the Arabs.

Nor was the president-elect let off a share of responsibility with the outgoing administration for stimulating a revival of the nation's foreign trade, usually the source of one-third or more of its total income. That meant renewed negotiations with a somewhat distraught European community on the one hand and added efforts to gain more concessions for American products from a reluctant Japan and an ever-suspicious China.

．　　．　　．

The Canada–United States–Mexico trade pact attracted the new president's attention almost immediately after election day. He worried about the diversion of a badly needed part of American business and industry to Mexico in search of cheaper labor, something he believed he ought to try to prevent with proposed treaty revisions before it was given to the Senate for ratification. He also had to come to grips with the always difficult position between Israel and its Arab neighbors when it came to selecting State Department appointees who would have to deal with the problems of the Middle East. As always, such civil rights issues as the continual struggle against apartheid in the Union of South Africa could not be avoided.

Only a month after election day, however, the president-elect had to face an entirely new problem: the humanitarian issue of relieving the suffering of the people of Somalia, wracked by starvation amid a murderous civil war. It was of some importance, although not a major consideration, that the tortured nation on the horn of East Africa lay just across the Red Sea from the Saudi Arabian peninsula, the major source of foreign oil for the United States.

Without preliminary consultation, the issue was posed for the incoming president when President Bush, at the request of the UN Security Council on December 4, 1992, a month after election day, ordered twenty-eight thousand American troops into Somalia to protect and feed millions of Somalis. Clinton observed that the United States could have only one president at a time, that Bush was still the chief executive, and he supported the president's move to lead an international armed force into the beleaguered African country.

Although the outgoing president welcomed his successful rival's support, he tried to assure the nation that the American forces would be replaced by others and brought home before Clinton's inauguration. That was not the way the more honest Pentagon saw it. In fact, at the time of the Clinton inaugural, only a token first contingent of 950 of the troops in Somalia had been loaded aboard aircraft for a flight back to their American base after being replaced by Australians.

The president-elect inherited a far more serious problem from Bush in the incipient warfare, technically on behalf of the UN, against Saddam Hussein in Iraq. This had to do with Saddam's continual defiance of UN resolutions passed by the Security Council that directed Iraq to safeguard incoming UN inspection teams whose mission was to locate and destroy installations where Saddam was trying to produce atomic and chemical weapons.

For several weeks, Saddam played a cat-and-mouse game with President Bush and the large complement of American aircraft he had ordered to police "no-fly zones" over north and south Iraq. Here, there was an added objective, the protection of Iraq's Kurdish population in the north "no-fly" area from Saddam's persecution and, similarly in the south, an air guard against the dictator's assault on the Moslem shi'ites, most of the population in that protected zone. When Saddam moved some of his antiaircraft batteries on the edge of these

zones to threaten the American and allied air patrols that were enforcing order, President Bush, as commander in chief, authorized American aircraft to bomb the opposition.

That was done repeatedly in the president's final days in the
White House. Moreover, when several of Saddam's aircraft invaded
the "no-fly" zones, they were shot down. What developed was a
small war, but a war nevertheless, conducted only on the authority of
the commander in chief.

The niceties of the constitutional provision giving Congress sole
power to declare war once again were ignored, as had previously
been the case in Grenada and Panama. The commander in chief thus
asserted his precedence over Congress to wage war, and a meek Senate and House, even though both remained under Democratic control,
didn't even protest this determined Republican president. Whatever
Bush's faults, and they were many in the closing days of his fifty
years of service to the nation, he was no coward.

As for the president-elect, he also gave a good account of himself in this minicrisis in the Middle East. When it came to his attention that his support for the president was a necessity in this foreign
challenge during the transition of power at the White House, he gave
full support to the military action against Saddam. In the first of
several statements thereafter, he warned the Iraqi again not to try to
take advantage of a change in administration and attempt to divide
support for the president.

So the American-allied raids over Iraqi air space continued right
up to and through the inauguration of the new president together with
the economic blockade against Iraq to force Saddam's compliance
with UN resolutions. The first sign of weakening in Baghdad was the
issuance of a unilateral cease-fire from Saddam's headquarters, which
didn't amount to much because his radar operations still tried to lock
antiaircraft fire on the American-allied air patrols over the "no-fly"
zones and touched off repeated bombings as a result.

That marked the baptism of fire for the new commander in chief
who, in his youth, had led some of the student antiwar protests
against the American conflict in Vietnam. However, he was not as
quick to join with Bush and the British in taking sides in the complicated and bloody brawl over the fate of Serbian and opposing forces
in Bosnia-Herzegovina. Much depended on the success of mediation
efforts in which former Secretary of State Cyrus Vance participated.
These seemed to recommend a "wait-and-see" policy for the new
president at least until after he entered the White House.

This, too, was the position he had to take to ease the problem of

dealing with the attempts of shiploads of Haitians fleeing their home-
land and trying to enter the United States illegally. Pending his assumption of the presidency, he had no choice other than to support
the Bush-imposed Coast Guard blockade of the American coastline
against the Haitian sailing vessels.

Thus the new president learned before the dawn of his inaugural
day that he could not easily separate his responsibilities for both foreign and domestic policies. Whatever he meant to do to revive the
home front, he also would have to see to it that the nation's leadership of the free world was maintained. This, too, was in the American interest.

At another inaugural for a young Democratic President thirty-two
years before, John F. Kennedy had set the proper tone for the Arkansan who had been inspired by him and was to follow him. These
were the words of the Kennedy inaugural: "Let the word go forth
from this time and place, to friend and foe alike, that the torch has
been passed to a new generation of Americans—born in this century,
tempered by war, disciplined by a hard and bitter peace, proud of our
ancient heritage . . . . Let us begin anew, remembering on both sides
that civility is not a sign of weakness and sincerity is always subject
to proof . . . . All this will not be finished in the first hundred days.
Nor will it be finished in the first thousand days, nor in the life of this
administration, nor even perhaps in our lifetime on this planet. But
let us begin . . . . And so, my fellow-Americans, ask not what your
country can do for you—ask what you can do for your country . . . .
My fellow-citizens of the world: ask not what America will do for
you, but what together we can do for the freedom of man."

.   .   .

Much in the inaugural address of William Jefferson Clinton on
January 20, 1993, built upon and extended the aims, ideals and purposes with which Kennedy moved and inspired the America of his
time. For Clinton's, too, was a new generation, representing as he
did the quiet different American populace born after World War II.

Kennedy had had his poet, Robert Frost, who spoke his mind at
his inaugural with these lines:

> Such as we were we gave ourselves outright
> (The deed of gift was many deeds of war)
> To the land vaguely realizing westward,
> But still unstoried, artless, unenhanced,
> Such as she was, such as she will become . . .

269

For the new generation at the Clinton inaugural, his poet, Maya Angelou, expressed the feelings of this new generation that also sought to renew the nation in a quite different way:

> Here, on the pulse of this new day
> You may have the grace to look upward and out
> And into your sister's eyes, and into
> Your brother's face, your country
> And say simply
> Very simply
> With hope—
> Good morning.

In style and attitude, the two young presidents a generation apart displayed the differences marked by the words of the poets who spoke at their respective inaugurals. The certainties of the American future invoked by Frost ("Such as she was, such as she will become") gave way to Angelou's expression of hope for a renewed America yet to come ("look upward and out / . . . / And say simply / Very simply / With hope— / Good Morning.").

If Clinton was less jubilant and challenging than Kennedy in the tone of his inaugural, the message of the two presidents a generation apart was substantially the same.

To celebrate "the mystery of renewal"—in the Arkansan's words —would require a vigorous people "to force the spring" and summon up "the vision and courage to reinvent America." He went on with more certainty, "There is nothing wrong with America that cannot be cured by what is right with America." To do so, he warned, "will require sacrifice" and then came that same summons Kennedy had addressed to the American people:

"We must do what America does best: offer more opportunity to all and demand more responsibility from all. It is time to break the bad habit of expecting something for nothing from our Government or from each other. Let us take more responsibility for not only for ourselves and our families but for our communities and our country."

The new president was well aware that change at home was not enough. Like Kennedy and a retinue of other presidents of this century he saw that while another old order was passing, the new world may have been more free but less stable. He rephrased the Truman Doctrine of support for the cause of freedom the world over as follows: "Our hopes our hearts, our hands are with those on every continent who are building democracy and freedom. Their cause is

America's cause." Thereupon, he challenged a new generation of young Americans to "a season of service," to rededicate themselves "to the very idea of America" and concluded: "We have heard the trumpets, we have changed the guard. And now, each in our own way, and with God's help, we must answer the call."

It remained for the future to determine what could be done to revive the economy and create a better quality of life at home while advancing the cause of a free world. On that inauguration day of 1993, however, the leader of still another new American generation once again had committed the nation to change and renewal, to service and sacrifice, and to uphold the cherished ideals and purposes of its founders.

Once again, a new president that crisp and sunny January day gave the command, "Forward!" It remained for a whole great nation to respond.

Epilogue

The Changing Face of American Politics

When Bill Clinton became the first of the nation's presidents in the post-cold war era, he defined himself to the public as a centrist rather than the liberal Democrat many believed him to be.

The Republican leadership wasn't impressed. To such foes, he was the same type of Democrat they'd kept out of the White House for twenty-five years with but two exceptions—Jimmy Carter was one and he was the other.

Yet, before Clinton's first year in office ended, these doubting Republicans were making common cause with him against the majority of liberal Democrats in the House who had deserted their leader. This became the coalition that sealed into law the NAFTA treaty binding the United States, Canada, and Mexico into a pact that sharply reduced remaining trade barriers between them.

Equally important soon afterward, when the Republicans filibustered in Congress to kill the Brady gun control bill that had been pending for seven years, an outburst of public wrath broke their opposition. Instead, they joined the president and the Democrats in a unanimous declaration in Congress that made the bill law.

In these and other ways that critical first year of the Clinton administration, the forty-six-year-old president—third youngest in history after Theodore Roosevelt and John F. Kennedy—certified his credentials to the public as the different kind of Democrat he claimed to be.

He was, in effect, the product of a different age, one in which the country itself now was changing even though Congress and the two-party system were slow to change with it. Following the end of the cold war with the collapse of the Soviet Union on Christmas Day,

1991, the American people were bound to insist that their needs had to come first.

And no wonder. An uncertain economy had created more than 10 million jobless, 30 million partly employed and eligible for food stamps, and millions more who either were on welfare or homeless. One of the worst crime waves in the nation's history was claiming thousands of lives and millions in stolen property, along with the human wreckage of mounting drug abuse. Victims of natural disasters in Florida and the Midwest were receiving scant help to assuage their misery. In such critical areas as public education, health care, and the environment, remedial action also was needed.

In these circumstances, what President Clinton had determined to do upon entering the White House was to move the nation forward, as he had pledged to do during the campaign. But it was almost a year before he was able to produce any significant sign of progress toward an ill-defined goal.

· · ·

Despite the president's brave talk about a bright future for the American people in a better country and a peaceful world, he made scant progress in the opening phase of his administration. He seemed to be bogged down in furious contests over homosexuals in the military, a failed program to stimulate the creation of new jobs, military problems he had inherited in Somalia and Bosnia-Herzegovina, a scandal in the White House travel office, a fatal shootout between government agents and a cult leader's private army outside Waco, Texas, and long delays in his oft-promised plan for health care reform.

When many conservative Democrats in Congress opposed him in a pitched battle over his first budget, he was lucky to escape a major disaster by pulling out a one-vote victory. It saved his administration, but it also forced him to begin running a government on what amounted to sufferance.

After all, he had been elected as a minority president in the three-way race against President Bush and the billionaire Texas independent, Ross Perot. Almost from the outset, this forty-second chief executive had seen his ratings in the polls fall far more often than they had increased in the early months of his administration. In the Senate, he had a narrow margin of Democrats over Republicans that made him hostage, in effect, to the conservative members of his party. And in the House, despite its large Democratic majority, the liberal leadership wasn't as supportive of the president as it should have been.

Just about the only area in which he showed progress was the one in which he had the least experience, foreign affairs. When he ordered a punitive air strike against Saddam Hussein's Iraqi intelligence headquarters on June 26, 1993, he won a 66 percent approval rating in a *New York Times*-CBS News poll for that decision and a 50 percent level for the way he was handling his job at the White House. In addition, he received public approval for his work at the 1993 Tokyo meeting of the Big Seven industrial leaders, and managed to maintain a shaky partnership with the Russian president, Boris Yeltsin.

But in Haiti, President Clinton failed to persuade the military junta to accept the legally elected President Aristide. In the murderous Serb attempt to wipe out the Muslims in beleaguered Sarajevo, there was little he could do except to support the UN's humanitarian efforts to feed the helpless victims of the war. And in Somalia, Congress finally decided to force him to withdraw American troops by March 31, 1994.

The most costly disappointment of all, however, was the long delay in presenting the proposed comprehensive health care plan that had been so important a factor in his election. An unwieldy combination of politicians, medical and other scientific people, and hangers-on appeared unable for months to agree on specifics, despite continual prodding by the first lady, Hillary Rodham Clinton.

Even the modest backing that had emerged in Congress and elsewhere was insensibly reduced by widespread fear among elderly Americans that their Medicare and Social Security benefits might be reduced. It was hard for the administration to sell them on the argument that their needs would be met by the benefits that would be made available to them under the new Clinton program.

Meanwhile, alternative health reform programs were being produced in profusion by Republicans, conservative Democrats, the various industrial and professional associations involved in protecting the nation's health, and an odd assortment of piecemeal suggestions. In this extremity, toward fall, the president let it be known that he wanted to give priority to NAFTA, the North American Free Trade Agreement linking the United States, Canada, and Mexico. What he had been doing earlier in his stay in the White House, he explained, was to try to produce more favorable conditions from Mexico, and he now was satisfied that the proposed pact was a good deal for the United States.

Ross Perot, one of his principal opponents, scoffed at the president's assurances. The Texan predicted the treaty would send millions of American jobs south of the border to low-paid Mexicans, a belief that was shared by the leaders of the AFL-CIO. Worse still, most of the liberal Democrats in the House balked at the president's leadership and refused to support the pact.

Few presidents of this century had been placed in so disagreeable a position within the first year of their service, but Clinton wouldn't give in. He wanted to win with NAFTA even if it alienated labor, the liberal Democrats, and others among the traditional allies of a Democratic president. Health care came second—and undoubtedly would be irretrievably lost if NAFTA failed.

.   .   .

As late as Labor Day that first year, Clinton hadn't opened a campaign to save NAFTA. Rumors spread on Capitol Hill that he had caved in and wouldn't put up a fight after all. In the interim, he presided at the White House over the surprise peace accord agreed to by Israel and the Palestine Liberation Organization.

It happened that three former presidents attended the White House ceremony at which the Middle East peace effort was announced. And it was then, by happy chance, that Clinton received the first boost for his NAFTA campaign when all three of his predecessors backed him. At last, on September 22, he began what seemed like a hopeless effort to keep the treaty alive. How he won in the House by thirty-four votes has since become a classic in the uses of White House influence. It also established him at last as a first-rate political operative in the White House who seemed to be at his best when he had to fight the hardest.

If there remained any doubt about the president's ability to produce results in a crisis, given even a limited amount of time to work, his victory in persuading Congress to pass the Brady gun control bill should have provided additional evidence. It occurred on November 24, just a week after the Republican-Democratic coalition in Congress put over the NAFTA treaty. The bill set up a mandatory waiting period for the purchase of handguns, mainly because public anger caused the Republicans to break the filibuster through which they had twice been able to block passage.

This was a triumph, too, for President Reagan's press secretary, Jim Brady, who was shot at the same time as his chief in an attempted assassination in 1981. During the seven years during which

Brady and his wife had campaigned for the gun control bill bearing his name, he had been confined to a wheel chair. On the day that President Clinton paid tribute to both the Bradys at the White House while signing the bill into law, Jim was still strong enough to give the thumbs up sign.

.　　.　　.

There was still another way, late that first year in the White House, in which President Clinton served the nation. On the eve of the Thanksgiving holiday, when more Americans travel than at any other time over a twelve-month period, striking flight attendants turned to the president in an effort to oblige their employer, American Airlines, to agree to binding arbitration to end the walkout. It was a pretty good sign that the rank and file still had a lot more confidence in him than the bosses of the AFL-CIO, who had sworn vengeance against him and those who had supported him in putting over the NAFTA treaty.

Clinton justified the strikers' confidence in him. With very little delay, mainly through the airline's cooperation, he was able to announce that the strike had been settled, and that aircraft would be flying soon enough to take care of holiday travel.

To cap the climax, that same week, during a hasty trip to Seattle for an Asian summit with the leaders of China, Taiwan, Indonesia, South Korea, and other newly prosperous nations on the Pacific rim, the president once again demonstrated his diplomatic skill. He made no extravagant claims for the promotion of American trade abroad, which was his basic purpose, but he managed to set in motion the same kind of stimulus for freer trade in the Pacific that had brought the leading nations of Europe together in a common trading bloc. He was playing for long-term gains for American business and industry, and the increase it would bring in employment and other benefits to the home front.

There was one other event that also attracted attention directly after the Asian summit, when the president met privately with President Jiang Zemin of China, the representative of Beijing's aging leadership. The purpose this time was to serve notice on China that its $20 billion trade surplus with the United States depended on real progress toward the observance of human rights within the coming year. It was not something the masters of Beijing could easily shrug aside, and it also demonstrated that there was a limit to what Clinton would do to bring bigger and better trade benefits to the United States at a time when they were badly needed. It was, all in all, a good way to end the first year of a different kind of Democratic administration that had begun under such disturbing conditions and wound up in a skyrocketing burst of success.

. . .

It was the economy, finally, that would determine to a very large extent whether Bill Clinton's presidency would succeed or fail. The health reform plan, as it developed from 1994 on with the approaching midterm elections, would be important, just as the bare idea had been in his 1992 run for the presidency. But, as had so often been shown in previous administrations in this century, the nation's economic well-being invariably was of the first importance to the electorate.

From Franklin Roosevelt to Ronald Reagan, successive American presidents had dealt with setbacks on the economic front in various ways. FDR's New Deal expedients, ranging from leaf raking to vast public works, were the most famous, if not at all times the most admired and successful. Reagan's decision on a major national arms buildup was by far the most expensive and the most productive of good times, as witness the record Reagan boom of the 1980s.

Neither of these options, among others, were open to President Clinton in dealing with a slow-growth economy after a long recession. The massive national debt, the interest on which was the nation's major expense along with national defense and entitlements, made it impossible for the new administration to provide more than a five-year, $500 billion program that, in effect, would merely hold the line against large further costs in that area.

For Clinton, therefore, it became a triumph of sorts when the nation's rate of unemployment dropped below 7 percent for a time in his first year.

Even so, both industry and government still had scheduled layoffs or forced retirements of employees for several years in advance. Expedients such as retraining for the jobless or shifts of employment opportunities in growth industries offered only slight hope of either a Reagan-type recovery or even a longer-term New Deal effort at readjusting the nation's 120-million work force. The option credited to the Bush presidency of merely waiting for something to turn up (Bush denied it) was hopeless under such circumstances. Moreover, nobody wanted another war as the price of stimulating jobs.

What Clinton and Alan Greenspan, the Federal Reserve chairman, were left with was the relatively slow and difficult adjustment of the nation's financial structure to the economic realities of the era. For most of the Clinton first year, all the right choices seem to have been made. Interest rates were kept low so that money could be made available for business loans, especially to small businesses that provided most of the nation's employment.

As for tax increases, Clinton already had learned that these were decidedly risky even when he tried to restrict them to people who could best afford to pay—always a difficult choice. This is why he reverted to attempts to stimulate more American trade abroad, currently the source of a third of the nation's income, but there was a limit to what he could do with the Japanese, owners of the biggest annual trade balance in dealings with the United States. Even a new scandal free Japanese premier couldn't do much to open up his country to more American products.

Instead, the United States began offering special inducements to boost tourism for foreigners, among other innovations. A problem soon developed with rising attacks on prosperous-looking tourists in Florida, including a number of murders. As a growth industry, tourism had its disadvantages in a crime-ridden society.

In any event, the economy continued to be slow to develop in the creation of new industries, new plants, new jobs. It may have seemed unreasonable for much of the public to continue to blame the president for a condition that he had done nothing to create. This, however, was the way the political system still worked in America, despite all the other changes that had come to the president, Congress and other elements of the nation's governance, party politics, and the electorate itself.

· · ·

President Clinton is not the first nonconformist president to break with some of the leaders of his own party over issues deeply affecting the national interest in changing times. Confronted with that kind of rebellion within his own Republican Party against both his mutual security program and his Reciprocal Trade Agreements Act before the midterm elections of 1954, President Eisenhower wondered if he belonged "in this kind of Republican Party." He was known to have speculated privately about the possibility of founding a new socially-oriented internationalist party that would be conservative in its economic approach but more flexible in dealing with the ills of American society.

Ike tried to avert conflicts over the Republican leadership post in the Senate and other party appointments, but seldom was spared. At one time, when he announced he could not balance a post-Korean War budget, he was publicly reproached by the then Senate leader, Senator Robert A. Taft, who cried, "You're taking us down the same road Truman traveled. It's a repudiation of everything we promised in the campaign."

It was this that influenced Ike's efforts to reach bipartisan solutions to Congressional issues whenever possible. On February 10, 1954, he said: "I don't believe in bitter partisanship. I never believe that all wisdom is confined to one of the great parties, and I certainly have never in general terms criticized the other party, that is, to include its great membership. I believe there are good Americans in both parties, and I believe that the great mass of both parties is fundamentally and naturally sound."*

Despite his arguments within his own party and the battles he had to fight to win Congressional approval of the issues that seemed important to him, President Eisenhower did not do too badly in the 1954 mid-term elections and won reelection in 1956 for a second term. It remains for the American people to decide whether President Clinton, as a nonconformist Democratic chief executive, who has followed Ike's nonpartisan behavior to some extent in his first year, will receive similar treatment at the polls four years later.

*Louis W. Koenig, *The Chief Executive* (New York: Harcourt, Brace and World, 1964) 115–16.

About the Author

John Hohenberg has been a national and foreign correspondent, a university professor, a soldier, an administrator of the Pulitzer Prizes for twenty-two years, and the author of fourteen previous books. In his fifteenth, he tells the story of what he calls "the incredible, the unbelievable, the hundred-to-one shot" campaign that made William Jefferson Clinton the forty-second president of the United States.

Professor Hohenberg has won many honors in an adventurous lifetime including three Distinguished Service awards from the Society of Professional Journalists and a Pulitzer Prize Special Award in 1976 for his services to American journalism. For one of his books, *Between Two Worlds,* he was sent to Vietnam during that nine-year war to do a book for the Council on Foreign Relations and fortunately missed the bombing of his hotel, the Caravelle in Saigon, by ten minutes.

Later, the Ford Foundation supported another of his major works, *New Era in the Pacific,* an analysis of American foreign policy in dealings with Japan, China, and India, among other countries. He also served thereafter as an American specialist for the State Department and the U.S. Information Agency in two successive visits to ten Asian countries from Pakistan and India to Japan.

Another of his books, *Foreign Correspondence: The Great Reporters and Their Times,* also won several journalism awards and was given page one reviews in the *Times of London*'s *Literary Supplement* and the *New York Times Book Review*.

His textbook, *The Professional Journalist,* ran through five editions and was translated into a dozen foreign languages including Spanish, Japanese, Chinese, and Arabic.

Professor Hohenberg was born in New York City, grew up in Seattle, and was graduated from Columbia University's journalism school as a Pulitzer Traveling Scholar in Europe, during which he undertook graduate study at the University of Vienna. Thereafter he worked for several New York newspapers for more than twenty years including six years as a diplomatic and foreign correspondent after his World War II army service. In 1950, he was appointed a professor at Columbia's Graduate School of Journalism and four years later became, in addition, the Pulitzer Prize's administrator, posts he held until 1976, when he left Columbia for teaching assignments elsewhere.

He served successively from 1976 through 1987 as the Meeman Distinguished Professor at the University of Tennessee, the Newhouse Distinguished Professor at Syracuse University, the Gannett Professional in Residence at the University of Kansas, the Gannett Distinguished Professor at the University of Florida, a visiting professor at Miami University, a senior specialist at the East-West Center of the University of Hawaii, and a visiting professor at the Chinese University of Hong Kong.

There also have been shorter assignments for teaching and lecturing in this country and abroad, including that of Nieman lecturer at Harvard and another lectureship at Dartmouth. His autobiography, *You're Getting the Best of Me* is among his latest works.